INTIMATE FAMILY MOMENTS

INTIMATE FAMILY MOMENTS

Dr. David & Teresa Ferguson
Dr. Paul & Vicky Warren
& Terri Ferguson

VICTOR BOOKS

A DIVISION OF SCRIPTURE PRESS PUBLICATIONS INC.
USA CANADA ENGLAND

INTIMATE
·LIFE·

All Scripture is from the *New American Standard Bible,* © the Lockman Foundation 1960, 1962, 1963, 1968, 1971, 1972, 1973, 1975, 1977.

Editing: Barbara Williams
Design: Scott Rattray

Library of Congress Cataloging-in-Publication Data

Intimate family moments / by David & Teresa Ferguson . . . [et al.],
    p. cm.
   ISBN 1-56476-524-5
   1. Family—Religious life. 2. Family recreation. 3. Families—Prayer-books and devotions—English. 4. Christian education—Activity programs. I. Ferguson, David, 1947–   .
  BV4526.2.I55 1995
  248.4—dc20
                                   95-20641
                                        CIP

---

1 2 3 4 5 6 7 8 9 10 Printing/Year 99 98 97 96 95

Dedication

"The land is still ours because we have sought the Lord our God; we sought Him and He has given us rest."

—2 Chronicles 14:7

Marriages and families are HIS land!

This resource is offered with special dedication to . . .

- The Lord, who *"is intimate with the upright"* — Proverbs 3:32.
- The **Intimate Life** network of churches and other ministries who are colaboring to establish comprehensive, ongoing ministry which deepens intimacy with God, in marriage, family, and the church. While using **Intimate Life** publications and other resources, homes, churches, and communities are being "fortified" against such enemies as divorce, abuse, and neglect — providing places of refuge, security, and rest.

"Let the one who is taught the Word share all good things with him who teaches."

—Galatians 6:6

- The **Intimate Life** ministry associates is a network of pastors, ministers, and other Christian leaders who seek to walk intimately with God and with others in their marriages, families, and churches. As these associates faithfully teach the Word, they benefit from specific **Intimate Life** principles and then are able to impart these principles to others. The Galatians 6:6 ministry includes "Intimacy Retreats" and other events for ministry couples in key cities in the United States, the United Kingdom, Europe, and other countries.

For further information on how you might be a part of making an impact on marriages and families in your church or community, contact:

Intimate Life Ministries
P.O. Box 201808
Austin, Texas 78720-1808

Telephone: U.S. 800+881-8008
or 512+795-0498
FAX 512+795-0853
U.K. 080+096-6685

- *Center for Marriage and Family Intimacy* • *Intimacy Press*
- *Galatians 6:6 Ministry* • *Intimate Life Communications*
- *Intimacy Institute* • *Worship Connection*

Contents

Acknowledgments

We feel blessed to be part of *Intimate Family Moments* and pray that your families will be blessed by these "Lessons from Galilee." This has been a labor of love, and our hearts are filled with gratitude as we pause to reflect on those who labored with us.

First and foremost, thanks be to God who loves us unconditionally, desires an intimate relationship with us, and makes family intimacy possible.

To Dennis Gallaher for his creative contributions in making the Bible Dramas come alive! Dennis, your intimate walk with the Lord is evident in every work you pen! You're a cherished friend and brother in Christ.

To our son Matthew—the joy of our lives—for his loving heart, forgiving spirit, and sense of humor. As always, he stood by us with a generous measure of understanding, support, and sacrifice.

To our families and friends for their love, support, and sustaining prayers.

To Barb Williams for her editorial expertise and commitment to seeing this project come to fruition.

To David Horton and Victor Books—Thank you for catching the Intimate Life vision and for believing in this project.

—*Paul and Vicky Warren*

This book is a special testimony to the burden and creativity of our daughter Terri. Her insight into children and teens is only surpassed by her faithful walk with the Lord and commitment to His Word. Her age-graded learning activities make the Scripture come alive as she leads families to "experience biblical truth."

Special thanks are in order to our friend Dennis Gallaher, whose Bible Dramas make the passages come alive for the entire family.

We've desired to put these "Lessons from Galilee" into print for several years. God has kept us patiently waiting for just the time when Dennis could join us with his creative writing skills. Dennis and his wife, Jan, serve with us as Intimate Life ministry associates. Many are blessed through their walk of faith and example of victorious living in spite of difficult obstacles.

We've been blessed by the friendship of our "journeymates," Paul and Vicky Warren, and the supportive encouragement of Dave Horton at Victor Books.

—*David and Teresa Ferguson*

It has been my privilege to work closely with members of my family during this project. Thank you Dad, Mom, Robin, Ike, Eric, and Meleah for so many of our own "intimate family moments."

Paul and Vicky Warren, you have been constant sources of encouragement and support. I appreciate your transparency and willingness to live out the Intimate Life Principles.

Dennis and Jan Gallaher, you two have been such an inspiration to so many. I consider it a special gift to be able to see the testimony of your lives as you communicate the joy of knowing our Lord. Dennis, I appreciate your ability to write both with passion and creativity. Your support and encouragement along this "writing road" means more than you will ever know.

I owe many thanks to Chuck and Stacy, Marty, Mike, Karen, and Jay. Thank you all for sharing your life and love.

Lastly, I would like to honor the many children and young people that God as brought to touch my life. May God bless Ian, Jennifer, B.J., Tyrone, Brandy, Andre, Scott, Brian, Kristin, and Jenny. You and many others are truly gifts from the Lord.

—*Terri Ferguson*

Introduction

WE ARE HONORED that you have made the special effort to pick this book off the shelf. We are privileged to know that you've chosen this product out of hundreds of others. You may have even taken a few seconds to scan the material. But we feel as though we owe it to you to offer a few words of warning before you go any farther. This book may be different than you expect. In fact, this may be different from anything you've seen before. So we just want to say, right from the start:

If you're looking for a book that will help you keep the kids entertained while you get things done around the house, this is not the book for you. But if you're willing to get your hands dirty, your feet painted, and even wear a lamp shade on your head, all in the effort to experience life **with** your kids—then read on!

If you're looking for calm, low-key activities that will teach your kids how to behave more properly, this is not the product for you. But if you're looking for creative ways to engage your children and teens in discussions about scriptural principles, then you've found what you've been looking for!

Finally, if you're looking for quick answers and short sermons, we haven't included many of those. But if you're looking for a way to get to know your kids and let them get to know you, we do have that to offer. If you're willing to develop a relationship that requires an investment of time and produces a reward of great value, then . . . welcome to *Intimate Family Moments!*

The vision for this book came as we reflected on the reasons Christ came to this earth. The Bible tells us clearly that Christ came so that we could have a relationship with the Heavenly Father. During the three and one-half years He spent on this earth, the Lord's public ministry consisted of teaching the multitude of followers and demonstrating His power over the sin of this world. If we look closely, we notice that Christ also had a more private ministry, a more intimate ministry. It was His custom to retreat with His disciples to a separate place.

Jesus chose a special arena that enabled Him to teach the more fundamental issues of faith and the key lessons in life. It was through these private times with the Master Teacher that the disciples learned what they needed in order to face the challenge of "making disciples of all the nations."

We could think of Christ's ministry in this way: He impressed people from a distance, but He impacted lives up close. You may wonder how the Lord found time to give the disciples any private instruction. But when it came time for the disciples' training, He withdrew to a special place. When it came time for the disciples' training, it was time for a "Lesson from Galilee."

We hope that as you and your family withdraw together you will remember that these times may have eternal value. Because you see, you have just enrolled in a school that teaches the fundamental lessons of life. You will be studying the same curriculum as the Twelve who were chosen to build the church. And most importantly, you have the opportunity to establish an intimate relationship with the Divine Instructor.

The Purpose of Lessons from Galilee

The purpose of the Lessons from Galilee is to lead families on a journey toward an intimate relationship with the Savior and with one another.

Where and When to Use Lessons from Galilee

You will want to use this material anywhere families or groups of children/teens get together:

- Family night settings—when families come together for weekly evenings of fun and sharing
- Home devotions—when parents lead the family in times of Scripture focus
- Family Bible studies—at church, retreats, or camps
- Children or Youth Events—at church, school, or camps

How to Use Lessons from Galilee

Each unit contains four lessons that teach a fundamental truth. These lessons come from the disciples' experiences around the Sea of Galilee. The first lesson of each unit contains the key principle for the whole unit. This first lesson also gives the leader a short explanation of the Scripture passage. The other three lessons further develop this same principle. All lessons contain activities for four different age-groups. Each lesson contains these important features:

Key Scripture Passage—The Scripture passage on which the lesson is based has been included for you (NASB).

Leader Preparation—This section contains goals for each lesson and materials needed.

This family devotional is part of a series of books entitled *Intimate Life Series*. We have included two additional items in the Leader Preparation section that coincide with other products in this series. We have included the Intimacy Principle that applies to each lesson. This set of principles details God's plan for an intimate life with Him and with those He has created. A brief explanation of these principles is included in the appendix. Second, we have included a Disclosure Goal for each lesson. These goals are designed to guide parents on their journey toward an intimate relationship with their children. By following these goals for disclosure, parents will gain a better sense of what they should say and when. (See Appendix, pp. 337–38)

Bible Drama—Fictional stories have been created in order to make concepts appealing and understandable for children.

Projects with Preschoolers—This section contains activities appropriate for ages 4–5.

Great Fun for Grade Schoolers—This section contains activities appropriate for ages 5–11.

Making It Real for Middle Schoolers—This section contains activities appropriate for ages 11–13.

High School Happenings—This section contains activities appropriate for ages 13–17.

Some activities will be repeated in more than one age-group. Instructions will be given the first time, and you will be referred to that section thereafter.

Please note that the Bible Dramas have been written at approximately a sixth-grade reading level. Therefore, these stories may be too juvenile for junior high and high school students. Parents may want to retell the Bible Drama in their own words, making it age appropriate. You may also want to suggest that teens read the Bible Drama prior to the day of the lesson and then retell the story in their own words for the rest of the family.

You may want to work through the three units sequentially; the twelve lessons might serve as a semester's focus. Or you may want to study a particular topic for four weeks in order to address a specific family issue like "priorities" or "decision-making."

Structure of Each Section

The activities for each age-group are divided into three parts. These will be indicated by the following titles:

Letting Your Child Know You

Getting to Know Your Child

Becoming Caringly Involved

These three divisions reflect three different Hebrew words often translated as *intimacy*. Since the disciples were able to learn these lessons because of their intimate relationship with Christ, we thought it important to designate each section of our lesson to one element of intimacy. The three Hebrew words can be translated as "to know," "to disclose," and "to become caringly involved." The Book of Psalms tells us that God knows us and that He is caringly involved with our lives (Ps. 139:3, 13). Proverbs 3 reminds us that God discloses Himself to us so that we might know Him (Prov. 3:32). It seems only fitting to apply these three words to developing intimacy within our families. So when applied to parenting, the Hebrew words for intimacy challenge each of us to get to know our children, to let each child know us, and then to become caringly involved in their lives.

Guidelines for Lessons from Galilee

All family members participate in the lessons.
These activities are not for the kids to do and parents to watch. The lessons are designed to be "caught" rather than just taught. So parents will need to actively participate with their children. Wear the costumes. Play the games. Make every lesson something that you do together.

It is OK to talk and not to talk.
Give each family member the permission to participate in the activities that he or she chooses. Never try to force a child to share or be involved. Make sure that the lesson is structured so that everyone will find at least one activity that is appealing. Then invite all family members to join you. As the adult(s), model a willingness and an enthusiasm for doing things together, the children will feel more free to join in.

No lecturing or giving advice.
Children begin to dread anything that sounds like a lecture or advice-giving. Many times during these lessons you will see the words, "Discuss with your family. . . ." This means you will want to hear their views and respect their opinions. Be careful not to make

a habit of correcting answers or criticizing input. Also, guard against the tendency to speak for another family member. Let all talk for themselves.

Have fun together and enjoy being with one another.
These activities have been purposefully designed to teach biblical principles in an experiential style. They are for you to experience together. These activities are to provide you with ideas only. You may find it beneficial to quickly scan the activities in all four age-groups. As you scan the material in other age-groups, you might find an activity that would appeal to your family and can be adapted to fit the ages of your children. So feel free to custom design the Lessons from Galilee to fit the unique needs of your family.
Now, let's begin!

Unit One

A Lesson in Purpose

Unit Outline

HE FITS MY EMBRACE like a well-worn sweatshirt. Every night for as many years as I can remember, our "hug and pray" time has been a ritual. Here is what I pray:

Father, make Joseph into a man of God. Give him a heart that would serve You and You only. Give him a heart that would seek hard after You all the days of his life. Don't let him follow after anyone but You, O Lord! Make him into the man You have called him to be.

Yes, I know. He is really just a little boy going to bed. He probably doesn't understand what I'm praying. But every night I pray the same way. Oh, sure, I throw in some prayers about "good dreams" and "guardian angels around the bed." I pray for his next day at school and that he will be obedient—that sort of thing.

But when I pray for him, I am doing more than just following a family ritual. I am instilling a great truth into his young and tender heart. The truth is this:

God has a purpose for his life that is more important than anything else in the world!

I am telling him that his purpose is to be a man of God . . . a David, Joshua, Samuel, or Elijah. I am telling him that he is important to God.

Does he understand? I don't know. But what he does know is that his dad thinks being a man of God is pretty important stuff. And that pleasing his father means having a heart for God.

Tucked away in the deep folds of the prophecy of Isaiah is a beautiful truth. God is speaking through the prophet that He will gather back to Himself all those who belong to Him. *Everyone who is called by My name, [everyone] whom I have created for My glory* (Isa. 43:7).

Most of us spend time teaching our children that God calls us, "His children." But God goes a step farther than just saying we were created by Him. He declares that He creates us for His glory. In other words, simply by our obedience and love for God our lives declare the glory of God. It is God's divine design that our seemingly insignificant lives shout, "Hallelujah to the King of kings!"

Do you want to build worth and value into your child's life? Start telling him or her that her life declares the glory of God!

Instilling purpose, you see, can be passive or very directive. You can teach your children that God has a purpose for their lives and that purpose is to declare God's glory. Or you can passively sit back and hope that the message of the Gospel will somehow win out over the messages of the world.

That is why teaching children that they have great purpose must come first. No greater truth can ever be imparted. No other truth can have greater dividends.

So teach them that they have purpose. Teach them that the God of all heaven and earth knows them by name. He has a wonderful life filled with excitement planned for them. Teach them that knowing God and following Him is more important than anything else in the world!

After all, it is the one true purpose that we can count on.

Lesson 1

The purpose of knowing Jesus

Key Scripture Passage *And He went up to the mountain and summoned those whom He Himself wanted, and they came to Him. And He appointed twelve, that they might be with Him, and that He might send them out to preach, and to have authority to cast out the demons. And He appointed the Twelve: Simon (to whom He gave the name Peter), and James, the son of Zebedee, and John the brother of James (to them He gave the name Boanerges, which means, "Sons of Thunder"); and Andrew, and Philip, and Bartholomew, and Matthew, and Thomas, and James the son of Alphaeus, and Thaddaeus, and Simon the Canaanean; and Judas Iscariot, who also betrayed Him. — Mark 3:13-19*
(See also Luke 6:12-16)

Leader Preparation

This lesson introduces a unit on life purpose. What we believe to be our purpose will impact every other aspect of our lives. Our purpose determines our priorities and values, our decisions and commitments. Our life purpose influences the way we spend our time and our money.

In Christ's calling of the Twelve we find these three truths concerning life purpose:

We have the challenge to follow Him. *He went up . . . summoned those whom He Himself wanted . . . and they came.* Notice the order: Christ leads and the disciples follow. Christ calls and the disciples follow. We have the same call, the same Leader, and the same challenge to follow.

We have the privilege to be with Him. *And He appointed twelve, that they might be with Him.* Before the disciples got busy doing things, they had to first spend time with Christ. They needed to be with Him. Before we engage in the busyness of activity for Christ, we need to heed the challenge to "be still and know that He is God." Getting to know Christ must precede His doing great things through you.

We have the opportunity to share Him . . . *that He might send them out. . . .* The order is quite clear. After the twelve men spent time with Christ and learned about Him they could be called "disciples." Only then could they be called an "apostle"—one who is sent out. They would be sent out by Christ to share what they had experienced with Him.

Bible Drama

Peter was restless with waiting. He shook John from his sleep around the makeshift camp. "John? John! Are you asleep? Wake up!"

"Leave me alone, you big oaf!" John did not take kindly to the big, rude fisherman whose booming voice roused him from sleep. Peter just laughed. It was that deep, loud laugh that made him so likable. He had the kind of laugh that causes everyone to want to be in on the joke.

"No wonder Jesus calls you and your brother 'the Sons of Thunder,' little John! Ha! Does He know that you're so cranky when you wake up?"

By now everyone around the campfire was either laughing or yelling at Peter for waking them up too. But even at times of frustration, the little band of faithful followers had an unusual love for one another. Other people couldn't quite understand their devotion to each other.

Take Matthew, for example. Many in the group had known him for years. When he appeared on the outside of the crowd that first day, some had picked up stones to throw at him. He was hated because he stole from the people by claiming to collect Roman taxes. Everyone knew better and hated him for it.

Everyone except Jesus, that is. Jesus took him aside one day and simply talked with Matthew. He was never the same. And now he too followed Jesus wherever He went.

Matthew came close to console his friend, John. "Pay no attention to the big fisherman, John. He's just lonely and needs someone to talk with. And you just happen to be his choice!" Everyone laughed at the thought of Peter being lonely. Everyone laughed but Peter. Since Jesus had gone to the mountain the previous day, he had done little else but wait for His return.

All of the men were concerned actually. It had been a long time since Jesus had climbed the mountain to pray. And even though the Master went alone to pray often, the disciples always felt awkward when He wasn't with them. None of them knew why, but they all secretly wished that He would never leave them.

The campfire commotion died down, and the weary travelers soon were quietly absorbed by the glowing coals of fire. The silence was broken by Peter, as usual. "John, why don't you go up and see if He's all right? Maybe He's fallen or turned an ankle or something." By this time, Peter was putting the cloak on John and lifting him to his feet. Before he could protest, the whole crowd was urging him up the path to where Jesus was.

The light of the campfire faded. John shivered more from anticipation than cold. Would he be interrupting the Master? Would He be angry with him? John was lost in thought when he heard the Master's voice.

"Well, there you are! I've been waiting for you." The bright moonlight lit up Jesus' face just enough for John to see the welcome smile he had hoped for. *No sense in asking Him how He knew I was coming,* thought John. Long ago he had decided those kinds of questions didn't really have answers.

"Go and tell the others to come up here too," Jesus said. "Tell Peter, James, Andrew, Philip, Bartholomew, Matthew, Thomas, James, Thaddaeus, and Simon to come. Oh, yes. And tell Judas to come too."

The sun's effect was just being seen when John ran into the camp. And as he suspected, everyone had gone back to sleep. John saw his opportunity for some playful revenge. John leaned over the big fisherman. He was only inches from Peter's face when he yelled, "PETER! RISE AND SHINE! JESUS IS CALLING!" And boy, did Peter jump! He'd never gotten up so fast.

But the game was quickly over. The Master had summoned them to the mountain, the place where He had never allowed them to follow. The mountain was the place where He met with the Father, always alone, to pray. They walked up the mountain silently, in earnest single file. How important they were!

Jesus was cooking some breakfast when they arrived. "Men, I need to speak with you. Please sit down." Jesus seemed so intent, as if a big, new event was about to take place.

"I've been talking with My Father, and He has given Me permission to appoint you as special companions of Mine. From now on, each of you will be called My "apostles.""

Apostles! My, my. Each of the men turned the word over and over in his mind as they watched Jesus busy Himself around the little fire. And one by one, each one realized that he didn't have a clue as to what an apostle did.

Suddenly, all eyes were on Peter. When the group needed a spokesman, they all knew whom to pick. Obediently, Peter leaned over to speak to the Master. Jesus had that little grin on His face that said He knew exactly what was going on.

"Jesus, just what does it mean? 'Apostle' that is."

Jesus had a look that told the followers that everything that was taking place was planned and designed to teach them a valuable lesson. The Master simply sat down on a rock and looked lovingly at each of the twelve men, perched like children around His feet.

"What were each of you thinking when I left yesterday to talk with My Father? Weren't you all wishing that you could come with Me?" Each looked sheepishly around the circle. How did He always know what was in their hearts?

"Well, I enjoy being with you also. And that is why you will be My apostles. Because you know the joy of being with Me more than anybody else. And that is what you will do. You will be with Me and tell others of the joy of being a part of My Father's kingdom."

To the ragtag, little group of fishermen, tax collectors, and simple country folk that sat on the mountain that day, the words of the Master were the kindest words that had ever been said to them. No longer would they wonder if Jesus really wanted them around. No longer would they question whether their friendship was valuable to Him. No one had ever cared for them the way Jesus did. And what a joy it would be to invite others to know Him too!

Goal of Lesson 1: Families will realize that we are chosen to follow Christ, to be with Christ, and to share Christ.

Intimacy Principle: Intimacy is deepened through affectionate caring, vulnerable communication, joint accomplishment, and mutual giving.

Disclosure Goal: Adults will affirm their child by sharing about the process of choosing the child's name.

Projects with Preschoolers

Materials Needed: Pen and paper for Win, Lose, or Draw; outside area for playing Red Rover; ten twelve-ounce empty soda bottles; small rubber ball (if indoor bowling is played); stickers or some small token for each family member

Letting Your Child Know You Explain to your child the process by which you chose his name. How was the decision made? Describe your excitement about choosing the name for this newborn. Is there a special significance attached to the child's name? Is this a family name? Be sure to communicate how special your child is to you. Affirm the uniqueness of each child by remembering your careful decision about the name.

Getting to Know Your Child Ask your preschooler to tell you about a time when she was glad to be chosen—perhaps for a team at recess or to help the teacher. Invite her to share as many experiences as she can think of where she was happy to be chosen. Then ask her to share about one time when she was sad because she wasn't chosen. Explain that this Bible lesson is about a time when Jesus chose twelve special men. He chose them out of hundreds and hundreds of people. These men were chosen to be with Jesus all the time and to tell other people about Him. They were His twelve closest friends. He called them "disciples" or "apostles."

Becoming Caringly Involved Read the Bible Drama out loud to your family or allow an older child to read for you. When you finish, discuss the answers to these questions together.
- Do you think the disciples were glad to be chosen?
- What would you have done if you were one of the disciples listening to Jesus?

Explain that our family has been chosen too. Just like the disciples, we have been chosen by Jesus. He has chosen us to follow Him, to be with Him, and to share Him. We are going to play some games together. In each of the games you will have a chance to be chosen. Play the following games together.

Follow the Leader

Play "Follow the Leader" with your family. Let each member have a chance to be the leader. Be sure to make this game creative. Walk backward or hop like a frog as you move through the house. Roll on the bed or lead the family in and out of the shower. You might want to end the game by turning flips on the sofa. Remind the family that Jesus has chosen our family to follow Him—just like the game. We want to follow Jesus wherever He wants us to go.

Red Rover, Red Rover

Next, play games that focus on how important it is to be chosen to be a part of a team. If you have five or more family members or friends who can join you, play the game "Red Rover." This game will need to be played outside. Divide into two teams. Flip a coin to see which team goes first. Each team joins hands and faces each other. Leave a good running distance between the two teams.

The team that goes first decides on a member of the opposing team that they would like to join them. They announce to the opposing team, "Red Rover, Red Rover, Let _____ come over."

The person who has been called lets go of his teammates' hands and runs toward the opposing team. He/she tries to run and break through the opposing team's hands. If he succeeds in breaking through, he gets to choose one member of the opposing team to take back to his own team. If he does not succeed in breaking through, he must stay and join the opposing team. Each team takes turns calling players to come over. The team that has all the players wins the game.

If your family has less than five people, play one of these games together: "Mother, May I?" basketball, miniature golf, croquet, or play indoor bowling (explained in Great Fun for Grade Schoolers). Ask family members how it feels to be chosen. How does it feel when someone wants you to be on his team? Jesus has chosen us to be with Him. He wants us to be on His team.

Win, Lose, or Draw

Finally, play a game that emphasizes sharing with others. Play "Win, Lose, or Draw." Write words that describe simple pictures on strips of paper (tree, house, apple, car, etc.). Let everyone have a chance to choose one of the slips of paper and then, without talking, draw the word that is on the paper. Family members try to guess what has been drawn. Each person "wins" if a family member is able to guess the word that is drawn. One adult may want to whisper the word to the children who aren't able to read. Emphasize the importance of the game. You win by sharing with others. You share what you know by drawing pictures. Jesus has chosen us to share with others about Him. We were created to tell other people what we know about Jesus.

Closing the Lesson

Prior to closing the lesson make the following arrangements. Tape a sticker or some small token to the bottom of each person's seat at the table or around the living room. Ask everyone to sit in these seats as you begin this closing. Close the lesson by asking each family member to tell what part he or she liked best about tonight's activity. Did she like being chosen? Tell your family members that you are going to give stickers to all the people that Jesus has chosen. Only the special people that Jesus has chosen will receive these stickers. Ask each family member to look under his or her chair—one person at a time. As they find their stickers, remind them that they have been chosen by Jesus. Just like the disciples in the story, Jesus has chosen each of us to follow Him. Each of us gets to be with Him. Each one of us has been chosen to share with others about Him.

Great Fun for Grade Schoolers

Materials Needed: Ten twelve-ounce empty soda bottles; small rubber ball; paper and pens or markers

Letting Your Child Know You Share about the decision-making process that you went through to name each child. What were the important factors as you considered names for each child? Did you want to include a family name? Did you consider possible nicknames or pet names? Explain the careful consideration that went into choosing each child's name. Explain why their name was chosen above the rest.

Getting to Know Your Child Ask your family members to relate a time when they were glad to be chosen. They might have been glad to be chosen for a team, selected in a contest, or chosen to help the teacher. Ask them to tell about this experience and how good it felt to be chosen. Invite each person to share the reasons why it felt good to be chosen. Then compare this with a time when you weren't chosen. How did that feel? How was it different? Explain that today's lesson is about a time when Jesus chose twelve men to be His disciples. He chose these twelve men out of hundreds of others. They were the ones chosen to follow Jesus and those who got to be with Jesus all the time. The word "disciple" means "follower" or "learner." The disciples were the ones who followed Jesus wherever He went.

Becoming Caringly Involved Read the Bible Drama out loud or ask another family member to read for you. Then as a family, discuss the answers to the following questions:
  • How do you think the disciples felt as they listened to

Jesus choose them as His followers? What were they thinking?

- What would you have done if you were one of the disciples who was chosen to follow Jesus?

Play games together that emphasize being chosen. Explain that each of the following games illustrate the three tasks of the disciples. They were chosen to follow Jesus. They were chosen to be with Jesus, and they were chosen to share about Jesus.

Jesus Says

Play "Simon Says" together as a family, except as you play exchange the word "Simon" for "Jesus." Let one of the adults begin the game as the leader. The rest of the family is supposed to follow the leader's instructions, but they are only to follow the instructions that are preceded by the words, "Jesus says . . ." For example, the leader might say, "Jesus says touch your nose; Jesus says pat your head; Jesus says hop on one foot." The other family members must follow these instructions.

If the leader gives an instruction without the preceding words, "Jesus says . . ." then the players must ignore the instruction. If the leader only says, "Hop on two feet," the players who do not ignore this instruction are out of the game. You will want to give the instructions at an appropriate pace. Older elementary students will want to be challenged by a fast-paced game. Take turns being the leader. When the game is over, emphasize this point. The disciples were called to follow Jesus. Our family has been called to follow Jesus. We were supposed to follow Jesus' instructions in the game. Jesus wants us to follow His instructions every day.

Indoor Bowling

You will need to prepare the materials for this game ahead of time. Play indoor bowling with your family. Gather ten twelve-ounce plastic soda bottles and rinse them out. Fill each bottle with water and make sure the cap closes securely. Use a small rubber ball for a bowling ball. Find a large area or hallway in your house that would serve as a bowling lane. Set the bottles up in a diamond formation like bowling pins. Choose teams and then keep score of how many pins each team can knock down. Let each team bowl five times. If there are enough family members, let each person take turns choosing who they want to be on their team. At the end of the game, emphasize this point. Jesus chose twelve men to be with Him. Jesus has chosen us to be with Him too. You were chosen to be on a team. Jesus has chosen us because He wants us to be "on His team." He wants us to be with Him.

Win, Lose, or Draw

See Preschool section for explanation of this activity. Select words that will be sufficiently challenging for grade schoolers.

Closing the Lesson

Close the lesson by asking each family member to tell about his favorite part of the evening. What did he like best? If he could choose one thing to do again, what would that be? Hold hands and pray together. Thank Jesus for choosing your family. Thank Jesus for letting your family follow Him, be with Him, and share Him.

Making It Real for Middle Schoolers

Materials Needed: Various objects from the living room or kitchen; one roll of ribbon or soft string (approximately fifteen–twenty feet in length); watch with a second hand or a kitchen timer; paper and pens

Letting Your Child Know You Introduce this lesson by telling your children about the decision process you went through as you chose their names. What factors were considered? How did you arrive at the names you chose? Affirm your children's uniqueness by sharing how you carefully chose their names. Second, share with your children the inadequacies you felt about being a parent. What challenges seemed most difficult to face? What did you think you would do well as a parent? What things were you unsure of?

Getting to Know Your Child Ask your family members to share about a time when they were happy to be chosen. They might tell about a time when they were chosen for a team, chosen as a friend, asked to help an adult they admired, or chosen to win in a contest. Invite each person to tell about this event and then explain why it felt so good to be chosen. Why was it important for you to be chosen? Explain that this first lesson is about a time when Jesus chose twelve men to be His disciples. These twelve men were willing to leave their families, jobs, and friends in order to follow Christ. They considered it a great privilege to be chosen as Christ's disciples. Christ had a special purpose for these twelve men. He talks about this purpose in the following Bible Drama.

Becoming Caringly Involved Before you read the Bible Drama, play the game, "What's Wrong with This Picture?"

What's Wrong with This Picture?

Ask all the family members to wait outside of the room. While they are waiting, choose eight to ten objects from the room that are in plain view. Rearrange these objects so that they are no longer serving their purpose—they are not doing what they were created to do. Remember, the crazier the better. Be as sneaky or as challenging as you think appropriate. For example:

- use a lamp shade for a hat or a fruit bowl
- take off your socks and use them to tie back curtains
- use a magazine as a dinner plate
- try using a banana to stir your coffee

After you have these objects arranged, invite your family back into the room. Tell them that their challenge is to find "What's Wrong with This Picture?" They must identify the ten items that are wrong. All of these items are not serving their purpose. These items are not doing what they were created to do. Give each person a pen and something to write on. While family members work alone, see who can identify the ten items first.

You may want to let other family members try setting up for this game again. Let someone else have a chance to challenge others' observation skills. After you have completed this game, make the following statements. We were able to identify what was wrong because the items were not serving their purpose. We arranged them so that each item was not doing what it was created to do. As a family, we also have a purpose. We have been created for a unique reason. Our purpose for being here is the same as Christ's disciples. The story for this lesson reveals our purpose.

Ask a family member to read the Bible Drama aloud to the family or retell the Bible Drama in your own words. Then as a family, discuss the answer to these questions:

- What would you be thinking if you had just heard Jesus say the same things to you? What would you be feeling?
- What was Jesus calling the disciples to do? What special purpose did He have in mind?

Explain that Christ called the disciples for a unique purpose. He called the Twelve so that they could follow Him, spend time with Him, and then eventually share with others about Christ. Christ has called our family for this same purpose. That's the reason we are here—to fulfill these same three purposes.

Amoeba Race

For the next activity, ask all family members to stand up and get as close to one another as possible. Begin wrapping a piece of ribbon around the entire family. Be sure to join the huddle yourself. Tie the ribbon at waist level so that it doesn't rub against anyone's skin. Wrap the ribbon tightly enough so that movement is a challenge, but not impossible. When you have tied the ribbon tightly, give these instructions.

Announce to the family that this is an "Amoeba Race." You have just created the "amoeba" and now it's time to race. Moving together like an "amoeba," the family must move through each room of the house. You want to move as quickly, but as safely as possible. Take one practice run, time yourselves, and then try to beat this practice time by thirty seconds. Set a timer or check the second hand on your watch. Then go for it!

As you complete the activity and all have had a chance to catch their breath, make these statements. Jesus gives us a three-part purpose, just as He gave the disciples. We have the privilege of being with Him or getting close to Him. We are also here to follow Jesus. The game we just played illustrates these two parts of our purpose.

In order to race the "amoeba" we had to stay close to one another. We definitely got to know each other a little better than we did before! The times that we were communicating with one another and not trying to do our own thing were the times when we could move the "amoeba" the best. The same is true of our relationship with Christ. The closer we are to Him, the more we get to know Him, and the more we communicate with Him, the better we are able to maneuver through life.

We also had to follow a designated leader. That leader helped us know the best direction to go. Jesus invites us to fulfill this calling. He invites us to get to know Him and follow His directions. He always knows the best way to go. Jesus then encourages us to share Him with others.

Win, Lose, or Draw

See Preschool section for an activity that illustrates our purpose to share Him. Select words that will be sufficiently challenging for middle schoolers.

Closing the Lesson

Close the lesson by asking everyone to choose the one part of the evening that they liked best. Ask everyone to share what activity they liked and the reasons why. Next, explain that the disciples probably felt overwhelmed at the thought of being Christ's apostles. They were undoubtedly a little scared or uncertain about what was ahead. They needed courage. We need courage as well. It takes courage to follow Jesus because many times we don't know what's ahead. It takes courage to be with Jesus, to make getting to know Him a priority. It also takes courage to share with others about Jesus. Ask family members to join you in prayer. As you pray, ask God for the courage to fulfill your purpose.

High School Happenings

Materials Needed: Various items from the living room or kitchen; white construction paper and markers or crayons; one roll of ribbon or soft string (approximately fifteen-twenty feet in length); watch with a second hand or kitchen timer; copies of the worksheet entitled "Portrait of Purpose"

Letting Your Child Know You Introduce this lesson by telling your teenager about the decision process you went through as you chose his name. What factors were considered? What made you choose this name above all the rest? Affirm your teen's uniqueness by sharing how carefully you chose his name. Second, share with your teen the inadequacies you felt about being a parent. What challenges seemed most difficult for you? What did you think you would do well as a parent? What things were you uncertain about?

Getting to Know Your Child Ask your family to share about times when they were glad to be chosen. They might want to tell about a time when they were selected for a team, asked to help an adult they admired, selected as a winner in a contest, etc. Invite each person to tell about this event and then explain why it felt so good to be chosen. Why was it so important to them? When everyone has had a chance to share, explain that this first lesson is about a time when Jesus chose twelve men to be His apostles. Jesus selected these twelve men for a unique purpose. These men were willing to leave their families, jobs, and friends in order to follow Christ. This lesson explains what Christ asks them to do. This lesson explains their purpose. It also explains our purpose.

Becoming Caringly Involved Play the game, "What's Wrong with This Picture?" See Grade School section.

Foot Art

Ask family members to take off their shoes and socks. Place a crayon or marker and a piece of construction paper in front of each family member. Don't forget one for yourself. After everyone is barefooted, announce this contest of skill. We are going to see who can do these simple tasks with the most accuracy. Tell everyone the four tasks listed below. Then give the final instruction: All of these tasks must be completed using only your feet.

- Pick up a crayon or marker and write your name.
- Fold the paper in half and crease it firmly.
- Pick up the paper and put it on the table.
- Pick up the crayon or marker and give it to the person on your left.

When everyone has completed these tasks, ask the following question. Our feet were obviously not created for these tasks, but what were our feet created to do? Allow time for responses, then point out that when our feet were doing something they weren't created to do, things just weren't quite right. When we are doing something with our lives that we weren't created to do, things are just not quite right. We were created to follow Christ, to hear Jesus' plan for our lives in Scripture, and then to follow in His footsteps.

Amoeba Race

See Middle School section.

Closing the Lesson

Close the lesson by giving everyone a copy of the worksheet entitled, "Portrait of Purpose." This worksheet serves as an assessment tool. Ask each family member to look at the illustration and ask:

(1) Am I following Christ? If so, what is different about my life since I have trusted Christ as my Savior? If not, am I interested in talking with someone about that? Now draw shoes or a symbol on the feet of the portrait that represents your answer.

(2) Am I spending time with Christ? Have I made it a priority in my life to get to know Him? Do I have a seven-day-a-week relationship with Christ or a Sunday-only relationship? What am I doing well in pursuit of a relationship with Christ? What do I need to work on? Draw a symbol that represents your answers. Draw this symbol in or near the heart of the portrait.

(3) Am I looking for opportunities to share what I have experienced? How do my lifestyle, words, actions, and attitudes share my relationship with Christ? Draw a symbol or picture that represents your answers. Draw this picture in or on the hands of the portrait.

Ask family members to fill in this worksheet privately. Each adult should share their answers to these questions. Be careful not to preach to others, just share about yourself. Invite your teens to share, but give them the freedom not to share as well. Close the lesson by praying for each family member. Call each person by name. Ask God to show them how much He loves them and wants them to follow Him. Pray for the wisdom to lead the family. Ask God to give you the grace to be a godly parent.

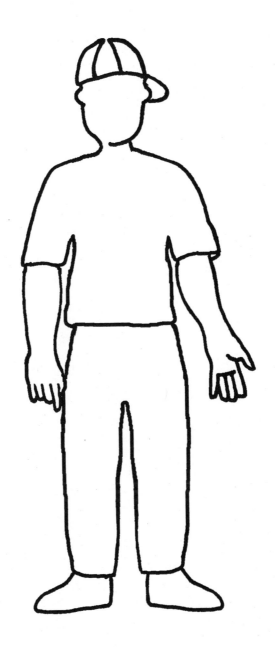

Lesson 2

Our family is here to follow Jesus

Key Scripture Passage *Jesus therefore lifting up His eyes, and seeing that a great multitude was coming to Him, said to Philip, "Where are we to buy bread, that these may eat?"—John 6:5*

One of His disciples, Andrew, Simon Peter's brother, said to Him, "There is a lad here, who has five barley loaves, and two fish; but what are these for so many people?" Jesus said, "Have the people sit down." Now there was much grass in the place. So the men sat down, in number about five thousand. Jesus therefore took the loaves; and having given thanks, He distributed to those who were seated; likewise also of the fish as much as they wanted. And when they were filled, He said to His disciples, "Gather up the leftover fragments that nothing may be lost." And so they gathered them up, and filled twelve baskets with fragments from the five barley loaves, which were left over by those who had eaten.—John 6:8-13

Bible Drama

What was it like to follow Jesus? What was it like to be so close to Him that you could actually be a helper in His miracles? One little boy had that opportunity in the countryside around Galilee. What a day it was for a little boy whose name might have been Seth!

"Seth, Seth! It's time to get up. Now don't let me have to tell you again to get out of that bed!"

It was too early for Seth, especially since he knew what the day would bring. School was never his favorite and today was no different. First would be the chores of feeding the family cow and the little donkey that he loved to ride. Next, the simple breakfast of grape juice and the flat bread called "matzoh." Then off to the synagogue school where he and his friends from the village would memorize the Hebrew Torah and recite the traditions that the old rabbi would tell them.

Seth ran out of the house hoping to get to the play yard before lessons began. Halfway down the road he heard his mother's voice chasing after him. "Seth! Your lunch! Come back and get your lunch!" Running back to the house, Seth grabbed the little bunch of dried fish and bread that was the lunch of the simple village folks around the Sea of Galilee.

As Seth approached the synagogue, he saw old Rabbi Micah watching all his friends as they played in the yard. Seth couldn't help but smile as he got closer. Deep down inside, Seth really liked his friends and school. He especially liked the old rabbi. In fact, Rabbi Micah was more like a grandfather than a teacher to the boys. And he had such a love for God that he made the boys want to be just like him.

Inside the little stone building, the boys found their places. "Boys, today we are going to do something very special. A teacher of the Torah has come to our area and is out in the countryside. His name is Jesus and today we will all go to hear Him teach. Now line up at the door and let's get going."

What a surprise! Never before had the boys left the little school and the endless repetition of the Torah. Old Rabbi Micah must be very impressed with this teacher.

The entire village seemed as if it was emptying out into the countryside. Everyone had left their jobs and homes to hear the stories of the Teacher. As they came to the top of the hill, they looked and saw what seemed to be a sea of people. The people surrounded a man perched on top of a big rock.

"Now boys, I want you to be on your very best behavior today," said Rabbi Micah. "Try to stay together and . . ." But it was too late! Like kids at a carnival, the boys were already chattering away and making their way into the sea of people. Every boy was trying to get as close as he could to the action.

It took awhile, but Seth managed to get right to the feet of Jesus to hear His stories. Very quietly, he sat. Well, at least most of the time. Never before had he heard anyone tell stories that touched his heart like Jesus. The day seemed to disappear in a few moments!

By now the sun was going down. It was time to go. Seth realized that the day had been so exciting that he had forgotten to eat the lunch he had carried with him. Unfolding the little sack, the fish and bread looked so good to the hungry boy. But before he could take a bite, a man called out to him.

"Young man! Young man! Don't eat that fish! Wait a minute,

please! The Teacher has need of your lunch. Would you mind sharing it with Him?"

Over in the distance, Seth could see Jesus smiling and waving at him. Seth was scared. His little lunch was only enough for one little boy. How could he have enough to share?

When they got to Jesus, Seth was shaking with excitement. "Seth," Jesus already knew his name, "would you like to help feed all of these people?" Why, there must have been 5,000 people there that day! How could his five little bread cakes and two small fish feed all of these people?

But Seth felt something in his heart. Something was telling him to just do what Jesus asked. "Yes, Jesus," he said, "I would sure like to help." With that, he held up the little sack with his lunch in it to the Lord.

Jesus looked up to heaven and prayed, "Father, thank You for this food You have given to us. And bless My friend Seth, who is here to help Me today." Jesus took the sack and emptied it into a basket and His disciples began to pass the basket around. But something was wonderfully mysterious. Seth couldn't believe his eyes. Everyone took both bread and fish out of the basket and yet the basket never emptied. It was . . . a miracle!

Seth sat down next to Jesus, who was eating His fish and bread too. All through the meal, Jesus and Seth talked about his school and Jesus told him stories about when He was a little boy. He was the kindest and wisest man Seth had ever met. In fact, Jesus was the kind of man that Seth could follow anywhere. And he too, little boy that he was, was now a follower of Jesus.

Goal of Lesson 2: Families will learn that we are here to follow Jesus.

Intimacy Principle: Intimacy is a prerequisite for living a meaningful and abundant life.

Disclosure Goal: Parents of younger children will share about a time when they were lost or separated from their families. Parents of teens will share about a time when they faced temptation and tell about a person whom they admired. Parents will express their desire to protect their child and then share words of empathy.

Projects with Preschoolers

Materials Needed: Colored chalk; large white construction paper; two colors of tempera paint or some other washable paint; two disposable pie tins or other shallow pan; one marker

Letting Your Child Know You Introduce this lesson by sharing with your children a time when you were lost or separated from your family. How did you feel? What did you want to do? Who was able to help you? Did you feel safe or unsafe? Why? Next share with your children your concern for their protection. Explain that rules like, "holding my hand to cross the street, wearing a helmet when you ride your bike, or staying near me when we're in a crowded place" are made because we want to protect you. These rules are to keep you safe. Verbalize your love for your child. Tell him how important he is to you.

Getting to Know Your Child Ask your children to share about a time when they were lost or felt alone. How did this happen? What were you thinking? How did you feel? Did you feel safe or unsafe? Take this opportunity to share words of empathy with your child. Share your understanding for their feelings. Tell them how sad you feel when you know that they are afraid. Tell your child that you always want to keep her safe.

Explain that today's lesson is about a boy who followed Jesus and was able to help Jesus with a very important job. The boy's name is Seth. Seth found out that when you follow Jesus that is the safest place to be.

Becoming Caringly Involved Read the Bible Drama to your family. Invite everyone to participate in this discussion.
- Do you think you would have shared your lunch with Jesus? What would have been hard about doing that?
- What was the miracle that Jesus performed? What happened that was so wonderful?
- At the end of the story we read that Seth was proud to be a follower of Jesus. Why do you think he was proud to be called a follower of Jesus?

Jesus Says

Begin the activities this evening by playing a game of "Simon Says." But for this game exchange the word "Simon" for "Jesus." Let one of the adults begin the game as the leader. The rest of the family is supposed to follow the leader's instructions, but they are only to follow the instructions that are preceded by the words, "Jesus says . . ." For example, the leader might say, "Jesus says touch your nose, Jesus says pat your head, Jesus says hop on one foot." The other family members must follow these instructions.

If the leader gives an instruction without the preceding words "Jesus says . . ." then the players must ignore the instruction. If the leader only says, "Hop on two feet," the players who do not ignore this instruction are out of the game. You will want to give the instructions at an appropriate pace. Some children will want to be challenged by a fast-paced game. Be sure to take turns being the leader. At the end of the activity, explain that to win this game we had to follow the leader's directions. Jesus wants us to follow His directions too. He wants us to learn His stories from the Bible so that we will be able to follow His directions every day.

Hopscotch

For the next activity, take the family outside. Find a large stretch of flat pavement like the driveway or sidewalk and be sure to bring the colored chalk. Create your own hopscotch game board with the chalk. The game board can be as simple or as complicated as you think appropriate. Just make sure it is divided into sequentially numbered spaces. We suggest you start with a game board that has ten numbered spaces. Each number represents a place for you to land as you hop. If you wish, design the board with some squares that are side by side and others that stand alone. This will let players alternate between landing on both feet or landing on one foot as they hop.

Show your preschooler how to hop through the game board once. Turn around and hop back through. Then let them try. Once they have the idea, try out some of these variations:

- balance a rock under your chin or on top of your head as you hop

- make it a penalty for stepping on a line or outside the lines, player loses their turn
- see who can jump through the game board the fastest

For the final phase of hopscotch, try reciting this rhyme as you hop:
I want to follow Jesus. He's so kind.
I'll hear Bible stories. His words I'll mind.

Sit down with your family and make these final comments. We knew where to hop in the hopscotch game because we marked the squares. Jesus tells us where He wants us to go and what He wants us to do. He has "marked the way" for us to follow. We can know what Jesus wants us to do when we read His stories in the Bible.

Footprints

For the final activity of the evening, find a place outside or in the garage where you can work with paint. Fill two pie tins or shallow disposable pans with two different colors of paint. Place one large sheet of construction paper on the ground. An adult will need to demonstrate how to make footprints with the paint. Take off your shoes and socks. Then dip one foot at a time into one color of paint. Make two footprints near the top of the paper. Leave room for your child to put her footprints below, using the second color of paint. Let every child make their own footprint poster. Each poster should have two sets of prints. The large set of prints represents Christ's footprints. Your child's smaller set of prints represents that he or she is willing to follow Jesus. Be sure to make a poster of your own—with two sets of prints. Put all posters in a safe place to dry.

Closing the Lesson

When you have all supplies and feet cleaned up, carefully pick up your footprint posters. They won't be dry but you will need to put on the finishing touch. If children can and want to write for themselves, instruct them to put these words at the bottom of their poster. "Our family is here to follow Jesus." Finally, ask everyone to repeat these words after you say them. "I want to follow Jesus. He's so kind. I'll hear the Bible stories. His words I'll mind." Sign your name to your poster and return them to the safe place to dry. When completely dry, display them on the refrigerator or in some other prominent place at home.

Great Fun for Grade Schoolers

Materials Needed: One large sheet of white construction paper; used coffee or tea grounds; markers, crayons, pencils and pens; some kind of hidden treasure (chocolate coins, picnic dinner that includes fish and bread from Long John Silver's, candy, etc.). Prepare the paper for the treasure map prior to this lesson. Take a sheet of white construction paper and carefully burn the edges over the burner of the stove. Then take wet coffee or tea grounds and brush them over the paper. Let the paper dry completely. This will give an authentic look to the treasure map.

Letting Your Child Know You Introduce the lesson by sharing with your children a time when you were lost or separated from your family. Tell about a time when you were alone or unsafe. Explain your thoughts and feelings. What did you want to do? What decisions got you in this situation? Or what decisions got you out of the situation?

Getting to Know Your Child Ask your family to also share a time when they were lost or alone. What circumstances led up to this event? How did you feel? What were you thinking? Who was able to help? Take this opportunity to share empathy with your child. Verbalize your understanding of his feelings. Tell him that it makes you sad to think about him being afraid or alone. Tell your child that you love him. Tell him how important he is to you.

Explain that the Bible story for this lesson tells about a boy who becomes a follower of Jesus. He finds out that when you follow Jesus great things can happen. Listen for the miracle that Jesus performs. Jesus involves a young boy about your age when He performs this miracle.

Becoming Caringly Involved Read the Bible Drama or ask another member of the family to read for you. Invite everyone to participate in this discussion.

- Do you think you would have given your lunch to Jesus? Why or why not?
- What was the miracle that Jesus performed? What do you think the people said as they watched the miracle that day?
- The boy named Seth was proud to be a follower of Jesus. Why do you think he wanted to be called a follower of Jesus?

Treasure Hunt

Ask your family to think of all of the ways to complete this sentence: "I can follow . . ." Some responses might include, "I can follow directions," "I can follow the leader," etc. Let your family keep guessing or give them some hints until they say, "I can follow a map." Ask your children if they think they could follow a treasure map. Then make this announcement: That is exactly what we are going to do. We are going to follow a treasure map!

Pull out the pencils and erasers and work together on a map of a room in your house or a backyard map or even a neighborhood map. Explain that maps are drawn so that they give a bird's-eye view. So pretend that we are in an airplane looking down. What would we see? If you are drawing an indoor map then you'll want to include furniture, doors, windows, and toys. If you've decided on an outdoor map, then make sure you include trees, flowerbeds, fences, swing sets, and dog houses. Help your children draw their maps roughly to scale. Point out that the bigger objects should be big on the map too. Be sure that you include labels for the landmarks on your map—just in case it isn't clear later. When you are all pleased with the penciled version, let the children color the map with crayons or markers.

While the kids are coloring, hide the treasure somewhere in the mapped area. Make the treasure something appealing to your children. They may like chocolate coins or just their favorite kind of candy. After you've hidden the treasure and the kids have finished coloring the map, go to another room and complete the map. Put an X on the map to mark the hiding place. Then mark a starting point on the map. From the starting point, mark a trail on the map that the kids have to follow in order to find the treasure. If you want to make the hunt more challenging, you can hide a clue at the X mark instead of the treasure. The children have to solve the clue that tells them where to go next. A series of clues can lead them to the hidden treasure.

After your children have enjoyed a portion of their hidden treasure, gather together for some final thoughts. When we followed the map we found the hidden treasure. Jesus has also given us a map for living. The Bible is like a map. Jesus has given us the Bible so that we will know His plans for us. When we follow what the Bible says we find certain treasures: We learn about Jesus and how to follow Him.

Closing the Lesson

Close the lesson with this "ticklish" activity. Explain that the focus of this lesson is for our family to remember that we are here to follow Jesus. To make sure we don't forget this important point, we are going to write ourselves reminder messages. We are going to write the message, "I am here to follow Jesus." Ask your children what part of their body they use when they are following someone. Right! Your feet!

Make sure everyone takes off their shoes and socks. Divide into pairs. Partners take turns writing the reminder message on each other's feet. Use markers to write the message, "I am here to follow Jesus." After you have inspected your partner's penmanship and recovered from the laughter, close with a short prayer. Thank Jesus for giving us instructions in the Bible to help us follow Him. Let Jesus know that you want to follow Him because of your love for Him.

Making It Real for Middle Schoolers

Materials Needed: White construction paper or typing paper; crayons and markers; half sheets of typing paper; masking tape; index cards; pens and pencils

Letting Your Child Know You Introduce this lesson by asking family members to take a piece of typing paper or construction paper and draw a "Life Map." On this map, they are to put the important points or events of their lives. Maps may include pictures, symbols, or words. Encourage your family to be as creative as possible. Each person's map will be very different. However, ask your family to be sure to include two specific items. These are the only items that will be common to all. Mark one place on your map that signifies a time when you faced temptation. Second, mark one place on your map when you met or realized there was a person in your life whom you really admired.

When everyone has finished drawing their "Life Maps," parents should explain each point on their maps. Give explanations for symbols and pictures. Tell why you included the events you did. Tell about the temptation you faced. Tell why this temptation was difficult for you. Were you pulled in two different directions? Explain. Also tell about the person whom you admired. Explain why you admired this person. Focus on the example you saw from his life.

Getting to Know Your Child Invite your young person to tell about her life map. Give her the opportunity to explain the pictures and symbols that she has included. Ask for clarification, but be careful not to ask too many questions. Make certain that you create an environment that lets your child know that it is OK to talk and NOT to talk.

Invite your young person to share about the time when she felt tempted. Give her the freedom to share as much or as little as she chooses. Ask her to share about the person whom she admires(d). What attributes does this person have that are admirable? What do you see in this person that you might like to have said about you?

Becoming Caringly Involved Read the Bible Drama out loud or retell it in your own words. Then ask family members to join you in this discussion.

- Do you think you would have given your lunch to Jesus? Why or why not?
- What was the miracle that Jesus performed? Does this give you any idea about how Jesus felt about the people who were there that day? (He knew they had a need and He did something about it.)
- What do you think Seth was saying after the miracle? What about the people? What were the disciples thinking?

Explain that our family is here to follow Christ. We were created to have a relationship with Him. We can follow Christ in several different ways, including following His Words and following His example. The next activities are designed to illustrate two of the ways we follow Christ.

Friendly Followers

The first activity is called "Friendly Followers." Ask every family member to stand in a circle facing one another. While they remain facing forward, tape half sheets of typing paper to their backs. Then write one of the following words on each piece of paper:

love	prayer	kindness	forgiveness
eternal life	heaven	neighbor	cross

Instruct family members to stand in a tight circle—not looking at the words you are writing. Hand each person an index card and something to write with. Give these instructions. The object of this game is to follow each other around the room, trying to see what words have been written on your backs. When you see a word, write it on your index card. At the same time, however, you want to keep other people from seeing the word that is on your back. The game ends when one person has written down all the words from the other players' backs. Tell your family that if people stop moving during this game, you will count to ten and they must move from one side of the room to the other. Get ready, set, and go!

After you have declared a winner, ask everyone to be seated. Explain that we have the responsibility to follow the words of Jesus as well as His example. Ask your family if they can think of any of the words that Christ has said that we should follow. Here are a few ideas:

- *You have heard that it was said, "You shall love your neighbor, and hate your enemy." But I say to you, love your enemies, and pray for those who persecute you in order that you may be sons of your Father who is in heaven.* —Matthew 5:43-45
- *For if you forgive men for their transgressions, your Heavenly Father will also forgive you.* —Matthew 6:14

- *For God so loved the world, that He gave His only begotten Son, that whoever believes in Him should not perish, but have eternal life.* —John 3:16
- *I am the light of the world; he who follows Me shall not walk in the darkness, but shall have the light of life.* —John 8:12

Pick one or two of these verses to discuss. Don't make this into a sermon, but rather talk about the challenge of these verses. Why is it difficult to love your enemy? God forgives us if we ask, but why is it so hard to forgive others? God loved us so much that He sent His Son to die for us, but have we believed in Him?

Encourage your family to think about these words of Christ. He gave us some difficult challenges through these words, but He also makes a relationship with God available. It is this relationship that enables us to follow Christ's words.

Double Time Charades

For the next activity, explain that we are also here to follow Christ's example. We need to look closely at Christ's lifestyle and the way He conducted Himself. This next activity makes us look closely at the actions and example of one another.

Play "Double Time Charades" with your family. Give every person one index card and something to write with. Pass the Word List below to each family member. Ask them to choose ten words from this list, write them down on their index card, and check them off the list. Each word on the list should only be acted out once. The ten words chosen are the words that each person will act out. Every person will have two minutes to act out their words, while other family members guess these words. The person who gets the family to guess the most words within the two minutes, wins the game.

Double Time Charades
Word List

marbles	massage	knee	bubble
beard	accident	volcano	shampoo
tattoo	lick	dive	jump rope
perfume	wink	pucker	bend

husband	pitch	pancakes	attention
scarecrow	telephone	typewriter	camera
mouse	mosquito	crawl	spiral
thigh	suspenders	diaper	gong
tackle	bad breath	stuff	belly button
corn	stork	newspaper	hole
dizzy	binoculars	slingshot	spaghetti
dribble	knead	pose	nervous
neck	milk	deodorant	shoulder
mustache	hammer	punch	scarf
cheek	detective	fishing pole	mirror
measure	kangaroo	basketball	banana
sleeping bag	gallop	dozen	dimple
referee	spine	guillotine	dentist
pacifier	chopsticks	coffee	stapler
fat	earring	chicken pox	pigtail

After you have declared a winner for Charades, ask your family to join you in this discussion. In the game we just played, we were supposed to follow the example of the person who was acting. We have a similar task when we look at Jesus. We are here to follow His example, His actions, and lifestyle. In order to know what we're supposed to be following, we have to take a look through Scripture. Ask your family to name some of the ways that Christ shows us how to live. Some responses might be:

- Christ was sensitive to the needs of others. He noticed that the people in the Bible Drama were hungry. And He did something to meet their need.
- Jesus was willing to die on a cross for us. He loves us that much.
- Jesus didn't just hang out with the popular people. He cared about everyone. Jesus spent time with Zaccheus—a cheating tax collector, Peter—a common fisherman, former prostitutes, and lepers.
- When Jesus faced tough times He prayed. Jesus prayed when He needed relief from the stresses of the day. He was praying right before He was arrested and finally persecuted.

- Jesus wasn't afraid to show His feelings. When His friend Lazarus died, Christ began to cry. He showed us that relationships with people are most important.

Choose a few of these ideas and discuss them together. Talk about the example that Jesus gives us. What makes following His example difficult? Which lifestyle examples are easier to follow than others?

Closing the Lesson

Close the lesson with this reminder: We are here to follow Jesus. We are here to follow His words and His example. Think back to the person you described in your Life Map. You wanted to be like that person because you got to know him. You liked what you saw in that person! So, the best way to make sure that we follow Jesus is to get to know Him.

High School Happenings

Materials Needed: White construction paper or typing paper; crayons and markers; half sheets of typing paper; masking tape; index cards; pens and pencils

Letting Your Child Know You Introduce this lesson by asking family members to take a piece of typing paper or construction paper and draw a "Life Map." On this map, they are to put the important points or events of their lives. Maps may include pictures, symbols, or words. Encourage your family to be as creative as possible. Each person's map will be very different. However, ask your family to be sure to include two specific items. These are the only items that will be common to all. Mark one place on your map that signifies a time when you faced temptation. Second, mark one place on your map when you met or realized there was a person in your life whom you really admired.

When everyone has finished drawing his "Life Map," parents should explain each point on their maps. Give explanations for symbols and pictures. Tell why you included the events you did. Tell about the temptation you faced. Tell why this temptation was difficult for you. Were you pulled in two different directions? Explain. Also tell about the person whom you admired. Explain why you admired this person. Focus on the example you saw from her life.

Getting to Know Your Child Invite your teenager to tell about his Life Map. Give him the opportunity to explain the pictures and symbols that he has included. Ask for clarification, but be careful not to ask too many questions. Make certain that you create an environment that lets your child know that it is OK to talk and NOT to talk.

Invite your young person to share about the time when he felt tempted. Give him the freedom to share as much or as little as he chooses. Ask him to share about the person whom he admires(d). What attributes does this person have that are admirable? What qualities do you see in this person that you might like to have people say you have?

Becoming Caringly Involved Read the Bible Drama out loud or retell it in your own words. Then have this discussion.
- Do you think you would have given your lunch to Jesus? Why?
- What was the miracle that Jesus performed? Does this give you any idea about how Jesus felt about the people who were there that day? (He knew they had a need and He did something about it.)
- What do you think Seth was saying to himself after the miracle? What about the people? What were the disciples thinking?

Explain that our family is here to follow Christ. We were created to have a relationship with Him. We can follow Christ in several different ways, including following His Word and following His example. The next activities are designed to illustrate two of the ways we follow Christ.

Friendly Followers
See Middle School section.

Double Time Charades
See Middle School section.

Closing the Lesson

Close the lesson with this reminder: We are here to follow Jesus. We are here to follow His words and His example. Think back to the person that you described in your Life Map. You wanted to be like that person because you got to know him. You liked what you saw in that person! So, the best way to make sure that we follow Jesus is to get to know Him.

Lesson 3

Our family enjoys the privilege of being with Him

Key Scripture Passage *Now as they were traveling along, He entered a certain village; and a woman named Martha welcomed Him into her home. And she had a sister called Mary, who moreover was listening to the Lord's word, seated at His feet. But Martha was distracted with all her preparations; and she came up to Him, and said, "Lord, do You not care that my sister has left me to do all the serving alone? Then tell her to help me." But the Lord answered and said to her, "Martha, Martha, you are worried and bothered about so many things; but only a few things are necessary, really only one: for Mary has chosen the good part, which shall not be taken away from her."*
— *Luke 10:38-42*

Bible Drama

Some of Jesus' most devoted servants and friends were ladies who followed and obeyed Him. Two of them were sisters, Mary and Martha, who learned many lessons from walking with the Master. This story is about one of the most important lessons they learned.

"Mary! Mary! Where are you? My goodness, you are never where you should be. I need your help!" Mary and Martha were sisters who were quite different in almost every way. Martha was a doer and Mary was a dreamer. "Always dreaming," Martha would say, "never doing."

But one thing they had in common. No one knew of two sisters who loved each other more. And even though they were different, one wonderful thing was the same. Both of them loved Jesus above all else.

Mary was daydreaming under the big tree that gave shade to the livestock pen in the back of their home. She knew that her chores needed to be done, but it seemed like such a fine day just to dream. "Oh, Mary! There you are. Jesus is coming to our house this afternoon! So hurry and come in; there is much to do."

Mary began helping to prepare the most wonderful meal imaginable for their friend, Jesus. But as the time for Jesus to arrive drew closer, Martha's excitement turned to worry.

"What if Jesus doesn't like our stew? And just look at our little home! It will never hold all of our friends!"

Mary tried to quiet her older sister's fears as best she could. "Now, Martha, you know that Jesus is coming to see us, not our home! And don't you remember that He told you how much He enjoyed your cooking? You just wait until He tastes your stew. It will be the best He has ever had!"

But nothing seemed to calm Martha's fears. By the time Jesus arrived, Martha was more anxious than ever. She so wanted to make a good impression.

Jesus was all smiles and laughter as He entered the home. "Oh, Martha! I could smell your cooking all the way from the street! And your home is so full of love. I am so glad to be here." But Martha was too busy and too nervous to even hear what Jesus was saying.

Jesus sat down as all of the villagers gathered to listen to Him talk. Mary found a spot right in front where she could hear every word that Jesus said. Martha, though, was too busy trying to serve everyone to notice that Jesus was telling His stories. Poor Martha hustled and bustled to and from the kitchen in a tizzy, trying to impress all the guests.

But as she rushed from the kitchen with yet another pitcher of cool water, her foot slipped and the pitcher crashed to the floor. And the first one to help clean up was Jesus.

He knelt down next to Martha, whose tears were now mixing with the water on the floor. Such compassion He always had!

"Jesus, I am so sorry that I ruined Your day. If my sister, Mary, would help more, none of this would have happened."

Jesus was very quiet for a moment, as if He had something very important to say but did not want to hurt Martha's already wounded heart. After everything had been cleaned up, He and Martha were alone in the little kitchen.

"Martha, I know how hard you are trying to make everything nice for Me, but you need to learn an important lesson from your sister. You have been worried and troubled about many things, but only one thing is needed. The only thing that is really important is for you to enjoy being with Me as much as I enjoy being with you. So come in with Mary and sit by Me as I talk about My Father's kingdom."

Martha understood. All the work of getting ready for Jesus was good, but Mary knew when to stop and just be with Jesus. After all, the greatest privilege we have is to spend time with Him!

Goal of Lesson 3: Families will realize that Jesus is our friend. We have the privilege of being His friend too.

Intimacy Principle: Intimacy relationships are based upon mutual knowing and caring involvement.

Disclosure Goal: Parents of younger children will share their remembrances of childhood friends. Parents of teens will share examples of decision-making and reveal their own dreams or inadequacies during the teenage years.

Projects with Preschoolers

Materials Needed: Two scarves for dramatizing the Bible story

Letting Your Child Know You Introduce this lesson by telling your child about one of your own childhood friends. Remember when you were a preschooler. What special friend did you have? Tell your own children about the games you played, the house you lived in, and how you met this special friend.

Getting to Know Your Child Next, let your children tell about one of their friends. What fun things do they like to do together? What makes their friend special? Then say: Today's story is about having friends. We are going to meet two sisters who had a very special friend.

Read the Bible Drama out loud to your preschooler, then retell the story as you portray the characters of Mary and Martha. You will need two scarves for costumes. Each adult or an adult and an older child will need to tie a scarf around their heads as they say the following:

Martha: Hi, my name is Martha. I have a sister named Mary. I love my sister, but we are very different. I like to spend my time cooking and cleaning. I stay busy all the time. My sister is not like me; she likes to sit out by the tree and daydream. Always dreaming, never doing!

Mary: Hi, my name is Mary. My sister's name is Martha. I want to tell you about this special friend that we have. His name is Jesus. He came to visit us not too long ago. It was a very important day. My sister Martha was busy fixing the food and getting ready for Jesus. She was worried that things wouldn't turn out just right. I tried to say nice things that would calm her down, but she just got more worried.

Martha: I remember that day. I was worried. When Jesus got to our house, I was so anxious that I didn't even hear Jesus' kind words.

   My sister Mary sat down and listened to the great stories that Jesus could tell. She was glad to be with our special friend. She just wanted to be near Jesus.

Mary: Jesus is the best friend anyone could have. He always knew just what to say. He taught us an important lesson the day that He visited.

Martha: He sure did. As I was rushing around trying to serve everyone, I dropped a big pitcher of water all over the floor. I felt terrible; things weren't turning out the way I had planned. I started to cry. But Jesus said some kind words that I will never forget. He said, "Martha, you've been worried about a lot of things, but the really important thing is to enjoy spending time with one another." I'll never forget what a privilege it is to spend time with our friend Jesus.

As you finish retelling the Bible Drama, be sure to give your preschooler the opportunity to try on the scarf and pretend to be Mary or Martha too!

Becoming Caringly Involved Ask these questions as you discuss the Bible Drama together.

- Who in our family likes to stay busy all the time—like Martha?
- Who in our family likes to daydream—like Mary?
- What would you do if your brother or sister was supposed to be helping, but was daydreaming instead? What did Martha do?
- Jesus was a good friend to Mary and Martha. What did He say was most important for Martha to do?

Action Rhyme

This action rhyme encourages children to remember Jesus as their friend. Have the children stand facing you. Ask all family members to follow your actions as you say the rhyme.

> **I can talk to Jesus** (pretend to pray)
> **Jesus is my friend** (hold hands with person next to you)
> **I can walk with Jesus** (walk in place)
> **His love for me won't end** (cross hands over chest)
>
> **He's with me while at church** (peak fingertips like roof)
> **He's with me while I play** (pretend to throw ball or jump rope)
> **He's with me everywhere I go** (march in circle)
> **He loves me more each day** (cross hands over chest)

You may want to repeat the action rhyme until the children have learned it well. Take turns leading the action rhyme. You may also want to think of new motions or verses.

Closing the Lesson

Close the lesson by reminding family members of the best friend they shared about earlier. One of the best parts of having a good friend is being able to talk with her. Explain that Jesus is our friend too. We have the privilege of talking to Him any time and any place. Take turns going around the circle and finishing this sentence: I can talk to Jesus when. . . . Continue the activity until the family can't think of any more times or places when they can talk to Jesus.

Hold hands and pray together. Thank Jesus for being a good friend. Thank Him for always being there to listen to us. Thank Him for the privilege of being with Him.

Great Fun for Grade Schoolers

Materials Needed: White paper, cotton swabs, vinegar, a dry iron and a thick towel. Using one piece of the white paper, dip a cotton swab into the vinegar, and write the word "Jesus" in very large print. Save this paper for the appropriate time in the lesson. Have enough paper and cotton swabs so that each family member can do this activity later

Letting Your Child Know You Introduce this lesson by sharing with your children one of your own childhood friends. Remember when you were a grade schooler. What was the name of one of your special friends? What grade were you in? What kind of house did you live in? What fun things did you do together? What made this friend so special? In what ways were the two of you the same? In what ways were you different?

Getting to Know Your Child Next, let your children tell about their best friend. What do they like to do together? What makes this best friend so special? In what ways are they like their best friend? In what ways are they different from their friend? Explain that today's story is about friendship. Two sisters have a very special friend. They learn an important lesson when their friend comes to visit. See if you can discover what this important lesson might be.

Becoming Caringly Involved Read the Bible Drama out loud or have one of the children read the story. Then discuss the following questions.
   • How do you think Martha felt when Mary was supposed

to be helping and was daydreaming instead? How would you feel if your brother or sister was supposed to be helping and was daydreaming instead?

- Who in this family are the doers? Who in this family are the daydreamers?
- Did Jesus get mad at Martha when she dropped the pitcher? How did Jesus show that He was a good friend?
- What was Mary doing while Jesus was visiting? What was Martha doing while Jesus was visiting? What important lesson did Martha learn after talking with Jesus?

Guess Who's Coming to Dinner?

Take turns playing "Guess Who's Coming to Dinner?" Each family member thinks of a friend who they would enjoy spending time with. Then each player gives clues about their friend. Family members try to guess the friend's name. For example: "My friend has brown hair. My friend has blue eyes. He likes to play soccer. Guess who's coming for dinner?" Have each family member take at least two turns.

Talk about how much you like to spend time with the friends you've just mentioned. What do you like to do together? How often do you get to see this friend? What makes him such a good friend?

Think how silly it would be if your friend came to visit and you stayed in your room the whole time. Instead of playing with your friend, you spent the time cleaning out your closet. Would you ever do something like that? Why or why not? You wouldn't be taking advantage of the privilege of being with your friend. What character in the Bible Drama does this remind you of?

Mystery Friend

Explain that we have a friend who is always available for us to spend time with. He is never too busy to listen to us. He is always ready to spend time with us. We have the privilege of being with Him. Tell the children that this special friend's name is written on this white sheet of paper. Can you guess whose name is on the paper?

Place the paper with Jesus' name on a table where the children can see. Hold a warm, dry iron on the paper for approximately thirty seconds. Protect the surface of the table with the thick towel.

As you iron, let the children continue to guess the name on the paper. Make sure every child sees the name "Jesus" on the paper when you have finished. Explain: Jesus' name was on the paper but we couldn't see it until we ironed the paper. Let the children do this same activity themselves. They might want to write their own name, draw a picture, or write Jesus' name again. Let the papers dry and then iron the papers until the designs are revealed.

As the children finish their designs say: We couldn't see Jesus' name at first, but it was still there. Jesus is a very special friend. We can't see Him, but He is still here with us. He is always ready to listen to us. He wants us to talk with Him. He wants us to get to know Him. We have the privilege of being with Him. Discuss the way we can talk to Jesus (by praying to Him any time and any place). Discuss the ways you can get to know your friend Jesus (by reading about Him in the Bible and learning about Him in church).

Closing the Lesson

Close the lesson by letting each person share what they would like to tell their friend, Jesus. Some family members may also want to tell reasons why they think Jesus is such a good friend. End the time together by completing an acrostic that reminds us of the privilege of being with Jesus. Write the letters J-E-S-U-S vertically on a sheet of paper. Then, as a family, think of statements that begin with each letter and remind us of Jesus' friendship. For example:

J   Joins me everywhere I go

E   Enjoys the times I talk to Him

S   Says He'll never leave me

U   Understands my feelings

S   Such a good friend

At the end of this activity, hold hands and pray together. Let each person who wants to pray thank Jesus for the privilege of being with Him. Thank Him for being such a good friend.

Making It Real for Middle Schoolers

Materials Needed: Paper and pen for every family member

Letting Your Child Know You Introduce this lesson by telling your children about one of your own childhood friends. Remember when you were in middle school. Who was your closest friend? Tell what grade you were in and what kind of house you lived in. What fun things did you like to do with this friend? Did the two of you ever get into any trouble because of poor decision-making? What were your dreams at this age?

Getting to Know Your Child Next, let your child tell about her best friend. What are the favorite things they like to do together? Invite them to tell about their dreams. What hopes do they have for the future? Have they had a recent opportunity for decision-making? Invite your middle schooler to tell about this event. Explain that the story for this lesson tells about two sisters who were friends of Christ. One sister recognized the value of a friendship with Jesus and the other did not. Pay close attention to how Jesus handled the situation at Mary and Martha's home.

Becoming Caringly Involved Read the story out loud yourself or invite one of the children to read. Then ask family members to join you in discussing their answers to these questions:
- Which sister seemed to appreciate the value of a friendship with Jesus? How did she show this?
- Would you consider yourself a worrier or a daydreamer? Please explain why.
- Explain how Jesus related to Martha. Was He angry? irritated? put out? How did His response communicate friendship?
- Mary and Martha looked forward to seeing their friend, Jesus. Who do you look forward to seeing and why?

Close this discussion by reiterating *that a good friend is someone who you really want to spend time with.*

Sardines

Explain that the game the family is about to play is won when the family members get together—when you spend time with each other. Play the game "Sardines." This game is much like the game Hide and Seek. One person hides somewhere in the house and the rest of the family must look for her. The difference, however, is that once a family member finds the hiding person, they hide with her. Each family member continues to join the "hiders" as they are found. The last person to join the group becomes "it" on the next round.

After playing Sardines, reemphasize that a good friend is someone you want to spend time with. We enjoy being around our best friends. It is a privilege to be with them. Would you ever think about:

- inviting your best friend over for dinner? You haven't seen him in a month but you spend the whole evening cleaning your room? Why or why not?
- going over to your friend's house on Saturday to try out her new video game? Your friend is moving to another state in about a week, but you end up helping her mom instead of playing video games. Why or why not?

Students will probably give answers that show that it is most important to them to spend time with their friends. Explain that in these situations it would be silly not to take advantage of the privilege of being with their friends. We have this same privilege of spending time with Jesus.

Begin this family discussion. *In the Bible Drama, how did Jesus show that He was a good friend?* (He must have been fun to be around since Mary and Martha looked forward to His visit; He must have been good at giving encouragement because He gave Martha compliments on her cooking; He must have been easy to get along with, since the story said He was "all smiles and laughter"; He must have been kind since He was sensitive to Martha when she dropped the water pitcher; He must have been loyal because it seemed like He wanted to spend time with Mary and Martha most of all.)

Fabulous Friendship

Make up a recipe for a good friend. Begin by brainstorming all the characteristics that make a good friend. Then decide on the quantity needed for each ingredient. How much honesty is needed? How much loyalty is needed? etc. Let each family member come up with his own recipe. Then share them out loud with one another. If family members feel comfortable, have them explain the reasons they chose the ingredients for their recipe.

Your recipe might look like this when you're finished:

For a Fabulous Friendship

4 cups of kindness   4 tablespoons of a sense of humor
2 cups of loyalty   1/2 teaspoon of understanding
a sprinkle of individuality

Combine all ingredients together. Handle with care.

Closing the Lesson

Close this activity by going back to the story of Mary and Martha. They had a friend who was loyal, kind, sensitive, and compassionate. Jesus was a good friend to them. He is available to be our friend too. In fact, He is the perfect friend. He measures up to every person's recipe. How can we take advantage of the privilege of His friendship? (by talking to Him in prayer, by reading about Him in the Bible, by asking questions about Him, by learning about Him through the way He works in other people's lives)

Pray together as a family. Invite all family members who feel comfortable to pray out loud. Thank Jesus for His friendship. Thank Him for the way He is always available. Thank Him for the privilege of getting to talk to Him. Thank Him for the privilege of being with Him.

High School Happenings

Materials Needed: Paper and pen for brainstorming activity, displayed so that everyone can see

Letting Your Child Know You Introduce this lesson by telling your teenager about some of your own high school friendships. Remember your high school years. Who was your closest friend of the same sex? Who was your closest friend of the opposite sex? What grade were you in? What high school did you go to? What was the mascot? What did you do for fun with these friends? In what ways did you feel inadequate during these teenage years?

Getting to Know Your Child Invite your teenager to share about her own friendships. Who would she consider as her best, same-sex friend? Who is her closest opposite-sex friend? In what ways does she sometimes feel inadequate as a teenager? Explain that this lesson is about friendship. Two sisters are friends of Christ. One sister realizes the value of this friendship, the other does not.

Becoming Caringly Involved Read the Bible Drama out loud or ask one of the other family members to read. Then ask family members to join you in this discussion:

- Which sister seemed to appreciate the value of a friendship with Jesus? How did she show this?
- Would you consider yourself a worrier or a daydreamer? Please explain why.
- Explain how Jesus related to Martha. Was He angry? irritated? put out? How did His response communicate friendship?
- Mary and Martha looked forward to seeing their friend, Jesus. Who do you look forward to seeing and why?

For the first activity, play the following game together. Explain that this first activity reveals our preferences about friendships. There are no right or wrong answers to this game. For each question you will have to decide what you would rather do. Be sure to respect differences of opinion and just enjoy spending time with one another.

Would You Rather?

Designate one side of the room as "A" and the other side as "B." After you read each question, ask family members to move to the appropriate side of the room that matches their answers. Take turns reading the questions and be sure to have fun.

Would you rather your best friend (A) hang out *with you* at the mall or (B) just buy a book *for you* at the mall?

Would you rather (A) be invisible or (B) be able to travel through time?

Would you rather your friend (A) talk with you on the phone or (B) clean your room and hope to find the phone?

Would you rather (A) invent a cure for zits or (B) a cure for body odor?

Would you rather your friend (A) go to the movies *with you* or (B) have them secretly make a movie *of you?*

Would you rather be (A) held captive by aliens or (B) by a group of librarians?

Would you rather have your friend (A) go with you to Taco Bell or (B) have your friend give your phone number to the girl/guy who works at Taco Bell?

After this activity, ask family members to explain their answers. Each person gives the reasons behind their choice between "A" or "B." Pay special attention to the questions that have to do with friendship. Explain that most people want to spend time with their friend rather than have the friend do something for them. Most people would rather have the privilege of being with their friend rather than having their friend do them a favor. They want the friendship, not the favor.

Discuss any similarities between this thought and the story of Mary and Martha. What did Jesus say He wanted most from Martha? What was she worried about?

After hearing the story, what do you think Jesus wants from us? How are we sometimes like Martha? Answer this question yourself before you invite your teen to share. As the adult(s), take this opportunity to model vulnerability. For example, "Many times I am so worried about going to church and doing things for Jesus that I forget to talk to Him." Give everyone an opportunity to share his/her own response.

Guess Who's Coming to Dinner?

Next, play the game, "Guess Who's Coming to Dinner?" Each family member decides on one friend or celebrity that they would enjoy spending time with. This person must be someone they would feel privileged to spend time with. Participants may want to use props or costumes to portray the friend or celebrity they have chosen. A flashlight easily becomes a "microphone," a baseball glove gives a clue about a fellow teammate, and a pair of sunglasses goes with the image of a Hollywood actress. Each family member takes a turn giving clues about their friend or celebrity by assuming the identity of the person chosen. Clues are given as if they were the friend or celebrity. For example, one family member may want to spend time with the singer, Reba McEntire. He or she might say: Howdy ya'll. I'm the best country female vocalist around. My fiery red hair and performance with Vince Gil have made a name for me in country music—Guess who's coming to dinner? At the end of this activity, each participant also gives the reasons why he/she would like to spend time with this person.

Make a list of all of the reasons family members give for wanting to spend time with the person they've chosen. Why would it be a privilege to spend time with this person? Your list may consist of things such as:

- I've always wanted to meet someone with that much influence or power.
- They would be fun to be around. I like their sense of humor.
- They are famous; not everyone gets the chance to be around them.
- I've always wanted to meet a professional athlete; I have a lot of respect for what they do.

After the reasons have been given, begin to go through the list and see which reasons might also apply to Jesus. Why would it be a privilege for us to spend time with Him? Don't make this a lecture. As a group, try to come up with similar characteristics about Jesus that would show what a privilege it is to be with Him. For example:

- Jesus must have been an interesting person—He had groups of more than 5,000 people follow Him around.
- Jesus must have been considered powerful—He had rulers of entire kingdoms concerned with His whereabouts.
- Jesus only had a public ministry for 3 years, but people

are still talking about Him 2,000 years after He died. That fact alone is worth some respect.

- Jesus must have been fun to be around. The disciples never knew what He would do next—walk on water, feed thousands of people with only a few fish, or just hang out with the children at the lake.

Close this activity by emphasizing that it is indeed a privilege to know a friend like Jesus. It is a privilege to be able to talk with the Son of God. It would be sad for us to miss the opportunity to get to know such a friend.

Closing the Lesson

End the lesson by inviting everyone to complete the following sentences. *I realize now that Jesus wants my friendship, not my. . . . It is a privilege to know Jesus because of His. . . .* Again, parents will want to answer these questions first. For example: *I realize now that Jesus wants my friendship, not just my church attendance. It is a privilege to know Jesus because of His unconditional love for me.*

Pray together as a family. Invite members to pray out loud if they feel comfortable. Thank God that we have a friend who is powerful, interesting, talented, and approachable. Thank God that He sent His Son to earth so that we could have the privilege of getting to know Him. Thank God for the opportunity to talk with Jesus and get to know Jesus through the Scriptures. Thank God for the privilege of getting to be with Jesus.

Additional Family Night Suggestion Invite a guest for dinner this week. Let the entire family vote on who it will be. Decide on the menu (perhaps beef stew as in the Bible Drama), the evening's activity, and specific responsibilities for each person. Make sure everyone helps with the preparations. Make sure the guest has a specially decorated place at the dinner table. When the guest arrives, focus on enjoying his/her company. Don't let any family member just focus on the preparations. Afterward, discuss the privilege we have to know Jesus.

For younger kids, you may even want to pretend that this special guest is Jesus. What do you think He would like to eat? What would He like to do? Set a place for the "special guest"—Jesus. Welcome Him into your home. Pretend to tell Him about your day—just like you would a friend. Pretend to tell Him some funny anecdotes of family history—laugh together as friends. Ask your kids what questions they might want to ask Jesus. Talk about the privilege you have to be with Jesus.

Lesson 4

Our family has a purpose— to share Him

Key Scripture Passage *And they sailed to the country of the Garasenes, which is opposite Galilee. And when He had come out onto the land, a certain man from the city met Him who was possessed with demons; and who had not put on any clothing for a long time, and was not living in a house, but in the tombs. And seeing Jesus, he cried out and fell before Him, and said in a loud voice, "What do I have to do with You, Jesus, Son of the Most High God? I beg You, do not torment me." For He had been commanding the unclean spirit to come out of the man.—Luke 8:26-29*

And the people went out to see what had happened; and they came to Jesus, and found the man from whom the demons had gone out, sitting down at the feet of Jesus, clothed and in his right mind.—Luke 8:35

But the man from whom the demons had gone out was begging Him that he might accompany Him; but He sent him away, saying, "Return to your house and describe what great things God has done for you." And he departed, proclaiming throughout the whole city what great things Jesus had done for him. — Luke 8:38-39

Bible Drama

Have you ever wondered what it was like to be a follower of Jesus long ago? All of the disciples left behind their jobs and their homes to follow Jesus. But as they followed Jesus, the twelve disciples saw things that they had never seen before. In this exciting story, Jesus meets a demon-possessed man who becomes Jesus' friend.

One day, Jesus and His friends got into a boat and sailed across the Sea of Galilee. When they had pulled the boat up on the shore they heard the most horrible shriek! It was the most terrible sound they had ever heard! Far up the beach was a ragged looking man screaming at them and throwing rocks and dirt in the air.

Peter and the rest of the disciples were scared! "Jesus, this doesn't seem like a very good place to land," Peter said. "Let's row to a different spot to get out of the boat." But Jesus was already on the land and walking toward this demon-possessed man.

He was the most horrible looking man you can imagine! His body was covered with sores and caked with dirt. His hair was matted and big patches of it were gone, as if he had pulled it out in a rage. And his eyes were dark and full of evil, as if the devil himself was looking out of them.

Without warning, the demon-possessed man ran at Jesus screaming and flailing his arms in the air! Instead of running, Jesus just stood there. He was not afraid of anything. The man fell down at His feet and squirmed like a snake in the sand.

"I've heard of this man," cried John. "They say he is full of demons and stays chained in one of the caves where they bury the dead. Please, Jesus! Let's get out of here!"

Jesus wouldn't leave. Instead, He bent down in front of the man and spoke in a way that the disciples had never heard before. "All that is evil in this man, I command you to leave!"

With a loud cry, the man released a terrible evil that was inside of him. Everything became very quiet.

"Andrew, bring Me some water and a little food for our new friend. And John, bring Me your extra cloak. This man has nothing to wear!" All the disciples gathered around to help Jesus.

When it came time to leave, the man wanted to go with Jesus. "Jesus," he said, "You have done so much for me, and I want to follow You wherever You go. Please, let me come with You!"

Jesus looked at the man with great love and compassion. He knew that the man would always love Him and follow His commandments. But Jesus had a bigger job for the man—one that was more important than leaving his home to follow Jesus.

"No, friend. You cannot go with Me. The job I have for you is in your own town. It is too important. You must stay here, where your home and family are, and tell them all the great things that I have done for you!"

And that is just what the new friend of Jesus did. He went his way and proclaimed throughout the whole country the marvelous things that Jesus had done for him.

Goal of Lesson 4: Families will realize that our special job is to share with others about Jesus.

Intimacy Principle: Intimacy needs that are met affect our thinking, feeling, and behavior.

Disclosure Goal: Parents will share remembrances they have about particular jobs or household chores. Parents will affirm their child as they point out one job they do well.

Projects with Preschoolers

Materials Needed: Scissors and the six pictures of Jesus located at the end of this lesson; paper for letter writing, pens or pencils and crayons

Letting Your Child Know You Introduce this lesson by sharing with your preschooler about the special chores that you liked to do when you were a child. What things did you like to do to help around the house? What job made you feel big and important? What job did you not like to do? Tell about a funny incident that happened while you were trying to help. Finally, point out one job that your preschooler does well. Share your appreciation for their efforts as well as the completed task.

Getting to Know Your Child Ask your children about the special jobs they like to do. Which ones make them feel like they're grown up?

Which jobs make them feel like they're really helping Mom or Dad? Which jobs do they not like to do? Explain that today's lesson is about a man who was asked to do a very important job. Jesus gave him special instructions about the job he was supposed to do. Listen to the story. Try to find out about this important job.

Becoming Caringly Involved Read the Bible Drama out loud to your preschooler, paying close attention to the elements of action in the story. After you have read the story, involve the whole family in acting out this story. You will need someone to play the role of Jesus, the demon-possessed man, and at least one of the disciples. Here are the eight points of action in the Bible story. Try acting out the story a couple of times. Switch roles. Be sure to have each adult play the role of the demon-possessed man. Your children will love it!

1. Act out the steps of Jesus and His friends as they get into a rocking boat. Then pretend to row the boat across a great distance.

2. As Jesus and the disciples take steps out of the boat, the demon-possessed man screams and pretends to throw dirt and rocks. The disciples are scared and tell Jesus that they don't want to get out of the boat. Jesus isn't scared. He gets out of the boat first and walks toward the demon-possessed man. The disciples finally follow Jesus.

3. The demon-possessed man screams again and runs toward Jesus waving his arms in the air. When he gets to Jesus, he falls down on the ground and "squirms like a snake."

4. The disciples are even more scared and ask Jesus if they can leave.

5. Jesus bends down and talks to the demon-possessed man. He says in a loud voice, "I command all the evil in this man to leave."

6. The demon-possessed man is now quiet and lies very still on the ground.

7. Jesus asks His disciples to bring the man something to eat and something to wear. The disciples help the man stand up, put on the cloak, and give him something to eat.

8. Jesus and the disciples start to get back into the boat. The man asks if he can go with them. Jesus tells him no. It is more important that he stay and tell others about all that Jesus has done for him.

After acting out this story discuss these questions with your family.

- Have you ever felt scared—like the disciples? Tell about the time when you felt scared.
- Would you want to be with Jesus on a trip like this? Would you like to have met the demon-possessed man and seen Jesus help him? Why or why not?
- Jesus helped the demon-possessed man and then asked the man to stay with his family. What was the man's special job?

Hot or Cold

Invite all family members to join you in the game "Hot or Cold." Cut apart the six pictures of Jesus (located at the end of this lesson). Start with the family member whose birthday is closest to Christmas. Ask this person to hide the pictures of Jesus in the living room. The other family members must be out of the room. When the pictures are hidden the other family members are invited back into the room. They must find the pictures of Jesus. The "hider" selects one family member at a time and asks them to look for one picture. If the family member walks closer and closer to the picture, the "hider" says that he's getting "warm," "hot," or "sizzling." If a "looker" moves away from the picture, the "hider" announces that he's getting "cool," "cold," or "freezing." Emphasize that it is the "hider's" special job to share clues about the pictures of Jesus. Each family member finds at least one picture and then someone else takes a turn. After all six pictures have been found, let someone else become the "hider." Play until everyone has had a turn hiding the pictures.

At the end of the game explain that each one of us has played the game. We all had a chance to be the "hider." We all had the special job of sharing what we knew about the pictures of Jesus. God has given our whole family a special job. Our special job is to share what we know about Jesus with others.

As a family, talk about the important things that we can share about Jesus. What would we want to tell our friends about Jesus? (He is God's Son. Jesus loves you and me. Jesus is a very good friend. We can't see Him, but He's always here, etc.) Let each family member choose one extended family member or a friend that she would like to tell about Jesus. Then each person decides what she would like to tell this person. Finally, each family member writes a letter sharing these important points about Jesus. Have preschoolers dictate what they would like to say and parents write the letter for them. Preschoolers may want to draw a picture to go with the letter. Address and mail the letters this week.

Closing the Lesson

Close the lesson by holding hands and praying together. Thank Jesus for being a good friend. Thank Jesus for giving us such a special job, like the man in the story. Ask God to help you share the good news about Jesus with your friends.

Great Fun for Grade Schoolers

Materials Needed: Cassette tape recorder and cassette tape; butcher paper 2 feet x 11 inches; two paper towel tubes covered with decorative paper, glue; crayons or markers; ribbon or string approximately 12 inches in length

Letting Your Child Know You Introduce this lesson by telling your children about the chores or special jobs that you liked to do when you were young. Which jobs made you feel grown up? Were there certain tasks that were designated for you at mealtime or holiday gatherings? Think about the times when you wanted to help your mom or dad. What special jobs did you think were a privilege? Tell about a time when you made a mistake while trying to help. Tell about a time when you experienced success as you tried to help. Tell about a time when something funny happened while you were trying to help.

Getting to Know Your Child Ask your children to share about the jobs around the house that they like the least. Which ones do they not mind so much? If they could help you with a task that would make them feel very important, what would that be? Ask them to tell about a time when they were helping and they felt grown up. Explain that today's lesson is about a man who meets Jesus for the first time. After Jesus helps this man, He gives him a very important job. Listen to the story and try to remember what Jesus asks him to do.

Becoming Caringly Involved Read the story out loud or invite one of the children to read the Bible Drama. School-age children may enjoy acting out the story as well. Read the story through one time slowly. Then designate family members to act out the parts of Jesus, the demon-possessed man, and the disciples. (The eight elements of action are listed in the Preschool section of this lesson.) As you read the story a second time, allow time for family members to reenact the action scenes. Take turns reading the story and alternating roles. Make sure each adult plays the role of the demon-possessed man. Your children will love it!

After reading the story discuss the answers to these questions:

- Would you like to have been one of the disciples? Do you think it would have been easy or hard for you to step out of the boat? Please explain your answer.
- Have you ever been scared? Tell about that time.
- Jesus helped a lot of people, even the demon-possessed man. How would you like for Him to help you?
- Jesus gave the man an important job. What was that job?

Explain that Jesus has given our family the same job as the man in the story. He wants us to tell our family and friends about the great things that Jesus has done. Spend the next few moments brainstorming all the things that Jesus has done for your family. (Jesus died for us so that we can go to heaven with Him. Jesus listens to our prayers and answers "yes," "no," or "wait." We prayed for Jesus to heal Mom when she was sick and she got well. Jesus protected us during the storm, etc.)

Biblical Broadcast

For the next activity, family members will want to work in pairs or in groups of three. Each group will prepare a radio broadcast that reports the events of the Bible story. Each group will pretend they are news reporters for a local radio station. Their job is to interview the demon-possessed man from the Sea of Galilee. On your recording you will want to create dialogue between the reporter(s) and the demon-possessed man about the events at the Sea of Galilee. Each group will need to discuss what they would like to say in their radio broadcast and then record the information with a cassette recorder. You will have to take turns recording, if you have more than one group and only one tape recorder.

Remind your children of a few broadcasting phrases if they are not already aware. For instance; "Now back to you, John . . . Ladies and gentlemen . . . on the spot reporter. . . . We're live here at the Sea of Galilee." The opening lines of your recording might sound something like:

Good afternoon, ladies and gentlemen. This is Jonathan, live from the Sea of Galilee. We have heard reports of a terrific event that happened today at this very spot. We are standing near the Sea of Galilee just a little ways from the cemetery. We have a special guest with us today. Mr. _____ is here to tell us about his encounter with Jesus. Mr. _____, how did you meet this man called Jesus?

You will want to end each recorded interview by emphasizing the important job that Jesus gave to the man in the story. He was supposed to stay home and tell about the great things that Jesus had done.

After each group finishes recording their interviews, play them back for all to hear. Enjoy the creativeness of each family member. Be sure to point out each member's contributions. You may even want to make a copy of each tape at a later time and send it to a family member or friend. This could serve as an additional opportunity for your family to tell others about Jesus.

Closing the Lesson

Close the lesson by making a family scroll. Cut a piece of butcher paper 2 feet x 11 inches. Cover two paper towel tubes with colored paper. Glue the paper towel tubes to the ends of the butcher paper. At the top of the piece of butcher paper write this title: *Our Family Shares about Jesus.* On the butcher paper let each family member draw or write one thing they would like to share about Jesus. You may want to use the ideas brainstormed earlier. The final product should be a series of ideas that your family would like to share about Jesus—telling the great things He has done. When you're finished roll the scroll up from both ends. Tie the scroll with a piece of ribbon or string. Display it in a prominent place in your household.

Ask some special friends or family members to drop by your house this week. When they arrive, encourage your children to show and explain the family scroll. Talk about the special responsibility we have to share about Jesus.

Making It Real for Middle Schoolers

Materials Needed: Paper and pencil for "Secret Rescue" game

Letting Your Child Know You Introduce this lesson by telling your family members about the chores that you liked to do when you were young. What special responsibilities did you have at mealtime, family holidays, or just around the house? What jobs outside the home did you think were fun? made you feel important? Tell about a time when you tried to help and things didn't turn out as you hoped. Tell about a time when you were proud of the job you did.

Getting to Know Your Child Ask your middle schooler to share about a job that he liked to do when he was younger. Ask him to share the reasons why he liked this particular job. Then ask these questions: What job outside the home would you like to try? If you could work along with your parents at any task, what would that be? If you could have Mom or Dad's help with any task, what would that be? Would you like to get a job when you turn sixteen? What job would you like to have? Explain that this week's lesson is about a man who meets Jesus for the first time. Jesus helps this man and then gives him a very important job.

Becoming Caringly Involved Read the story out loud or invite one of the other family members to read the Bible Drama. After you've read through the story once, give these instructions. Assign every family member one of three roles. Designate one person as Jesus, one person as the demon-possessed man and at least one person as the disciple(s). Read through the story a second time. But as you read, the family members must perform the action that goes with their role. Every time they hear their "name" read, they must complete the appropriate action. The actions that match each name are as follows:

Demon-possessed Man—raise hands above your head, shake hands while screaming wildly

Disciple(s)—lift hands to your mouth and pretend to nervously bite fingernails

Jesus—flex arm muscles like a body builder

Secret Rescue

The next activity is called "Secret Rescue." Prior to the game, fold in half one piece of paper for every member of the family. On one of the pieces place an "x." Shuffle the papers so that no one knows which paper contains the "x." In this game every family member pretends to be trapped in a large cave waiting to be rescued. Let each person draw one of the slips of paper, look at it, and then return it to the pile. Make sure everyone keeps the contents of his/her paper a secret.

The person who gets the "x" on his paper is the "messenger"—the one who has received the message that help is on the way. It is his job to share with the other players that help will be arriving soon. The objective of the messenger is to rescue as many people as possible without being detected. The objective of the rest of the players is to try to identify the messenger.

This messenger has limitations about how he can communicate this good news. He can only tell one person at a time. In fact, if he is discovered as the messenger, the rescue mission may fail. So in order to maximize the chance for survival, the messenger tries to spread this good news but without being discovered. Finally, the messenger can only communicate by winking at people—no words.

All players get up and move around the room walking quietly. The messenger tries to spread his good news by catching someone's eye and winking at her. If the messenger does catch someone's eye, the person who received the message waits approximately ten seconds and then announces to the rest of the group, "I'm rescued." The person rescued continues to walk along with the other players. The messenger tries to rescue as many people as possible without being detected.

Meanwhile, the remaining members of the group are trying to guess who the messenger is. They are on the lookout for the person with this good news. If they suspect someone to be the messenger, they may announce "I have a guess." If they are correct the game is ended and a new round begun. If they are incorrect, they are lost in the cave and out of the game.

Play several rounds by redistributing the papers and designating a new messenger. The messenger who rescues the most people without being detected wins the game.

As this activity ends, emphasize this point. We had a special job as the messenger. Our purpose was to rescue our family members. The lesson today makes this same point. We have the same opportunity to help our family and friends by telling them about Christ. We have the special job of sharing with people about Him.

Closing the Lesson

Close the lesson by brainstorming about the great things Jesus has done for your family. (He died for us so that we could spend eternity with Him in heaven; Jesus protected Dad while he was out of the country; Jesus answered our prayer for help with finances; Jesus hears us any time that we pray to Him; etc.) Next, invite everyone to complete the sentence, "I'm glad that Jesus. . . ." With these same thoughts in mind, invite the family to join you in sentence prayers. Go around the circle giving everyone an opportunity to thank Jesus for what He has done. Close the prayer by asking God to give you and your family the courage to tell others about Jesus.

High School Happenings

Materials Needed: One slip of paper for each family member, pencil or pen, various props for talk show skit, several small packets of salt—from a fast-food restaurant

Letting Your Child Know You Introduce this lesson by telling your teenager about a job that you enjoyed as a teen. What part-time jobs did you have when you were a teen? How did you earn extra money? If you did work while going to high school, was it tough to keep up your grades? How well did you balance the demands on your time? Tell about a time when you felt proud of a job you accomplished. Tell about a time when you made a poor decision with regard to a job or responsibility. End this time by sharing with your teenager the admiration you have for their talents and gifts. What gifts do they possess that will make them successful in a work situation?

Getting to Know Your Child Invite your teen to tell what they would like about getting a job to earn extra money. Or what do they like about having a job to earn extra money. What would make a job enjoyable? What are or will be the positive and negative points of having a part-time job? What jobs do they feel equipped to do? Invite your teenager to share qualities they see in themselves that would help them in a work situation. Finally, explain that this week's lesson is about a man who meets Christ for the first time. Jesus makes such a tremendous impact on this man that he wants to leave his home and follow Christ. Jesus asks him to stay in his town and complete an even more important job.

Becoming Caringly Involved Introduce this lesson by playing the game "Secret Rescue" (explained in the Middle School section). As you finish the game, emphasize these points: We each played the part of messenger. We had a privilege and responsibility to share information. The lesson today is about something very similar. We have a privilege and a responsibility to share with others about Christ. We have the purpose of letting people know that help is available through Christ.

Read the Bible Drama out loud or invite one of the other family members to do so. Ask members to join you in a discussion about the following questions:

- What would your own response have been to this same situation? What if you had been one of the disciples who witnessed the events of the story? Would you have decided to get out of the boat? Why or why not?

- Think about how Jesus responded in this story. What impressions do you have about His response? Were you surprised? confused? impressed? etc.
- Jesus helped many people throughout His ministry. He even helped the man in this story. If you could ask for Jesus' help with one thing—what would that be?

Talk of the Town

Divide the family into pairs. Ask each pair to prepare a short skit as a television interview. Suggest that each pair choose one talk show that they would like to re-create. Talk shows might include "David Letterman," "Jay Leno," "Nightline," "Oprah," "Geraldo," "Donahue," etc. One person in each pair decides to be the talk show host and the other person becomes the demoniac from the Bible story.

Each pair works out the dialogue between the host and talk show guest. The guest has agreed to come on this talk show because he wants to tell others about what Jesus has done for him. Each pair will want to think up interview questions and responses. Then decide on any props or clothing items that might help re-create the talk show theme.

Give each pair approximately twenty minutes to prepare and then perform the interviews for one another. Encourage each pair to have the guest emphasize his desire to share with others about Jesus.

Closing the Lesson

Close the lesson by brainstorming about what Jesus has done for you as individuals and as a family. (For instance, Jesus died for me and that allows me to spend eternity in heaven. Jesus hears our family's prayers any time, any place. Jesus gave me the courage to participate in the state competition.) Then turn in your Bible to Matthew 5:13 and read the first phrase. *You are the salt of the earth.* Explain that these are Jesus' words. Salt brings out the flavor in food and salt is used as a preservative of food. Jesus wants us to know that we have the responsibility as the "salt" to bring the flavor of Christ to this world. We have the responsibility to bring the preserving qualities of Christ to those around us. Give every family member a packet of salt. Ask them to keep this small packet as a reminder of their purpose to share Christ with others.

Unit Two

A Lesson in Humility

Unit Outline

YEARS AGO, MY OLDEST son James had a passion for mowing the lawn. It's too bad that this was long before he was old enough to actually do it. I would pull the mower out of the garage and he would instantly be at my side.

"Can I mow the lawn, Dad? Please, let me try. I know I'm big enough now!" I knew that he wasn't big enough at all. Finally, though, I succumbed to the pressure.

The mower roared to life. And in the catbird seat was James, all three feet of him. Down the driveway he went, just like he had watched me do. He was planning to start near the street. And I could read his mind with every step.

"This is a piece of cake! Nothing to it!" Nothing, until he stepped from the driveway onto the thick St. Augustine grass, that is.

His little boy body put every ounce of strength into the task but to no avail. He really wasn't big enough to handle the job, no matter how much he wanted to be.

But suddenly the mower seemed to take off by itself. It glided through the grass like a fish through clear water. That's about the time he realized that I was standing behind him pushing the mower along with him. What he could not accomplish by himself, he could certainly do with my added strength.

Up and down the rows of shaggy grass we went, until the task was finally completed. Here is the childlike wisdom that came from James. "You see, Dad. I knew that I could mow the lawn. All I needed was a little help from you!" Amazing, isn't it? A child assumes that help from Dad is normal. They have a built-in humility that accepts help when the weeds of life get too high to deal with alone.

Along the way of growing up we seem to lose that humility. Maybe it's because of our sinful nature. Maybe it's because we are told to "be proud" of everything and anything. It happens, nonetheless, to every one of us. That's why it's important to capitalize on a child's built-in humility when he is small. It lets him know at an early age that moms and dads are there when the going gets tough. Because someday Mom and Dad will not be quite so available. God will be there as He always has, but humility is the key that unlocks His power in our lives.

A child who has learned the value of humility grows to be a teenager who trusts in God's strength more readily. And a teen who learns to trust in God's strength becomes an adult whose life is unpretentious and sincere. And a sincere adult is the living example that teaches children the great value of humility.

So teach your kids these great truths about the humble life because, by doing so, you'll impact your family for generations.

And that kind of thinking should humble every one of us.

Lesson 5

Humility: The challenge of walking with Jesus

Key Scripture Passage *And immediately He made His disciples get into the boat and go ahead of Him to the other side to Bethsaida, while He Himself was sending the multitudes away. And after bidding them farewell, He departed to the mountain to pray. And when it was evening, the boat was in the midst of the sea, and He was alone on the land. And seeing them straining at the oars, for the wind was against them, at about the fourth watch of the night, He came to them, walking on the sea; and He intended to pass by them. But when they saw Him walking on the sea, they supposed that it was a ghost, and cried out; for they all saw Him and were frightened. But immediately He spoke with them and said to them, "Take courage; it is I, do not be afraid." — Mark 6:45-50.*

And Peter answered Him and said, "Lord, if it is You, command me to come to You on the water."

And He said, "Come!" And Peter got out of the boat, and walked on the water and came toward Jesus. But seeing the wind, he became afraid, and beginning to sink, he cried out, saying, "Lord, save me!" And immediately Jesus stretched out His hand and took hold of him, and said to him, "O you of little faith, why did you doubt?" And when they got into the boat, the wind stopped. And those who were in the boat worshiped Him, saying, "You are certainly God's Son!"—Matthew 14:28-33

Leader Preparation

God promises in the Book of James, to *resist the proud, but [give] grace to the humble* (James 4:6). Humility, then, must certainly be worth looking into. But what exactly is it? Humility, is an attitude and a response of our heart. It is a response that says we vulnerably admit our neediness before God and then hope in His provision. It's this hope then that becomes the substance of our faith. These elements are linked in succession—when we admit our neediness, only then can we begin to hope for God's provision. As we hope for His provision, we exercise faith. And without faith, it is impossible to please God (Heb. 11:6). In Christ's experience with Peter on the Sea of Galilee, we find these truths concerning humility:

Christ allows circumstances in our lives that challenge us to acknowledge our neediness and foster dependency on God. These challenges facilitate the development of humility. The storm the disciples faced wasn't a fluke—it didn't catch Christ off guard. He knew there was going to be a storm and yet He told them to get into the boat. Christ wanted them to come face-to-face with their neediness. Jesus is very deliberate in putting challenges before us that highlight our limitations. Our "storms" are there to remind us of our need for Him and for other intimate relationships.

Next, we need to understand Christ's response to the storm. He wasn't merely trying to demonstrate His power over the forces of nature. Jesus let the storm rage. Our Lord appeared in the midst of the storm, but didn't stop it. Why not? Jesus wanted the disciples to learn some vital lessons. It may seem a little unusual, but Jesus loved His disciples so much that He wanted them in a situation that highlighted their neediness. He put them in a situation where their own skills and expertise were not enough. They had to say, "We need You, Lord." Christ also wanted to affirm their worth to the Heavenly Father. Christ orchestrated the events on the Sea of Galilee because He knew the disciples would need these lessons in order to fulfill their mission. Christ did all of this because He cared deeply about the twelve men in the boat. Our Savior wants the same for us. He wants us to be able to say, "I need You, Lord" and He wants us to know that He cares for us. **His focus on us and our needs affirms our worth to the Heavenly Father.** We are special to Him and we need Him.

We also learn from this Galilee experience of Jesus' attentiveness to our situation. The passage says that Christ saw the disciples on the water. Jesus couldn't see His friends with His physical eyes that night, but He was acutely aware of their situation. He saw with spiritual eyes; after all, it was about 3 o'clock in the morning. Our Lord was on top of a mountain while the disciples were in the middle of a lake. We also see that Christ not only noticed their predicament, but He took initiative to help them. *He* came to them. God notices our difficulties, is acutely aware of our needs, and committed to move forward with His provision. **It is His initiative to give that can relieve our fear that needs might not be met.** We need to look for His steps of initiative. Sometimes we're so busy concentrating on our "storm" that we miss the Lord's provision. He's right there, ready to give.

Lastly, Peter's experience on the water that day tells us that **when our neediness meets God's provision this is Scripture in action.** When Peter took those first steps out of the boat, he was living out a lesson of trust in the Lord. As Peter felt the hand of Christ pull him from the churning water, his need met God's provision. From that day forward, Peter undoubtedly had a new understanding of God's promise to be *our refuge . . . a very present help in trouble* (Ps. 46:1). Our storms challenge our weaknesses, confirm

God's attentiveness, and allow us to truly experience biblical truth. When God allows difficulties in our life He does so to show us our need for Him, our provision in Him, and our opportunity to fulfill biblical truths alongside Him.

Bible Drama

What a day! All the miracles of Elisha could not compare to what Jesus had done with the five loaves and two little fish. The weary disciples were gathering up the last of the baskets while the women made sack lunches for all the people who had traveled far to be near Jesus. What an exhausting day!

Finally, it was over. The people had gone about their way, and the Twelve were ready for a well-deserved rest. But Jesus had another idea.

"Men, I know it's been a long day but I want you to pack everything up and head back to the other side of the lake tonight. I'm going to get some quiet time with My Father on that mountain over there. I'll catch up with you later." With that, Jesus turned and walked toward the mountain before the disciples had a moment to protest.

No one was looking forward to the long trip across the lake in the little fishing boat that was beached in the sand. No one except Peter, that is. Peter was a fisherman, a man of the sea. He grew up loving everything about the sea and still secretly longed to return to his little fishing village and wet his nets each day. But since he had become a disciple of Jesus, there was very little time left to fish.

"Come on, men! Time's a wastin'! Let's get packed and in the water before the sun goes down." There's nothing like an excited sailor to charge up a group of men. Soon, Peter was telling all of his fishing stories, especially the scary ones about sea monsters and great storms. Peter made the stories come alive as if they were really true!

Twelve men pushed off from the beach at sunset while Jesus climbed the mountain to pray. The Master looked down at His faithful apostles now singing and rowing and laughing out into the big lake. "It's going to be a long night, Father," He whispered. "Thank You for watching over My men."

Hours passed and the sea turned angry. All the singing and laughing that had eased the men into the lake was no more. Even Peter, the best sailor any of them had ever known, seemed worried. And when Peter was concerned, the disciples knew that trouble was ahead.

The sky was dark with low-hung clouds that blocked out any

comfort from the stars or moon. And the wind seemed to go first this way and then that way. It never stayed the same, always contrary and howling with a terrible whine that stirred the water and pitched the little boat.

The men took turns at the oars as Peter stood at the helm trying his best to encourage them. "I've been in worse than this, friends! No need to worry; this is nothing compared to. . . ." But his words were suddenly cut short by a huge wave that swept over the boat and almost took Peter over the side! Dropping the oars, the disciples began bailing water from the little craft. The boat seemed to get smaller as the waves around them grew bigger.

"Grab the oars! Grab the oars! Don't let them float away!" yelled Peter, as he climbed back to his place. There was no hiding the fear in his voice now. Peter was scared, and that meant that the disciples were in serious trouble. All of the scary stories he told about men lost at sea seemed very real—too real for the friends of Jesus that night.

Hours passed. The wind grew stronger and more fierce than any of the men had known. The disciples' arms ached from pulling on the oars. Their voices grew hoarse from yelling above the howling wind. Their bodies shivered with cold even as they sweated from the strain of rowing. Peter knew that if they could just make it until dawn, they could find the shore. But with the boat slowly filling with water and the men so weary from rowing, dawn seemed forever away.

But what is that? Peter thought he saw something behind the wave. There it is again, closer this time. Peter looked to see if the others had seen it too. The look of terror told more than the words that were stuck in each throat. It was a ghost! And it was coming their way!

"Row, men! Row harder!" Peter yelled. But it was no use. The wind was blowing them toward the terrible creature that was now yelling at them above the waves. They were terrified and ready to jump overboard!

But what is the ghost saying? Peter could barely make out the words. The voice! It sounded like. . . . No, it couldn't be. . . . But, yes! It was Jesus!

"Courage, men! Courage, it's Me. Don't be afraid!" All of a sudden a great shout went up from the would-be sailors! Jesus had come to save them. There He was, standing on the water as if the lake was a giant bowl of Jell-O, rocking this way and that.

Suddenly, Peter got very excited—more excited than he had ever been. "Jesus, is it really You? Let me come out and walk on the water too!"

"Come on, Peter. Walk over to Me."

The other disciples were dumbfounded. Behold! There was Peter walking on the water toward Jesus. Up and down on the waves he went, laughing and shouting his way toward Jesus. Never before had he felt so brave!

But suddenly, a big wave blocked Peter's view of Jesus, then another wave and another. Peter began to look at the waves instead of Jesus. He began to sink. Too far from Jesus and too far from the boat, Peter was going down fast! He was going down too fast to do anything but cry out for help!

The Lord's strong grip took hold of him. Jesus pulled him from the waves that almost swallowed him.

"Oh, you of faint of heart! What came over you? Why did you look away from Me?"

What could Peter say? He was just glad that Jesus was there to rescue him. Even Peter, the mightiest sailor on the Sea of Galilee, couldn't walk on the water without Jesus at his side.

And as Peter and Jesus climbed into the boat, Peter and the disciples knew that Jesus was the one and only Master of the wind and the sea.

Goal of Lesson 5: Families will learn God allows difficulties in our lives in order to remind us of our need for Him and for other people.

Intimacy Principle: We all have physical, emotional, and spiritual needs that serve as the catalyst for intimacy.

Disclosure Goal: Parents of younger childen will share remembrances of a time when they were scared. Parents will tell how God helped them during these times. Parents of teens will share one success and one failure of their own teenage years.

Projects with Preschoolers

Materials Needed: A small pebble or stone, marble, golf ball, baseball, volleyball, basketball (or other objects that show proportion in size), crayons, and paper plates

Materials for the optional finger painting activity are: one envelope of unflavored instant gelatin, 1/4 cup hot water, 1/2 cup of cornstarch, 3 tablespoons sugar, 1 and 3/4 cups cold water, 1/4 cup liquid dishwashing soap, and food coloring

Letting Your Child Know You Begin this lesson by thinking back to a time when you were approximately five or six years of age. What were you scared of? Did you have a tough time getting to sleep at night? Did a movie or television show scare you? What fears do you remember as a child? Tell your preschooler how God helped you through those times. Did He provide you with people in your life to comfort you, keep you safe, or give you a hug? Did you pray to Him and find a listening and attentive ear?

Getting to Know Your Child Invite your child to share about a time when he was scared. What were the circumstances? Encourage your child to verbalize these feelings and provide an accepting atmosphere for him to do so. Then assist him in thinking about how God helped him during that time. Did God bring parents or friends that helped him feel safe? Did he pray to God? How did He answer this prayer? Did God help by bringing friends or family to make the scared feelings go away? Tell your family that this lesson is about a time when the disciples were really scared. They needed Jesus' help. Our story shows how important it is for us to know that when we feel scared our feelings are there to remind us that we need Jesus to help us.

Becoming Caringly Involved Read the Bible Drama out loud to your family. When you've finished reading, invite your family to join you in acting out this story. Find some toys that will represent the people of the story—Jesus, Peter, and the other disciples. Find some toy or item around the house that will serve as a boat for the make-believe disciples. If you have a blow-up pool or other large container that can be filled with water, use this for the Sea of Galilee. Otherwise, gather around the kitchen sink or bathtub. Re-create the Bible story with these main points of action:

- The disciples and Jesus are tired from working all day. They have just fed over 5,000 people.
- Jesus tells the disciples to get into the boat and go to the other side of the lake without Him.
- The disciples are tired but they get into the boat. They are good fishermen and good at sailing.
- Jesus goes up to the mountain and begins to pray.
- A great storm starts to rock the boat. The disciples are worried.
- The storm starts to get worse. The waves get bigger and water starts to get into the boat.
- The disciples see something coming across the water. They think it is a ghost and are scared.
- Peter recognizes Jesus and calls out to Him. Peter wants to walk out on the water too.
- Jesus invites Peter to walk out on the water. Peter steps out of the boat and walks toward Jesus.
- Peter looks at the waves instead of looking at Jesus. He begins to sink.
- Jesus saves Peter from the water. Jesus reminds Peter to always trust Him. Jesus reminds Peter that when tough times come Jesus is there to help.

After you have acted out the story, ask your family to participate in this discussion.

- The disciples thought that they could sail the boat in the storm without any problems. Were they right or wrong? Please explain.
- What did the disciples think they saw out on the water? How do you think they felt? How did they feel when they realized it was Jesus? How did Jesus help Peter?
- Do you think you would have gotten out of the boat like Peter did? Why or why not?

Bigger—Better—Best

For this activity you will need a small pebble, a marble, golf ball, baseball, volleyball, and basketball. Place the pebble on a table so that the whole family can see it. Ask your child to pretend that this pebble is a small ant or some other small insect. What animal is bigger than an ant? The child names a few animals such as mouse, cat, or dog. Then place the marble on the table. Let's pretend that this marble is our dog. What animal is bigger than our dog? The family may say things such as horse, tiger, or elephant. Place the golf ball on the table. Let's pretend that this golf ball is a big elephant. What animal is bigger than an elephant? The family may have many guesses. Continue the comparison of size, relating each ball to a different animal. Conclude with this statement. The biggest animal in the world is one of the giant whales that lives in the ocean. Ask your family if they can think of something or someone who is bigger than even the giant whale. Place the basketball on the table. Explain that God is bigger than the largest animal. He is bigger than the ant, the tiger, the elephant, and the giant whale.

Try this exercise again, but this time make comparisons of people. For example, you might put the pebble on the table and say: Let's compare people. Pretend this pebble is a tiny baby. Who in our family is bigger than a tiny baby? Continue with this comparison among your own family members or friends. End the comparison with Mom or Dad identified with the volleyball. Finally, place the basketball on the table, make this statement: Let's pretend that God is the basketball. God is even bigger than Mommy/Daddy. He's bigger than the baby. He's bigger than all the rest. *Make sure to identify Mom or Dad with the volleyball and God with the basketball each time you do this activity.*

Try this exercise a third time, but this time compare strength. For example, you might start with this statement: Think about Julie—she's our baby. Is Julie very strong? Let's pretend that this pebble is Julie. Who is stronger than Julie? Continue the comparison of strength. Identify the volleyball with Mom and/or Dad and then end with this statement. Who is stronger than all of these? Who is stronger than any superhero or cartoon character? God is stronger than all of these. Let's pretend this basketball is God. See how much stronger God is than all the others.

Finally, do the same exercise as you compare wisdom. For example, you might begin with this statement: Let's pretend this pebble is a brand-new baby that has just come home from the hospital. Do you think this baby is smart or very wise? Has this baby learned to recognize colors or count to ten? Who do you think is smarter or wiser than this baby? Continue the comparison of wisdom. As you end the comparison, match Mom and/or Dad with the volleyball and God with the basketball. End with these statements. Who do you think is the smartest, wisest person in the world? God is smarter and wiser than all these people. He's smarter than the baby. He's wiser than the second-grader and the doctor. God is wiser than Mom or Dad. Let's pretend this basketball is God. See how much wiser He is than all the rest? God is the biggest, the strongest, and the smartest of all.

How Much Do You Need?

For the next activity use the same supplies as in the previous activity. Invite your family to go outside with you. Make a large circle on the driveway with chalk or set up boundaries in the yard. Everyone must stand behind the boundary lines. Place the pebble, marble, golf ball, baseball, volleyball, and basketball in the center of the circle or playing field. Explain that you are going to call out a situation in which we need help and then everyone will run to the middle of the circle and grab one of the balls. I will say a sentence that tells about a time when we need help. After you hear the sentence and I count to three, run to the middle of the circle and pick up the object that shows how much help you need. For example, I might say: We are home one night and a great big storm comes with lots of lightning and thunder. We are scared. You want someone with you who is strong. How much strength do you need? Do you need someone who has this much strength (hold up the golf ball)? Or do you need someone who has this much strength (hold up the basketball)? Everyone should want the volleyball or basketball because Mom/Dad and God are the strongest of all.

Explain that you will say one sentence, count to three, and everyone will run to the circle, grab the ball they want, and then run back behind the line. Try this game several times, each time asking the person who gets the basketball, "Why did you choose the basketball?" Encourage children to verbalize such thoughts as, "I needed God's help. He is the strongest of all." Here are a few ideas for helping statements:

- We are scared because someone almost crashes into our car. We need someone who is very strong to help us not be afraid. How much strength do you need?
- We have to move to a new town and don't know which house to buy. We are a little scared. We need someone who is very smart. How much do we need?
- We are scared because we get lost in a strange town and can't find our way back to the hotel. We need someone who is very wise or very smart. How much help do we need?

Conclude this activity by reviewing these ideas. God is strongest. He can help us with any problem. God is smartest. He always knows the best plans. God loves us most of all. We can always count on Him to care for us.

Scared or Safe?

For this activity invite your family back inside. Give everyone a paper plate and ask them to draw a face on both sides of the paper plate. On one side they are to draw a face that shows how they feel when they are safe. On the other side they are to draw a scared face. Tell your family that you would like for them to listen to the sentences you are about to say. Then every family member will show how they would feel in this situation. You will show either the safe face or the scared face that has been drawn on the paper plate. Adults will want to participate as well. You might even want to add your own facial expressions to go along with the paper plates. Kids enjoy watching adults "having fun." Here are some possible sentences:

- You come home from playing outside and everyone is in the kitchen getting ready for dinner.
- You come home from playing outside and no one is home to meet you.
- You answer the telephone and hear your grandmother's voice.
- You hear a strange noise when you are in bed one night.

- Your friends come over and break one of your mom's china plates.
- Your best friend comes over to your house and the two of you play your favorite game.

Each time the family shows the scared faces make this point: When we are scared, those feelings remind us that we need God and we need each other. When we are afraid, those feelings are there to help us remember that we need God's help. We need the help of others too.

Closing the Lesson

Close the lesson by playing Hot Potato. Ask your family to sit on the floor with legs stretched out in a V-shape or Indian style. Sit so that legs or feet are touching, forming a circle with no gaps. Place the paper plate used in the previous activity in front of each person—scared face up. Using the basketball and volleyball play Hot Potato with these variations. Pass the basketball from one person to the next. The basketball must be picked up and set on the plate of the person next to you. Do not roll the basketball. Move the basketball as fast as you can. Stop the ball a few times and ask the person holding the ball to think of a time when she has been scared. She might complete this sentence, "I felt scared one time when. . . ." Remind her that those feelings are there to remind us that we need God. The disciples were scared when they were in the boat. Their feelings were there to remind them that they needed Jesus' help. Remind each person to look at the basketball and remember the first activity. See how big the basketball is? Look how much strength, wisdom, and love God has. That's how much help God has for you.

Make the Hot Potato game a little more difficult with these variations. Pass the volleyball at the same time as the basketball, but in a different direction. Or introduce the volleyball into the game, but roll the volleyball instead of passing it. The volleyball can be rolled across the circle in any direction, while the basketball must only be passed from person to person.

As you implement one of these two variations, stop the game whenever a person is "caught" with both balls. Ask the person to tell about a time when he was scared. Then ask that person to look at the two balls he has in front of him. The volleyball represented Mom/Dad and the basketball represented God in the earlier game. Remind each person of the love, strength, and help he has available. You have both Mom and/or Dad to help you and you have God to help you. See how much love you have? See how much strength you have? See how much wisdom you have?

End the game by joining hands and saying a prayer. Ask each person to complete these sentences as their prayer.

- "When I'm scared I remember that I need God's help."
- "Thank You, God, for helping me and giving Mom/Dad/ brother/Stepmom to help me too."

Note for Single Parents: You may want to encourage your preschooler to think of the volleyball as representing both biological parents. This may free the child from feeling torn between the two different households as they play these games.

Note for Blended Families: You may want to encourage your preschooler to think of the volleyball as representing both sets of parents. This may free the child from feeling torn between the two different households as they play these games.

Optional Activity Your children will love this chance to review the Bible Drama. If your bathroom tile will accommodate this activity, put your kids in the bathtub and let them finger paint on the tiles. Test the tub first to make sure the paints won't leave a residue in the bathtub. The paints should come clean with a powdered bathroom cleanser. Use the following recipe to make the finger paint.

Dissolve one envelope of unflavored instant gelatin in 1/4 cup hot water and let it sit for ten minutes. Combine cornstarch, sugar, and cold water in a saucepan and stir until smooth. Cook over medium-high heat, stirring the cornstarch mixture occasionally until thickened. Reduce the heat and add the gelatin mixture plus 1/4 cup of liquid dishwashing soap. Stir together until smooth. Cool thoroughly. Divide the mixture into small bowls and add several drops of different food coloring to each (*Family Fun*, December 1994, p. 24).

Tell your kids to draw one scene of the Bible Drama with their finger paints. They might want to draw the disciples in the boat with the big waves and stormy water. Your child may want to draw the scene where Peter and Jesus are walking on the water. Let your preschooler tell you about the scene she drew. Discuss the characters in each scene, how they were feeling, and how important it was for them to remember that they needed God's help.

Great Fun for Grade Schoolers

Materials Needed: White construction paper (9″ x 6″), large construction paper or art paper, markers or colored pencils, Post-it Notes, slips of paper, volleyball, basketball, and ice cubes

Letting Your Child Know You Begin this lesson by thinking back to a time when you were in elementary school. What were you scared of? Did you have a tough time getting to sleep at night? Was there a bully at school that scared you? Did a movie or television show frighten you? Tell your child how God helped you through those times. Did He provide you with people in your life to comfort you, keep you safe, or give you a hug? Did you pray to Him and find a listening and attentive ear? Share the scared time briefly with your child and focus on how God helped you through. Emphasize your need for His help in these situations.

Getting to Know Your Child Invite your child to share about a time when he was scared. What were the circumstances? Encourage your child to verbalize these feelings and provide an accepting atmosphere for him to do so. Then assist him in thinking about how God helped him during that time. Did God bring parents or friends who helped him feel safe? Did he pray to God? How did He answer this prayer? Did God help by bringing friends or family to make the scared feelings go away? Tell your family that today's lesson is about a time when the disciples were really scared. They needed Jesus' help. Our story shows how important it is for us to remember that we need Jesus. The times when we are scared can be reminders of how much we need God's help.

Becoming Caringly Involved Read the Bible Drama out loud to your family or ask one of the children to read it for you. After you have read the Bible Drama together, gather around the kitchen table for the next activity.

FAN-tastic Story Starter

Invite your family to make their own pictures that will help them retell the Bible Drama. You may want to make one picture ahead of time to use as an example. Gather these art supplies: one piece of white construction paper (9" x 6") for each person, one piece of large construction paper for each person, markers or colored pencils, glue, and several sheets of Post-it Notes. (Crayons will not work for this project.)

Each person folds the 9" x 6" sheet of paper accordion style to create a fan. Pinch and twist one end of the fan. The fan will be used as a sail for the sailboat. Position the fan on the large construction paper and then draw a large sailboat around the fan. Glue or staple the fan into position. Instruct everyone to draw the disciples that were in the boat—all except Peter and Jesus. You may want to refer to Lesson 1 for a list of disciples' names. Draw the strong waves and make the picture look like the boat is in a terrible storm.

Next, give each person one Post-it Note that has been cut in half. Instruct everyone to draw a picture of Peter on one half and a picture of Jesus on the other. When these steps are complete give everyone a chance to retell the Bible Drama in their own words. The characters of Peter and Jesus can be moved around on the picture to illustrate the points of action in the story.

To encourage everyone to listen carefully, make this challenge: As you retell the story, try to add one detail that was not included by the persons before you.

When you have finished retelling the Bible Drama, ask your family to join you in this discussion.

- The disciples thought that they could sail the boat without any problems. Were they right or wrong? Please explain.
- What did the disciples think they saw out on the water? How do you think they felt?
- What happened to Peter? What did Peter forget to do? Who helped Peter?
- Do you think you would have gotten out of the boat like Peter? Why or why not?

Feeling Charades

Begin the activity section of this lesson with a game of Feeling Charades. Write the numbers from 1 to 10 on slips of paper. Divide the family members into two teams—boys against the girls is always fun. Have each person draw a number and then act out the situation from this numbered list below. Each person acts out his/her situation for his team only. The team that guesses the most feelings correctly wins the game. Give approximately a two-minute time limit for each person's turn. Props and sound effects can be added, but no words. Each team tries to guess the situation and tell what feeling is portrayed. Younger children may need help reading the feeling situations and may need to do small bits of the written situation at a time.

1. You're lying in bed one night and hear a strange noise. **You are feeling scared.** You get up and stub your toe on the bed. **You are feeling hurt.**
2. You're hitting your baseball outside in the backyard. You accidentally hit the ball through the window. **You're feeling worried.**
3. You ride your bicycle to the park one afternoon. You lock up your bike and go to play soccer. When you come back you find that your bike has been stolen. **You feel sad.**
4. You are watching a tennis match. Your favorite tennis player is on the court and makes a few good shots. **You are excited.** Your player misses several shots in a row and loses the game. **You're feeling disappointed.**
5. You're driving in a car. You stop at a stop light. As you turn the corner, another car pulls out in front of you and you have to slam on the brakes. **You're feeling scared.**
6. You come home and unlock the front door. You are expecting to find your family home. You go from room to room calling out their names. You want to show them your good report card. You wave it in the air. They aren't home and **you're alone. You're feeling disappointed.**
7. You are walking down the street bouncing a basketball. Someone comes up behind you and tries to take your ball. He pushes you and knocks you down. He takes your basketball. **You're feeling angry.**

8. You have a thermometer in your mouth in order to take your temperature. You take it out to look at it and you have a fever—104 degrees. You rub your forehead because you have a headache. You take two aspirin with a glass of water. You take your temperature a second time and it isn't any better. **You are worried.**

As you finish the charades, explain that all of the situations we just acted out were difficult. They were hard to deal with; they didn't make us feel good. There will be times when we feel sad, angry, scared, or disappointed but we can always count on Jesus to help us. The tough times should be our reminder that we need Jesus' help. We also need the help of other people. Peter forgot that he needed Jesus' help. The storms made him scared. The storm was his reminder that he needed Jesus.

Make this activity a little more personal. Ask each person to think of a time in the last few weeks when he or she felt scared, sad, or worried. Ask each family member to complete these sentences:

> I felt scared one time when . . .
> I was worried one time when . . .
> I felt sad one time when . . .

Remind your family that those feelings are there to remind us of our need for God's help. Explain that the next activity focuses on two of the ways God provides for us. He helps us Himself and He gives us other people to help us during difficult times. He wants us to know that we don't have to handle difficult situations alone.

Hot Potato

For the next activity you will need a volleyball and a basketball. Invite everyone to sit on the floor. Start the activity by explaining that the basketball is going to represent God and all the ways that He helps us. You might want to brainstorm with your family about all the ways that God helps us. Some responses might be:

- God helps us by listening to us when we pray.
- God helps us by answering our prayers.
- God helps us by giving us the Bible to guide us.

• God helps us by changing things that happen around us.

Second, explain that God also helps us by giving us people who can help us too. The volleyball is going to represent the ways that we help each other as a family.

Ask your family to sit on the floor with legs stretched out in a V-shape or sit Indian style. Sit so that legs or feet are touching, forming a circle with no gaps. Using the basketball and volleyball play Hot Potato with these variations. Pass the basketball from one person to the next. The basketball must be picked up and set directly in front of the person next to you. Do not roll the basketball. Move the basketball as fast as you can. Stop the ball a few times and ask the person holding the ball to think again about the time when they were scared/sad/worried. Then they complete this sentence, "My sad/scared feelings help me remember I need God's help."

Now make the game a little more challenging. Introduce the volleyball into the game, but roll the volleyball around the circle instead of passing it. The volleyball can be rolled across the circle in any direction, while the basketball must only be passed from person to person. Move both balls around the circle as fast as possible.

Stop the game whenever a person is "caught" with both balls. Ask the person to think again about the time when they were scared, sad, or worried. Ask that person to look at the two balls they have in front of them. The volleyball represents the help of family members and the basketball represents God's help. Instruct this family member to hold the basketball and volleyball in the air. As they hold up the basketball they say, "My feelings remind me that God is my helper." As they raise up the volleyball they say, "My feelings remind me that I need help from other people." Remind the family that the disciples were scared when they were in the boat. Their feelings were there to remind them that they needed Jesus' help. We will have tough times too—times when we feel worried, sad, or scared. These feelings are there to remind us that we need God's help and we need the help of other people.

Closing the Lesson
Close the lesson with the following activity. If you have a creek or a lake near your home, you might want to complete this closing

activity there. If not, the bathtub or kitchen sink will be fine. Give each person a piece of ice and a cup to hold it in. Explain that in today's lesson we learned about Peter and his experience of walking on the water. Peter didn't remember that he needed Jesus' help. Peter was scared by the storms and waves but he didn't let those feelings remind him of his need for Jesus.

If we let our feelings remind us that we need God's help, here's what will happen. Throw one piece of ice into the water. What happened to the ice? It floats—it doesn't sink. God promises to help us. He promises to never leave us; He promises to keep us afloat during tough times. He won't let us sink. We can always talk to Him and pray to Him. He's always there for us. He gives us other people to help us through tough times too.

Close the lesson by having everyone throw their piece of ice into the water and say these words, "If I ask for God's help He will be there to help me. He will help me through any problem."

Making It Real for Middle Schoolers

Materials Needed: One Ping-Pong ball, several sheets of paper and scissors, lipstick or chapstick, one handheld can opener and several cans of vegetables, one pair of shoes with laces, broom and dust pan, several potatoes and potato peeler, a beach ball, permanent marker, one necktie and one rock for each person, one piece of ice

Letting Your Child Know You Introduce this lesson by thinking back to your own middle school years. What was one of your successes during those years? Did you make a team or a club you hoped for? Did you receive any award that you were proud of? Did you meet a friend that you were particularly fond of? Did you make great achievements in some academic subject? Did you learn a new skill during these years? Did you take a risk in school, church, or social settings? Share one of these successes with your middle schooler.

Second, share one of your failures. Think again about these same years. What was one experience where you did not succeed? When was there a time when you didn't make the grade or the team? Recount this lack of success for your child. Let them know that you remember what it means and feels like to try something and fail. Be sure you make this distinction: Failing at something you try, doesn't mean that *you* are a failure. Don't forget to actually say the feeling words, "I was really disappointed" or "I was embarrassed," etc.

Getting to Know Your Child Invite the rest of your family to also share one of their successes and failures. Ask your middle schooler to think back over the last two or three years of school. What does she consider one of her main successes? What new skill has she learned? How has her hard work in school really paid off? Has she made a team or club? Has there been a particularly difficult friendship or family situation that she resolved? How has she grown as a person in the last couple of years?

Also ask your middle schooler to share one of her failures. This may be more difficult for some, since it is more painful to talk about failures. Some adolescents may share only about a test that they failed or a class they did poorly in. Try to gently encourage additional sharing. What did they try last year (other than academics), that didn't turn out like she had hoped? Provide an open and accepting environment for responses. When everyone who is willing has participated, explain that this lesson is about an experience of the disciples. One of the disciples experienced tremendous success and a significant failure within a matter of minutes. Jesus wanted Peter to learn an important lesson. God sometimes allows difficulties to come into our lives. These difficulties remind us that we need His help.

Becoming Caringly Involved Ask one of your family members to read the Bible Drama or read it out loud yourself. Discuss these questions together.

- Do you think you would have stepped out of the boat and tried to walk to Jesus? Why or why not?
- What were the different feelings that the disciples had during this Galilee experience? How did they feel when they first got into the boat? when the storm came? when they thought they saw a ghost? when they realized it was Jesus? when Peter walked on the water?
- Why didn't Jesus just calm the storm? He allowed the storm to continue raging. Do you sometimes wonder why God allows difficult times to happen in your life?

Ping-Pong Blow

Begin the activity section of this lesson by asking everyone to gather around a coffee table or the kitchen table. Divide the family into two teams and position the teams across from each other. Place a Ping-Pong ball in the middle of the table. Tell your family that the objective of this game is to blow the Ping-Pong ball off the table. You want to blow the Ping-Pong ball off the side of the opposing team. No hands or body-blocks are acceptable ways of preventing the ball from falling off your side of the table—only lung power! Play this game a few times, and when everyone has caught their breath, ask these questions. Were you able to prevent the ball from falling off your side of the table without the help of your teammates? Were you able to defend your side all alone? In this situation we needed other people's help. The disciples were very skilled fishermen. They thought they could handle the storm all on their own. What reminder did Jesus want to give them? Jesus wanted them to realize that their own skill, expertise, and strength wasn't enough. Jesus wanted the disciples to remember that they needed God's help. And sometimes God's help comes through other people!

Challenge Chain

To further develop this point, ask family members to participate in the following activity. Divide up into pairs. If there is an odd number in your family, one group of three will have to work together for this activity. Ask each pair to tape their hands together. Using masking tape, tape one person's right hand together with their partner's left hand. If you have a group of three, the middle person will have both of her hands taped. Make sure you and your partner are the last to be taped, so that you can distribute the rest of the materials. Tell each pair that they are to work together to perform the following tasks. The tasks have been ordered by level of difficulty. The least difficult tasks are first. Individuals can only use the hands that are not taped.

1. Fold a paper airplane.
2. Apply lipstick or chapstick to both partners' lips.
3. Cut out a circle from a piece of construction paper.
4. Open a can of vegetables with handheld can opener.

5. Untie and then retie a person's shoe.
6. Sweep the kitchen floor using a broom and dust pan.
7. Peel a potato or carrot.

After everyone has completed the tasks above, ask these questions. As the tasks got harder, what did you notice about your ability to complete the jobs alone? Emphasize the point that the more difficult the task, the more we relied on our partner. The harder the situation the more aware we were of our need for assistance. Explain that this is exactly how the Lord operates with us. He allows difficult situations into our lives. These situations point out our need for His assistance. When we're in the middle of a challenging situation we are most aware of the need for His help. The challenging situation helps us remember that sometimes God's help comes to us through others.

Toss Up

For this next activity you will need a medium- to large-sized ball. The ball will be thrown in the house so a beachball might work best. Write these sentences directly on the outside of the ball with a felt-tipped pen. "I was worried when. . . ." "I felt sad when. . . ." "The most difficult time this year has been. . . ." "I was disappointed when. . . ." "I felt angry when. . . ."

Invite your family to sit with you in the living room. Ask someone to toss the beachball to you. Look to see where your thumbs have touched the ball. Answer the questions that are closest to your thumbs. As you answer the questions, make sure to give vulnerable and sincere responses. Give brief statements about the difficult situations that produced these feelings. This will encourage your young person to do the same. Toss the beachball to another person and ask him to look where his thumbs have touched the ball. They are to answer those two questions. Continue tossing the ball to each family member until everyone has answered at least four questions.

Explain to your family that God allows difficult times in our lives to show us that we need His help and we need the help of others. The feelings we have just shared resulted from tough times in our own lives. God helps us in many ways. He helps us directly by hearing and answering our prayers and providing the Bible to guide us. God also helps us by giving us people in our lives that help us too.

Rocky and Rambo

Begin this last activity by giving everyone a small rock and a necktie. Ask your family to tie the neckties around their foreheads (like Rambo) and hold the rocks in their hands. Introduce this activity by saying: When difficult things happen in our lives, we sometimes decide to respond like Rocky or Rambo. Sylvester Stallone is famous for his tough guy, do-it-all-alone image. Brainstorm some of the tactics of these characters if your family is familiar with Stallone's movies. You might emphasize these points: As Rambo, Stallone single-handedly defeated whole armies of enemy soldiers. As Rocky, he defied the odds by beating many formidable opponents. In one movie he changed the hearts of thousands of Russian citizens with a single boxing match. These are just movies, however, in real life it doesn't quite work this way. But too often we try the same tactics as Rocky and Rambo. When times get tough, we try to handle it all alone.

With the neckties around your foreheads, brainstorm about some of your own Rambo or Rocky tactics. How do we try to handle situations without the help of others? How do we try to act like tough guys? If you need help getting this discussion started, try the following activity. Ask every family member to pick a number between 1 and 6. Go around to each family member and read the statement below that matches the number they've chosen. Each person must decide if that statement describes him or not. They must give reasons for their answers. Before any individual can take off his necktie he must first identify one way that he tries to handle life on his own. Once a person has admitted his "Rambo" tactic he may remove his necktie.

1. I don't talk to anyone when I'm upset. I keep it all inside.
2. I try to pretend everything is fine—even when I'm very upset.
3. I don't ever want anyone's advice or help with my problems.
4. I worry constantly about things that I have no control over.
5. When I've had a bad day, I go in my room and want everyone to stay out.

6. Rather than tell anyone that I'm upset, I'll try to stay busy so I don't have to think about it.

Explain that God did not design us to be able to handle life alone. We were created to need His help and to need other people. End this activity by identifying alternatives to the statements above. What can we do instead? How can I show my willingness to need others in my life?

Closing the Lesson

Close the lesson by asking everyone to bring their rock and gather around a body of water. If you have a lake or a creek near your home, you may want to do this activity there. If not, ask everyone to join you around the bathtub or kitchen sink. Reemphasize that God did not design us to handle life alone. He made us so that we would have a need for Him and for other people. Our feelings of sadness, fear, or worry are there to remind us of our need for help. It is OK to need help. In fact, we were designed to be that way.

Explain that Peter forgot that he needed Christ's help, just like we forget sometimes. Let me show you what happened to Peter. Take your rock and throw it into the water. Pause a moment and say: Peter forgot about his need for God's help and look what happened. The Bible tells us that he began to sink. When we forget that we've been created to need God's help and the help of others we'll sink too. If we try to be Rambo or Rocky, we're sunk. Ask family members to try it. Ask them to throw their rocks in the water one at a time. Pause briefly between each person.

Finally, take a piece of ice and hold it in your hand. Say these words: When we remember that we need God's help and the help of others, something different happens. When we remember that we can't handle life all alone and ask for help, watch what happens. Throw the ice into the water. Remind your family that God promises to keep us afloat. He promises to help us through any tough time. He has provided us with people who will be there for us too.

Invite everyone to join you in a short prayer. Invite your family to verbalize their prayers. Tell God that you know that you need His help and the help of others. You might want to tell Him that you are willing to drop the Rambo idea of doing-it-all-alone.

Thank God for His help. Thank Him for specific people that are in your life and are available for you.

High School Happenings

Materials Needed: One Ping-Pong ball, several sheets of paper and scissors, fingernail polish, one jacket with a zip-up front, one magazine and one rubber band, one bed sheet, one raw egg for every two people, several balloons, beachball, permanent marker, one necktie and one rock for every person and several ice cubes

Letting Your Child Know You Introduce this lesson by thinking back to your own high school years. What was one of your successes during those years? Did you make a team or a club you hoped for? Did you receive any award that you were proud of? Did you meet a friend that you were particularly fond of? Did you make great achievements in some academic subject? Did you learn a new skill during these years? Did you take a risk in school, church, or social settings? Share one of these successes with your teenager.

Second, share one of your failures. Think again about these same years. What was one experience where you did not succeed? When was there a time when you didn't make the grade or the team? Recount this lack of success for your child. Let them know that you remember what it means and feels like to try something and fail. Be sure to make this distinction: failing at something you try doesn't mean *you* are a failure. Don't forget to actually say the feeling words, "I was really disappointed" or "I was embarrassed," etc.

Getting to Know Your Child Invite the rest of your family to also share one of their successes and failures. Ask your teenager to think back over the last two or three years of school. What does she consider one of her main successes? What new skill has she learned? Has her hard work in school really paid off? Has she made a team or club? Has there been a particularly difficult friendship or family situation that she resolved? How has she grown as a person in the last couple of years?

Also ask your high schooler to share one of his failures. This may be more difficult for some, since it is more painful to talk about failures. Some adolescents may share only about a test that they failed or a class they did poorly in. Try to gently encourage additional sharing. What did they try last year (other than academics), that didn't turn out like they had hoped? Provide an open and accepting environment for responses. When everyone who is willing has participated, explain that this lesson is about an experience of the disciples. One of the disciples experienced a tremendous success and failure within a matter of minutes. Jesus wanted Peter to learn an important lesson. God allows difficulties in our lives sometimes. These difficulties serve to remind us that we need God's help.

Becoming Caringly Involved Ask one of your family members to read the Bible Drama or read it out loud yourself. Discuss these questions together.

- Do you think you would have stepped out of the boat and tried to walk to Jesus? Why or why not?
- What were the different feelings that the disciples had during this Galilee experience? How did they feel when they first got into the boat? when the storm came? when they thought they saw a ghost? when they realized it was Jesus? when Peter walked on the water?
- Why didn't Jesus just calm the storm? He allowed the storm to continue raging. Do you sometimes wonder why God allows difficult times to happen in your life?

Ping-Pong Blow

See Middle School section for explanation of this activity.

Challenge Chain

To further develop this point, ask family members to participate in the following activity.

Divide into pairs. If there is an odd number in your family, one group of three will have to work together for this activity. Ask each pair to tape their hands together. Using masking tape, tape one person's right hand together with their partner's left hand. If you have a group of three, the middle person will have both of their hands taped. Make sure you and your partner are the last to be taped, so that you can distribute the rest of the materials. Tell each pair that they are to work together to perform the following tasks. The tasks have been ordered by level of difficulty. The least difficult tasks are first. Individuals can only use the hands that are not taped.

1. Cut out a heart from a piece of construction paper.
2. Apply fingernail polish to one hand of each partner.
3. Zip up the zipper on a jacket or winter coat.
4. Roll up a magazine and put a rubber band around it.
5. Fold a bed sheet (neatly).
6. Crack an egg and separate the yolk from the white.
7. Blow up a balloon and tie it.

After everyone has completed the tasks above, ask these questions. As the tasks got harder, what did you notice about your ability to complete the jobs alone? Emphasize the point that the more difficult the task, the more we relied on our partner. The harder the situation the more aware we were of our need for assistance. Explain that this is exactly how the Lord operates with us. He allows difficult situations into our lives. These situations point out our need for His assistance. When we're in the middle of a challenging situation we are most aware of the need for His help. The challenging situation helps us remember that sometimes God's help comes to us through others.

Toss Up
See Middle School section for explanation of this activity.

Rocky and Rambo
Begin this last activity by giving everyone a rock and a necktie. Ask your family to tie the neckties around their forehead (like Rambo) and hold the rock in their hand. Introduce this activity by saying: When difficult things happen in our lives, we sometimes decide to respond like Rocky or Rambo. Sylvester Stallone is famous for his tough guy, do-it-all-alone image. Brainstorm some of the tactics of these characters if your family is familiar with Stallone's movies. You might emphasize these points: As Rambo, Stallone single-handedly defeated whole armies of enemy soldiers. As Rocky, he defied the odds by beating many formidable opponents. In one

movie he changed the hearts of thousands of Russian citizens with a single boxing match. These are just movies, however, in real life it doesn't quite work that way. But too often we try the same tactics as Rocky and Rambo. When times get tough, we try to handle it all alone.

With the neckties around your forehead and the rocks still in your hands, brainstorm about some of your own Rambo or Rocky tactics. How do we try to handle situations without any help from others? How do we try to act like tough guys? Some of your responses might sound like:

- I don't talk to anyone when I'm upset. I keep it all inside.
- I try to pretend everything is fine—even when I'm very upset.
- I don't ever want anyone's advice or help with my problems.
- I worry constantly about things that I have no control over.
- When I've had a bad day, I go in my room and want everyone to stay out.
- Rather than tell anyone that I'm upset, I'll try to stay busy so I don't have to think about it.

After everyone has given their response, talk about what you might do instead of the responses above. How can you show your willingness to need the help of others? When each person has identified one alternative to their "Rambo" response, they may take off their neckties. When each necktie comes off, give these instructions: Loosen and untie any knots that are in the necktie. Hold one end of the necktie and ask a person across the circle to hold the opposite end. Make sure your family is sitting in a small circle. Explain that God did not design us to be able to handle life alone. We were created to need His help and to need other people.

By the time you finish, you should have several neckties crossing the circle. Make these closing comments: As you can see by looking at the neckties, we have a good support system here. We were each willing to say, I can't handle life completely alone, I need other people. When that happens, we create a network of support. God is the hub of this circle (point to the middle) and each tie represents our willingness to give and to be given to.

Closing the Lesson

Close the lesson by asking everyone to bring their rock and gather around some body of water. If you have a lake or a creek near your home, you may want to do this activity there. If not, ask everyone to join you around the bathtub or kitchen sink. Reemphasize that God did not design us to handle life alone. He made us so that we would have a need for Him and for other people. Our feelings of sadness, fear, or worry are there to remind us of our need for help. It is OK to need help. In fact, we were designed to be that way.

Explain that Peter forgot that he needed Christ's help, just like we forget sometimes. Let me show you what happened to Peter. Take your rock and throw it into the water. Pause a moment, and say: Peter forgot about his need for God's help and look what happened. The Bible tells us that he began to sink. When we forget that we've been created to need God's help and the help of others we'll sink too. If we try to be Rambo or Rocky, we're sunk. Ask each family member to try it. Ask them to throw their rocks in the water one at a time. Pause briefly between each person.

Finally, take a piece of ice and hold it in your hand. Say these words: When we remember that we need God's help and the help of others, something different happens. When we remember that we can't handle life all alone and ask for help, watch what happens. Throw the ice into the water. Remind your family that God promises to keep us afloat. He promises to help us through any tough time. He has provided us with people who will be there for us too.

Invite everyone to join you in a short prayer. Invite your family to verbalize their prayers. Tell God that you know that you need His help and the help of others. You might want to tell Him that you are willing to drop the Rambo ideas of doing-it-all-alone. Thank God for His help. Thank Him for specific people that are in your life and are available for you.

Lesson 6

Humility begins at the point of need

Key Scripture Passage *And when He had come back to Capernaum several days afterward, it was heard that He was at home. And many were gathered together, so that there was no longer room, even near the door; and He was speaking the word to them. And they came, bringing to Him a paralytic, carried by four men. And being unable to get to Him on account of the crowd, they removed the roof above Him; and when they had dug an opening, they let down the pallet on which the paralytic was lying. And Jesus seeing their faith said to the paralytic, "My son, your sins are forgiven."*

But there were some of the scribes sitting there and reasoning in their hearts, "Why does this man speak that way? He is blaspheming; who can forgive sins but God alone?" And immediately Jesus, perceiving in His spirit that they were reasoning that way within themselves, said to them, "Why are you reasoning about these things in your hearts?

Which is easier, to say to the paralytic, 'Your sins are forgiven'; or to say, 'Arise, and take up your pallet and walk'? But in order that you may know that the Son of Man has authority on earth to forgive sins"—He said to the paralytic, "I say to you, rise, take up your pallet and go home."—Mark 2:1-11

Bible Drama

Charging into the home of his lifelong friend, Joel barely slowed his pace enough to talk. "Quick, Samuel. Jesse needs us!" The panic in Joel's voice was enough for Samuel to act quickly. No need to ask what the problem was. Joel's concern was enough to act on.

Jesse was their lifelong friend. When they were young boys, the three had disobeyed their parents and climbed a big hill outside of their village. Tragically, Jesse had fallen onto the rocks below. He never walked again. The pain and guilt that the other boys felt welded their bond of friendship throughout their lives. When Jesse needed something, anything, he knew that he could count on Samuel and Joel. But what could cause such a panic on this hot afternoon in the sleepy town of Capernaum?

Now twenty years later, the two men rounded the corner and saw their pitiful looking friend. Each day, his family would place him on the busiest street in the village to beg for money from those who passed by. His little clay dish collected the few coins that the wealthy would toss in. He looked so wretched lying there on the street. The pang of guilt and sorrow struck the two men each time they saw their friend.

"Please help a poor cripple, sir! Please have mercy on a wretched sinner! Alms, alms for the poor!" Jesse's voice could barely be heard above the noise of the marketplace. And people were so used to seeing him, hardly anyone bothered to throw coins in his dish any longer. He often wished he could just die and be done with life. Surely God must hate him, he thought. Why else would God leave him to suffer so?

The comfort of his dear friends' voices caused a smile to break out on his face. For the first time, Joel told the whole story behind his excitement. "Jesse! We have to take you to see a man who heals people! I saw Him with my very own eyes. Jesus heals the blind and the lame. I know if we can just get close to Him He will heal you too!"

With that, the two friends picked up the stretcher and ran to the house where Jesus was staying. But the house was so crowded! There was no getting close to the doorway to see Jesus. Samuel had an idea. "Quick! Get up on the roof!" By now, two other friends were helping lift the crippled man onto the roof of the house. Samuel was up on top, pulling at the big clay tiles and digging through the hard mud and straw that lay beneath the heavy shingle.

Down below, no one knew what the commotion was all about. Suddenly the bright sunlight broke through, along with a shower of dirt and straw. And it fell right on top of Jesus! Looking up, the Lord could see the four men lowering Jesse right through the roof!

Jesus was very impressed! Never before had He seen this kind of love—a love that would do anything to help a friend. It didn't matter what others thought, Samuel and Joel knew that their friend needed to be healed by Jesus and they would do anything to help.

As Jesse lay on the floor, Jesus looked first at him and then at the four friends looking down from the gaping hole in the roof. He knew that the men had served their friend well. They had humbled themselves in front of the whole village in order to get help from Jesus.

"Son," said Jesus, "your sins are forgiven." Jesse felt a warmth go throughout his body. A feeling that he had not felt since the fall. Then Jesus looked about the room at the shocked look of the people and bent down close to the crippled man. "Rise and walk! Take up your bed and go home!" And Jesse did!

There was rejoicing in Jesse's home that night. All of his friends came to see the great work of God. But the greatest work was done in the hearts of Jesse and his friends. They learned that God will do great things for those of a humble heart.

Goal of Lesson 6: Families will learn that we are all special to God, but we are not perfect. We all need God's help.

Intimacy Principle: We were created with a need for intimacy.

Disclosure Goal: Parents will model humility for their children by sharing an apology. Parents will tell the specific wrong, model an appropriate confession, and then verbalize their need for Jesus' help.

Projects with Preschoolers

Materials Needed: Cookie dough, gingerbread or people-shaped cookie cutter, white icing, assorted candy for decorating, coconut, food coloring (different colors of coconut can be used for hair; clothing and facial features can be created with red hots, licorice, jelly beans, etc.), one sheet of construction paper for every family member

Parents will also need to make one puppet for this lesson. We give instructions for a sock puppet, but feel free to choose others. For the sock puppet you will need: one old sock, construction paper, yarn, glue, and scissors. (Optional materials include buttons, felt, pompoms or wiggly eyes from the craft store.) You will also want to make a home for this puppet. Some ideas include an empty oatmeal box, strawberry basket, coffee can, etc.

Letting Your Child Know You Introduce this lesson by sharing an apology with your child. Prior to this lesson, spend some time reflecting on your relationship with each child. Has there been any recent or past issues where you have wronged your child and didn't apologize? Have there been promises unkept? unkind words said in anger? disrespect? impatience? a critical spirit? etc. Ask the Lord to show you any areas that may need confession. Then start the lesson by completing these sentences as you talk to each family member.

1. God has shown me that I was wrong when _____.
(*I lost my temper with you yesterday. My words were ugly.*) or (*I didn't keep my promise about going to McDonald's.*)

2. I know that must have made you feel _____ inside.
(*sad, angry, hurt, scared, etc.*)

3. Will you forgive me?

4. I am asking God to help me with _____.
(*my time. I want Him to help me keep my promises.*) or (*my words. I want Him to help me talk kindly to you.*)

Share this type of confession with each member of your family. Be careful not to rationalize or blame. For example, words such as, *I wouldn't have done that if* . . . would not be appropriate.

If you already practice confession and forgiveness in your family and all hurts have been talked through, then share one of your current prayers. What things are you still praying for God to help you with? Tell your children what areas Jesus is working on. How do you want Him to change you? In what areas do you still need God's help?

Getting to Know Your Child Ask your children to share about a time when they had to apologize. What were the circumstances? How did they feel? How do they think the other person was feeling? Help your child determine one area in which she needs Jesus' help. Does she need God's help in being a good friend? sharing television privileges? telling the truth? etc. Explain that today's lesson is about a man and his friends who weren't embarrassed to show that they needed Jesus' help. Jesus can help with any need we have, but we have to be willing to tell Him that we need help. We have to show humility—that means we remember that we are special, but that we aren't perfect. We all need Jesus.

Becoming Caringly Involved Read the Bible Drama to your family or ask an older child to read for you. Invite everyone to participate in this discussion.

- Do you have a special friend like the men in the story—a friend who you would do almost anything for? Tell the family about that friend and why he's so special.
- How did Jesse feel when he had to lie beside the road and beg for money? How did he feel when he saw his friends, Joel and Samuel? How did he feel when Jesus healed him?
- Jesus wants us to be humble. *Humble* means that we remember that we are special to God but we aren't perfect. We need His help. How did the men in the story show that they needed Jesus' help?

Special but Not Perfect

Begin this lesson's activities by making cookies together. Using ready-made or homemade cookie dough to cut out gingerbread-shaped cookies, cut out at least one cookie for each family member. Everyone will need their own cookie to decorate later. As the cookies are baking and cooling, discuss how each family member is special or unique. Your responses might sound like these: *Jessica is spe-*

cial because she shares with others so easily. Matthew is special because he is helpful. Jonathan is special because he is good at track and field. Stephanie is special because she is a good reader. Focus on personality traits, accomplishments, and character. Be sure to focus on the uniqueness of each individual and that God made us all different, but special.

When the cookies have cooled you will want to put icing on each cookie. A parent may want to do this for the whole family or you may want to let each person ice a cookie himself. Finish decorating the cookies using the coconut and candy. Tell your family to decorate their cookies to look as much like themselves as possible. As the family decorates each part of their cookies, they tell how God made them special. Ask your family to continue talking about how God has made each of us different. For example, as you decorate the hands of your cookie you may say: *God made my hands so that I can play baseball* or *God made my hands so that I can work in the garden.* Continue this process of decorating and sharing until the cookies are complete. Don't eat the cookies yet! It will be tough, but try to save them for the closing activity.

Now ask everyone to look at his finished cookie. Ask them if their cookies look exactly like them. Does the cookie look perfectly like the owner? Talk about the differences between the cookies and the owners. What is the same? What is different? Finally, explain that Jesus made us special just like the cookies. He made us so that we would all be different. He wants us to know that there is no one in the world exactly like us. We are each one of a kind. But Jesus also wants us to know that we are not perfect. There are some things about us that He wants to change and make better. Jesus made us special, but we also need His help because we are not perfect. When we remember these important things, Jesus calls us humble.

Willie the Worm

Prior to this lesson you will need to create a puppet that is named "Willie." You can make Willie by using an old sock, construction paper, yarn, and some glue. Cut an oval shape out of construction paper a little smaller than the size of your hand—this will be the puppet's mouth. Put the sock on your hand so your fingers are in the toe part of the sock and your thumb is in the heel. Fold the puppet's mouth in half. Glue it to the sock, between your thumb and fingers. Glue on two small construction-paper circles for eyes and nose. You can also use old buttons, pompoms, or wiggly eyes from the craft store. Finally, glue on yarn for hair. Willie also needs a home, so find an empty oatmeal box, strawberry basket, or coffee can (be careful of the edges). Cut out the bottom of one of these so that your arm will fit through. Put the puppet on your hand and then slip your hand through the hole in one of the empty containers. Now Willie can peek out of his home.

Children will often interact with a puppet in ways they might not with an adult, so be sure to make Willie "come alive." Practice making Willie show different faces or feelings. Create a different voice that goes along with Willie's words so your children can distinguish when you are talking or when Willie is talking. Don't worry about trying to become a ventriloquist—just make the character of Willie distinguishable from yourself.

Tell your children that a special guest is coming over today and he should be arriving soon. This guest was a friend of Jesus' a long time ago. He's been around a very long time and has agreed to come over and visit with us. Go to the door to check and see if he's arrived, step outside and pick up the puppet that you have already prepared. Arrange the puppet and his house on your hand and return to your family. Introduce Willie to the family and let Willie explain why he's been invited. For example:

Parent: Hi, everyone! I'd like for you to meet my friend, Willie. He's kind of shy (Willie peeks out of his house) so let's tell him that we are glad he's here. Maybe we can convince him to come out and talk with us.

Willie: Oh, hi. My name is Willie. Your mom told me that your family has been talking about Jesus and how much we all need His help. Well, I know that I've needed His help plenty of times. I'm here to tell you about the times when I've needed Jesus.

Have Willie recount times that he's needed Jesus. Make Willie's situations similar to (but not exactly like) tough times or difficulties that your own children have experienced. Some of the situations Willie might tell about are:

I needed Jesus when I felt sad because my dog died.

I needed Jesus when I felt scared and needed someone to help me feel safe.

I needed Jesus when I had a hard time sharing with my brother.

I needed Jesus when I felt embarrassed at school.

I needed Jesus when someone hurt my feelings.

I needed Jesus when I didn't feel like being nice to my sister.

As Willie interacts with your children, make sure he asks your children if they have ever needed Jesus' help too. Invite your children to tell Willie about a time or situation that was hard for them. Encourage your children to verbalize their need for Jesus.

Close the time with Willie by having Willie remind the children about a song they probably know—"Jesus Loves Me." Remind them of the words to this song that say, *we are weak but He is strong*. Willie explains that this is what it means to be humble—to remember that we are weak but He is strong and that Jesus loves us. Willie sings the song, "Jesus Loves Me" with the family and then says good-bye.

Helper Tag

For the final activity, play the game Helper Tag. Each person except the person designated as "IT" will need one sheet of rolled up construction paper. This game will need to be played outside. Designate one person to be "IT." IT chases all the other family members around the yard; when a person is tagged she must freeze in that spot. That person stays frozen unless she is helped by another family member. In order to become unfrozen, you must kneel on the ground and say, "I need a helper." If another family member hears you, runs to you, and then taps you on the head with their rolled up construction paper, then you may get up and continue to play. IT tries to tag all the other players. The last person frozen or the person that is tagged twice becomes IT during the next game.

Paper Airplane Prayers

Before you go inside ask everyone to sit down in a circle. Pass out one crayon and one sheet of construction paper to each person. Review some of the ways we need Jesus' help. Elicit individual responses such as, *I need God's help when I get scared at night*. Then ask everyone to write this need or draw a picture on their construction paper that represents this need. After the sentences or pictures are completed, fold all construction papers into paper airplanes. Explain that just like the men in the Bible Drama, we are going to show the world that we are not embarrassed to admit that we need Jesus' help. We know that Jesus cares about us so much that He will always help us. Instruct family members to try to fly their airplanes as high and as far as possible, but each time they throw their planes, they must say *I need God's help. Thank You, God, for loving me and helping me.*

Closing the Lesson

At the end of the game ask everyone to return inside. Pass out the cookies and as you eat them make these comments: During our game of tag, we could get up and continue playing the game if we said certain words. What were those words? But we couldn't get up until someone did something for us. What did they have to do? Jesus wants to hear those certain words from us too. He wants us to be willing to say, "God, I need a helper." He promises to help us and to make us like Him. Jesus loves us and cares for us so much. We are all special to Jesus. Jesus will do great things for people who have a humble heart.

Great Fun for Grade Schoolers

Materials Needed: Ink pad, construction paper, jumbo craft sticks, one set of shoestrings or thick yarn for each person, glue, and markers

Letting Your Child Know You Introduce this lesson by sharing an apology with your child. Prior to this lesson, spend some time reflecting on your relationship with each child. Has there been any recent or past issues where you have wronged your child and didn't apologize? Have there been promises unkept? unkind words said in anger? disrespect? impatience? a critical spirit? etc. Ask the Lord to show you any areas that may need confession. Then start the lesson by completing these sentences as you talk to each family member.

1. God has shown me that I was wrong when _____.
(I lost my temper with you yesterday. My words were ugly.) or *(I didn't keep my promise about going to the park.)*

2. I know that must have made you feel _____ inside.
(sad, angry, hurt, scared, etc.)

3. Will you forgive me?

4. I am asking God to help me with _____.
(my time. I want Him to help me keep my promises.) or *(my words. I want Him to help me talk kindly to you.)*

Share this type of confession with each member of your family. Be careful not to rationalize or blame. For example, words such as, *I wouldn't have done that if* . . . would not be appropriate.

If you already practice confession and forgiveness in your family and all hurts have been talked through, then share one of your current prayers. What things are you still praying for God to help you with? Tell your children what Jesus still wants to change in you. In what areas do you still need God's help?

Getting to Know Your Child Ask your children to share about a time when they had to apologize. What were the circumstances? How did they feel? How do they think the other person was feeling? Help your child determine one area in which he needs Jesus' help. Does he need God's help in being a good friend? sharing television privileges? telling the truth? Explain that today's lesson is about a man and his friends who weren't embarrassed to show that they needed Jesus' help. Jesus can help with any need we have, but we have to be willing to tell Him that we need help. We have to show humility—that means we remember that we are special, but that we aren't perfect.

Becoming Caringly Involved Read the Bible Drama together, then discuss your answers to the following questions:
- The men in the story were willing to do almost anything for their friend. Who is your special friend? Please explain why this person is important to you.

- Pretend that you are one of Jesse's friends and you want him to see Jesus. If you saw the huge crowd surrounding the house, what would you have done? Please explain.
- If you could ask Jesus to help you with anything in the world, what would that be?

You're Thumb-body!

Begin the activity section of this lesson by completing the following art activity. Give every person two sheets of white construction paper. Make sure everyone has access to an ink pad. Ask family members to practice making their fingerprints on only one of the sheets of paper. Try to make the prints as clear as possible. As you practice, notice the differences and similarities between fingerprints. Notice that no one has exactly the same prints as you. God has created you like no one else. You are special. You are unique.

Once you have perfected the technique of making clear fingerprints, try making these prints into self-portraits. With a pen add a head, arms, legs, and facial features. Try combining different sizes of prints to create animals or objects. Experiment with the shape and position of prints, then add details with a pen.

Finally, on the second sheet of construction paper ask everyone to write this title: I'm Thumb-body Special! Discuss the things that make each person special. What do they do well? What are each person's strengths? What positive character traits can be attributed to each person? Make certain that everyone has at least five strengths identified. As you identify these strengths, each person makes a fingerprint picture to represent this strength. (Parents may want to refer to the Appendix for a list of Fifty Character Qualities.)

Before you start the next activity, explain to your family that God wants us to remember that He has made us all very different. We are special to Him and He has given us many talents. But God also wants us to remember that we need Him. We need His help. We can't do everything by ourselves. We are going to play a game that shows us the kind of attitude that God wants to see in us.

Helper Tag

See Preschool section for explanation of activity.

After you've played the game Helper Tag review these points: In the game we just played, what did we have to do before we could become unfrozen and continue playing the game? We had to announce that we needed a helper and wait for one of our family members to help us. God wants us to have this same attitude with Him. He wants us to remember that we need a Helper; we need Him to help us. We need to be willing to say to God, "I need Your help" and then wait for Him to help us. In the Bible Drama we learned about a man who needed Jesus' help. He and his friends weren't embarrassed or too proud to say that they needed Jesus' help. In fact, they were so sure that Jesus could help Jesse that they crawled up on the roof and lowered him through the ceiling of the house. We're going to make something to remind us of how we need Jesus' help too. In Jesus' day the men probably lowered their friend through the roof with ropes or long pieces of cloth. If we were going to lower someone through our roof today, we might use a rope or a ladder. We're going to make our own ladders that will remind us of our need for Jesus.

Ladder of Needs

Gather the materials for this activity: jumbo craft sticks, one set of shoestrings or thick yarn for each person, glue, and dark-colored markers. As you pass out the craft sticks, ask everyone to think about times when they need Jesus' help. The man in the story needed Jesus to heal him. Most of us don't have a serious illness but we still have times when we need Jesus to help us. Model for your children statements that reflect your need for Jesus. For example:

> I need Jesus' help with my temper; I want Him to help me be more patient.
> I need Jesus to help me when I'm away on business trips; sometimes I get lonely.

Assist your children in thinking of times when they need Jesus to help them. When they have decided on an idea, they write one word or phrase of that idea onto a craft stick. Try to come up with at least four or five different ideas for each person. Make sure all the ideas have been written on the craft sticks, but save one craft stick for the top of the ladder. The top craft stick should say, "I Need Jesus." Now assemble the ladder. Place the shoelaces in two vertical lines on the table. Arrange the craft sticks in the order that you want them to be glued. The "I Need Jesus" craft stick should be first, approximately 2½ inches from the top of the shoestrings. Glue the craft sticks to the yarn or shoestrings. Let them dry overnight. When they have dried you can tie the top ends of the shoestrings together and the ladders are ready to hang. Hang them on the refrigerator or let everyone hang them in their own rooms.

Closing the Lesson

As you close the lesson, go back over the needs that have been written on the craft sticks. Pray together as a family. Ask for God's help in each area that is listed. Tell God that you want to be humble—you want to remember that you are special but that you need His help.

Humble or Not Optional Activity

Explain to your family that this activity shows us more about what it means to be humble. Jesus wants us to have a heart that is humble. Humble means that we remember that God thinks we're special but not more special than anyone else. Humble means we remember that we are not perfect. Humble means we remember that we need Jesus to help us and change us.

For this activity, designate one corner of the room as the "Humble Corner" and another corner of the room as the "Not Corner." Tell your family that you are going to read some words out loud; they are to listen to the words carefully. If they think the words sound like someone who is humble, they run to the "Humble Corner." If they think the words sound like someone who is not humble, they run to the "Not Corner." Read the sentences aloud once before you begin the game. Make sure you add inflection to your voice as you read. Say the humble words with sensitivity and warmth. Say the proud words with a haughty attitude. As a group, identify the statements as humble or not humble before you begin the game. Use the movement to each corner as review. Players always start from the center of the room before the next sentence is read. Read the following statements:

- I know I'm good at soccer, but I always need to listen to the coach.
- I don't need to say "I'm sorry" to her; she's no good anyway.
- I know God loves me, and He loves my brother/sister too.
- I don't need any help from Jesus; I'm fine just the way I am!
- When I do things wrong, I tell God that I am sorry.

Close this activity by reading each statement again. Talk about why a statement does or does not sound like someone who is humble.

Making It Real for Middle Schoolers

Materials Needed: One old T-shirt for each person, markers or fabric paint, marshmallows, chocolate sauce, one package of uncooked spaghetti, one package of gumdrops (varied sizes)

Letting Your Child Know You Introduce this lesson by sharing an apology with your child. Prior to this lesson, spend some time reflecting on your relationship with each child. Has there been any recent or past issues where you have wronged your child and didn't apologize? Have there been promises unkept? unkind words said in anger? disrespect? impatience? a critical spirit? etc. Ask the Lord to show you any areas that may need confession. Then start the lesson by completing these sentences as you talk to each family member.

1. God has shown me that I was wrong when _____.
(I spoke with you so harshly. My words were critical.) or *(I didn't respect your privacy on the phone.)*

2. I know that must have made you feel _____ inside.
(sad, angry, hurt, scared, etc.)

3. Will you forgive me?

4. I am asking God to help me with _____.
(knowing how to show you respect and consideration.) or *(my words. I want Him to help me talk kindly to you.)*

Share this type of confession with each member of your family. Be careful not to rationalize or blame. For example, words such as, *I wouldn't have done that if . . .* would not be appropriate.

If you already practice confession and forgiveness in your family and all hurts have been talked through, then share one of your current prayers. What things are you still praying for God to help you with? Tell your children what Jesus still wants to change in you. In what areas do you still need God's help?

Getting to Know Your Child Ask your teenager to recount a time when he had to apologize to a friend. What were the circumstances? What made it difficult to apologize? How did the other person respond? What does forgiveness mean to him?

Explain that this lesson teaches some important principles about humility. Humility begins when people acknowledge their limitations. The Bible Drama for this lesson tells about a man and his friends who weren't ashamed to admit their needs. They showed great humility but great boldness as well. Invite your family to listen to the story and pay close attention to how the men could be seen as humble and bold at the same time.

Becoming Caringly Involved Read the Bible Drama with your family. As you finish reading discuss the answers to these questions:

- The friends in the story were willing to do almost anything for Jesse. Who is the special friend in your life? Explain why he means so much to you.
- How might these men be labeled "humble" and "bold" at the same time?
- Would most of your friends see humility as a positive trait? Why or why not?

Inside and Out

Ask every family member to find an old T-shirt or sweatshirt for this activity. (It must be an item of clothing that they will not mind writing on. The more holes or stains the better.) Gather plenty of markers or fabric paint and then find room to create. Ask everyone to create a T-shirt that tells about their strengths, both inside and outside. On the outside of the T-shirt encourage family members to write words or draw symbols that show their outside strengths—things they do well, accomplishments, or physical characteristics that they like about themselves. When that step is completed, invite everyone to turn their T-shirts inside out and write words or draw symbols that reflect their inner strengths. On the inside of the T-shirt write personality traits that are positive—character qualities that make you unique and statements that tell about the "you" that maybe nobody gets to see. (See Appendix for a list of Fifty Character Qualities.) Encourage your teenager to write or draw as many strengths as possible. As you're working alongside one another, it may be important to help your teenager think of additional things that make her special. You will also want to let her know that it is all right to write seemingly opposite strengths such as "quiet" and "loud" or "laid back" and "intense." Sometimes we exhibit different characteristics depending on the circumstance.

As you complete your T-shirts, invite everyone to share what they've drawn. Make this a time of affirming one another's strengths. Ask everyone to take a good look at their T-shirts again. Are they without flaws? Is there one T-shirt that is perfect? Some may have holes or stains, others may be faded or worn. Other T-shirts may be missing sleeves or pockets. All of the shirts have their imperfections. Emphasize this point. God created each of us with very unique strengths and talents, but He also created us human. Since we are human we have limitations, imperfections, or needs. God wants to develop in us a humble heart. Being humble means: I learn the balance between knowing I'm special to God and at the same time knowing that I have areas that need God's help.

This Shirt Is Like Me

Continue to use the shirt as a discussion tool. Ask your family to think about areas in their lives that need God's help. Think of your weak points or areas of weakness. Talk about qualities of the shirt that describe your limitations. Complete the sentence, *This shirt is like me because . . .*

- it looks tired and worn out. Sometimes I don't have a stick-to-it quality. I give up before the job is finished.
- it is missing a button. I'm missing flexibility. I don't handle it well if things don't go as I planned.

- it has a hole in it—a blowout. I explode if I'm having a bad day.
- it has a stain on it—I dropped some ketchup on it. I sometimes "drop the ball" when it comes to my homework.

Make this a lighthearted but sincere discussion. Guard against the tendency to point out weaknesses in others. Let each person take responsibility for him/herself.

Explain to your family that God wants us to know that He loves us very much. He created us uniquely different from anyone else. God gave us strengths as well as limitations. He is always ready to help with these limitations. Because God cares for us, He is available to help us with our weaknesses. All we have to do is ask.

Before you begin the next activity, make this important proposition to your teenagers. Explain that they are about to participate in a very important contest of wits. You will give a short explanation and description of what it means to be proud and what it means to be humble. The more carefully they listen, the more effective they will be in the contest.

Pride Goes before the Fall

This next activity will test the sportsmanship of parents, but we hope the lessons will be worth the mess! Explain to your family that you are about to give an explanation of what the Bible says about people who are proud and those who are humble. At the end of the explanation each person will be tested. The test will consist of five questions or statements. They are to identify whether the statement matches someone who is proud or someone who is humble. For each correct answer, they will be able to illustrate this principle, "Pride goes before a fall."

A parent will lay on the floor that has been covered with plenty of newspapers. The teenager is given five statements or questions that he/she must identify as humble or proud. If the teenager answers correctly, he can dip one marshmallow into a bowl of chocolate syrup and try to drop it into the parent's mouth. Only five marshmallows can be dropped by each person.

Here's the explanation: The Bible tells us in Proverbs that pride comes before the fall. In other words, people who are arrogant are destined for trouble (Prov. 16:18). Therefore, pride is the opposite of humility. God also tells us that He turns His back on the proud but gives grace or favor to those that are humble (James 4:6).

A person who is proud:
- tries to pretend that he doesn't need anybody.
- doesn't ever need to apologize because she is more important than the person she offended.
- doesn't listen to others' advice, opinion, or input.
- tries to live his life without Jesus.
- thinks her own strengths and abilities will enable her to handle anything that comes along—she never needs help from anyone.
- thinks that his ideas, preferences must always come first.

A humble person:
- realizes that she has strengths but that she can't do everything alone.
- knows that he must apologize if he offends someone—their feelings are just as important as his.
- is willing to hear another person's advice or point of view.
- knows that she needs Jesus in her life.
- knows that God has given him many strengths but that he needs other people too.
- shares her ideas and preferences but considers others' ideas and preferences just as valuable.

Before you start the quiz, you might want to review these statements. Ask your family to think of examples that might illustrate each one. Discuss them thoroughly, so that everyone has a clear understanding of the concepts. When you think everyone is ready, start the quiz. We've provided some quiz questions, but feel free to add your own.

Pride Goes before the Fall
Pop Quiz

Tell whether this sounds like someone who is proud or someone who is humble.

1. I don't have to listen to the coach; he's got nothing to say that I don't already know. (proud)
2. I don't have to cope with the stress of my best friend moving all by myself. I can talk with somebody. (humble)
3. God and I don't have much to talk about. I can pretty much handle things on my own. (proud)
4. I'll apologize whenever they apologize to me first. (proud)
5. I want to talk to my school counselor or youth pastor about this decision. I'm pretty confused. (humble)
6. I need to tell God that I'm sorry for some things and I've got to ask for His forgiveness. (humble)
7. I'm not going to go for tutoring after school. That teacher's stupid! I hate her class. (proud)
8. I better ask my sister if she's going to need the car before I finalize my plans. (humble)
9. I don't want anyone to come to my game this weekend. I don't care if they come or not. (proud)
10. It doesn't matter how I talk to them. I don't owe them anything! (proud)

After the young people have been tested, they will probably be well acquainted with the concepts. They may want to test you— this, of course, is your opportunity to get even with the marshmallows. So, enjoy it! Once the floor and your faces have been sufficiently cleaned, ask everyone to find a place at the kitchen table.

A Tower of Humility

Place a package of uncooked spaghetti and a package of gumdrops on the table. Assorted sizes of gumdrops work best. Ask your family to work together to build a tower using only the spaghetti and gumdrops. Work on your tower for approximately fifteen minutes. As you build the tower, notice how difficult it is to build this structure without assistance. Sometimes it takes more than one set of hands to manipulate the materials. Take note of how you need the other members of the family.

Closing the Lesson

After you have completed your tower to your family's satisfaction, make these closing remarks. Explain that this tower could be called a tower of humility because it is built out of strengths and out of limitations. We could say that the gumdrops are the strong points of the tower and the spaghetti are the needs. The tower could not have been built without both. God wants us to recognize those same two things in ourselves. He's created us with strengths and needs.

Second, as we worked together to build this tower we found that it required everybody's help. We needed an extra set of hands to hold the spaghetti while fixing the gumdrops. We needed assistance. We needed each other. God wants to teach us that He loves us so much that He is always ready to help in our limitations and meet our needs. He helps us Himself and He brings people into our lives to give us assistance.

Close this time in prayer. Think back to the areas of weakness that you identified earlier. Assign prayer partners for each family member. Each person is asked to pray out loud for one other member of the family. Pray and ask God to help that person with her area of weakness. Each teenager has the option of praying for himself. However, parents will want to verbalize prayers for God to change their hearts and lives. It will make a great impact for your children to hear your prayers of humility to God.

High School Happenings

Materials Needed: An old T-shirt for each person, markers or fabric paint, marshmallows, chocolate sauce, one package uncooked spaghetti, and one package of gumdrops (varied sizes)

Letting Your Child Know You Introduce this lesson by sharing an apology with your teenager. Prior to this lesson, spend some time reflecting on your relationship with each family member. Has there been any recent or past issues where you have wronged your teen and didn't apologize? Have there been promises unkept? unkind words said in anger? disrespect? impatience? a critical spirit? etc. Ask the Lord to show you any areas that may need confession. Then start the lesson by completing these sentences as you talk to each family member.

1. God has shown me that I was wrong when _____.
(I spoke so harshly to you yesterday.) or *(I didn't respect your privacy.)*

2. I know that must have made you feel _____ inside. *(sad, angry, hurt, scared, etc.)*

3. Will you forgive me?

4. I am asking God to help me with _____.
(my patience. I want Him to help me choose my words carefully.) or *(knowing how to show you respect and consideration.)*
Share this type of confession with each member of your family. Be careful not to rationalize or blame. For example, words such as, *I wouldn't have done that if . . .* would not be appropriate.

If you already practice confession and forgiveness in your family and all hurts have been talked through, then share with them the things that you are still praying for God to help you with. Tell your children what Jesus still wants to change in you. In what areas do you still need God's help?

Getting to Know Your Child Ask your teenager to recount a time when she had to apologize to a friend. What were the circumstances? What made it difficult to apologize? How did the other person respond? What does forgiveness mean to them? How does humility tie into forgiveness?

Explain that this lesson teaches some important principles about humility. Humility begins when people acknowledge their limitations. The Bible Drama for this lesson tells about a man and his friends who weren't ashamed to admit their needs. They showed great humility but great boldness as well. Invite your family to listen to the story and pay close attention to how the men could be seen as humble and bold at the same time.

Becoming Caringly Involved Read the Bible Drama together with your family. As you finish reading discuss the answers to these questions:
- The friends in the story were willing to do most anything for Jesse. Is there anyone that you would do almost anything for? Who is that person? Explain why he is so special to you.
- How might these men be labeled "humble" and "bold" at the same time?

- Would most of your friends see humility as a positive trait? Why or why not?

Inside and Out

Ask every family member to find an old T-shirt or sweatshirt for this activity. (It must be an item of clothing that they will not mind writing on; the more holes or stains the better.) Gather plenty of markers or fabric paint and then find room to create. Ask everyone to create a T-shirt that tells about their strengths, both inside and outside. On the outside of the T-shirt encourage family members to write words or draw symbols that show their outside strengths—things they do well, accomplishments, or physical characteristics that they like about themselves.

When that step is completed, invite everyone to turn their T-shirt inside out and write words or draw symbols that reflect their inner strengths. On the inside of the T-shirt write personality traits that are positive, character qualities that make you unique, and statements that tell about the "you" that nobody gets to see. We've listed sixteen character qualities that teens may want to choose from. Encourage your teenager to write or draw as many strengths as possible. Also encourage your family to write at least two feelings they may feel but do not show. Do you feel afraid or worried but try not to show it? Do you feel sad or angry and keep it inside?

Character Qualities

Fair	Generous	Flexible	Loyal
Dependable	Creative	Bold	Enthusiastic
Patient	Responsible	Truthful	Sensitive
Understanding	Persuasive	Neat	Forgiving

As you're working alongside one another, it may be important to help your teenager think of additional things that make him/her special. You will also want to let them know that it is all right to write seemingly opposite strengths such as "quiet" and "loud" or "laid back" and "intense." Sometimes we exhibit different characteristics depending on the circumstance.

As you complete your T-shirts, invite everyone to share what they've drawn. Make this a time of affirming one another's strengths. Ask everyone to take a good look at their T-shirt again. Is it without flaws? Is there one T-shirt that is perfect? Some may have holes or stains, others may be faded or worn. Other T-shirts may be missing sleeves or pockets. All the shirts have their imperfections. Emphasize this point. God created each of us with very unique strengths and talents, but He also created us human. Since we are human we have limitations, imperfections, or needs. God wants to develop in us a humble heart. Humility means: I learn the balance between knowing that I am special to God and at the same time knowing that I have areas that need God's help.

This Shirt Is Like Me
See Middle School section for an explanation of this activity.

Pride Goes before the Fall
See Middle School section for an explanation of this activity. Then you may want to use the Pop Quiz from the Middle School section as well as the Pop Quiz given here.

Pride Goes before the Fall
Pop Quiz
Tell whether this sounds like someone who is proud or someone who is humble.

1. I don't need to listen to that lady. The school counselor doesn't even know what she's talking about. I can figure this out on my own. (proud)
2. I don't have to cope with the stress of breaking up with my boyfriend/girlfriend alone. I can talk with somebody about it. (humble)
3. God and I don't have much to talk about. I don't need anyone else telling me what to do. (proud)
4. I'll talk to her whenever she apologizes. (proud)
5. I'm feeling overwhelmed by these decisions about college and work. I think I'll try to talk with Dad tonight. (humble)
6. I need God to forgive me. I really blew it last weekend. (humble)
7. There's no way I'm going to work today. I'm going out. My boss is such a jerk. He scheduled me to work on a Friday! (proud)

8. I'd better ask my sister if I can borrow that shirt. (humble)
9. I shouldn't have to clean up the bathroom. It's just too bad if other people have to go in there. (proud)
10. I don't care what you say! I can take care of myself. (proud)

After the young people have been tested they will probably be well acquainted with the concepts. They may want to test you—this of course is your opportunity to get even with the marshmallows. So, enjoy it! Once the floor and your faces have been sufficiently cleaned, ask everyone to find a place at the kitchen table.

Optional Discussion Some teenagers will be ready for a more in-depth look at emotional needs. This discussion is designed to look briefly at four emotional needs. Ask your family to think again about the men in the Bible Drama. Jesse's friends lowered him through the roof of the house because they wanted Jesse to be healed. They were willing to admit the need and then were bold enough to ask the One (Jesus) who could meet the need. Explain to your family that most of the time we don't have a physical need that is as serious as paralysis, but we still have needs that should be brought to Jesus. In this lesson we are going to talk about four of these needs. Everyone needs acceptance, support, comfort, and forgiveness. God created us with these needs—it is OK to have them. He's designed important ways for these needs to be met. Sometimes we ought to bring these needs to Jesus when we pray. He can meet the need Himself. At other times God involves the people in our lives to meet the needs.

Spend the next few minutes discussing the meaning of each need and then situations when you have experienced this need—past or present. Model these statements for your family. Invite others to participate, but don't insist that they share. These responses require a great deal of vulnerability. For example:

- When I have a need for *acceptance* that means I need to know that someone is going to like me, that they're going to give me a positive response. *I was needing acceptance when I started my new job. I didn't know if I would fit in.*
- When I have a need for *support* that means I need to know that I have someone who is around to share the good times as well as the tough times of my life. *I need*

your dad's support as I teach the Sunday School class. I need to know that he's behind me and that he's praying for me as I prepare.

- When I have a need for *comfort* that means I need to know that someone cares when I'm hurting. *I needed God's comfort last fall when Grandpa died. It was important to know that God cared about me and that He knew I was sad about Grandpa's death. God showed me some Scriptures that let me know He loves me and notices when I'm hurting. He also sent family and friends to comfort me.*

- When I have a need for *forgiveness* that means I need to know that I have been released from the wrong I've done. *I asked for God's forgiveness today for losing my temper. I also needed to apologize to that person. I needed to ask for his forgiveness as well.*

After you share your needs, invite your family to share times when they have experienced this need as well. Be sure to provide a very accepting, nonjudgmental atmosphere for this discussion. As you conclude your sharing, take out the items for the last activity.

A Tower of Humility
See Middle School section for an explanation of this activity.

Closing the Lesson
After you have completed your tower to your family's satisfaction, make these closing remarks. Explain that this tower could be called a tower of humility because it is built out of strengths and out of limitations. We could say that the gumdrops are the strong points of the tower and the spaghetti are the needs. The tower could not have been built without both. God wants us to recognize those same two things in ourselves. He's created us with strengths and needs.

Second, as we worked together to build this tower we found that it required everybody's help. We needed an extra set of hands to hold the spaghetti while fixing the gumdrops. We needed assistance. We needed each other. God wants to teach us that He loves us so much that He is always ready to help in our limitations and meet our needs. He helps us Himself or brings people into our lives to give us assistance.

Close this time in prayer. Think back to the areas of weakness that you identified earlier. Assign prayer partners for each family member. Each person is asked to pray out loud for one other member of the family. Pray and ask God to help that person with her area of weakness. Each teenager has the option of praying for herself. However, parents will want to verbalize prayers for God to change their heart and life. It will make a great impact for your children to hear your prayers of humility to God.

Lesson 7

Humility brings the provision of Jesus

Key Scripture Passage *And He entered and was passing through Jericho. And behold, there was a man called by the name of Zaccheus; and he was a chief tax-gatherer, and he was rich. And he was trying to see who Jesus was, and he was unable because of the crowd, for he was small in stature.*

And he ran on ahead and climbed up into a sycamore tree in order to see Him, for He was about to pass through that way. And when Jesus came to the place, He looked up and said to him, "Zaccheus, hurry and come down, for today I must stay at your house."

And he hurried and came down, and received Him gladly. — Luke 19:1-6

Bible Drama

Walking as close to the road as possible, the little round man never ventured a look up from the dirt path in front of him.

"Little thief," they would say. "Rob any widows lately?" The town's people would yell across the road at him. Occasionally, children would throw rocks. And the name-calling was constant.

His mother had named him Zaccheus after her father. It was a special name meaning "pure," but the little man felt anything but pure. You see, Zaccheus was a tax collector. And tax collectors, or "publicans" as the Jews called them, were hated by everyone.

Every day, Zaccheus would walk to the city gate and arrive just as the huge door was swung open. The merchants who brought goods into the city to sell would be lined up and anxious to get to the marketplace. But the merchants had to first deal with Zaccheus, the tax man.

"What do we have today?" Zaccheus would sneer to the merchant. Zaccheus' helpers would begin rifling through the cart full of goods, to make sure there was nothing hidden that could bring more taxes. Many times they would also help themselves to a portion of the merchant's goods. Zaccheus and his helpers would steal whatever they could from the merchant.

"Well, today I will be kind to you," he would announce. "I'll only charge you half a shekel for our Roman guardians and half a shekel for me!"

The merchant would be outraged. In order to make any money from his produce, he would have to sell it for twice what it was worth because of the high tax. But he could do nothing but pay. Zaccheus could charge whatever he wanted, no matter how unjust it was.

Deep down inside, Zaccheus hated what he did. But all of the town's people despised him. It was the only way he could get back at them for their cruelty. It was a horrible and lonely life that he lived.

Wait! What's that? There seems to be a commotion in the street. Everyone from the city is swarming to the city gate. Zaccheus was surrounded in an instant, yet he was so short that he couldn't see what was happening. Everyone around him was shouting a man's name and it sounded like . . . yes, it was the name of Jesus!

Zaccheus had heard of this great man from the travelers who passed his gate. In fact, he heard that another publican named Matthew had actually become His good friend. But how could he see over all of these people?

The sycamore tree! Zaccheus could climb the big-limbed tree and surely get a glimpse of Jesus. As he started to climb, the crowd around him started to laugh out loud.

"Look at the fat, little man climbing the tree! Ha! Ha!" Now they were all pointing and throwing stones at him. The shame and anger welled up inside of him. But he felt something else rise up inside him — something he had not felt for a long time. Zaccheus really wanted to be what his name meant. Zaccheus wanted to have his heart made pure. And if anyone could tell him how to do that, it must be Jesus.

No matter how shameful it seemed to others, he was going to get as high in the tree as possible to see Jesus. And maybe, just *maybe*, Jesus would notice him. Even though the crowd jeered and threw stones, the wee little man kept climbing.

"Zaccheus! Zaccheus, you come down from that tree!" The voice was different from the others. Gripping the tree tightly, Zaccheus turned to see who was yelling at him. Lo and behold, it was Jesus!

"Zaccheus, I would like to have lunch at your house today. I've heard Matthew tell of how difficult your job can be. I thought that you might need a friend to talk to!"

Zaccheus almost fell out of the tree. Never before had anyone wanted to come to his house. Never before had anyone wanted to talk with him! Tears came to Zaccheus' eyes, as the people stood dumbfounded by Jesus' words of kindness.

No one knows exactly what Jesus and Zaccheus talked about that day. But what happened afterward is very clear. Zaccheus got his wish. His heart was made pure, and he returned all the money he had ever stolen.

And from that day forward, the little town of Jericho had the happiest tax collector in all of Israel!

Goal of Lesson 7: Families will learn that God knows what we need even before we ask for it. God "goes first" in meeting our needs.

Intimacy Principle: Intimacy is experienced through humility and faith.

Disclosure Goal: Parents of younger children will share a time when they said or heard words that were unkind. Parents of teens will tell about an awkward situation and tell how they handled the experience.

Projects with Preschoolers

Materials Needed: Three coins and a small basket or container for each person, a box and gift wrapping supplies for every two people, several magnets (simple refrigerator magnets are fine) and an assortment of magnetic and nonmagnetic items (paper clips, marbles, coins, nails, string, cotton balls, etc.)

Letting Your Child Know You Tell your family about a childhood experience. Share about a time when you said words that hurt someone else's feelings. Did you ever call someone a name? Do you remember being unkind to a brother, sister, or peer? Did you ever say words that were mean or ugly? Share the situation with your family, but don't share the specific words that were used. Instead, emphasize the impact on the other person and how he must have felt. Explain that we all want our house to be a place where people say only words that are kind. We don't want to use words that hurt others' feelings.

Getting to Know Your Child Ask each family member to think of a time when a person *outside* the family said something that hurt his feelings. Did a friend ever call him a name? Has anyone in the neighborhood said words that were mean or ugly? How did those words make you feel? Did you like feeling this way? How do you think your friends would feel if you called them names? How would they feel if you said things that weren't nice? Explain that today's story is about a man whose name was Zaccheus. Zaccheus' neighbors didn't like him very much because he stole money from them. Zaccheus probably didn't have many friends in the town where he lived, and the people who knew him must have treated him unkindly. Zaccheus needed a friend. In this story, a famous man comes to the town of Jericho and selects one person to be His friend. Everyone is surprised because this famous man chooses Zaccheus (of all people) to be His friend!

Becoming Caringly Involved If the weather permits, take your family outside to read this Bible Drama. Find a good spot under a tree and ask your family to have a seat. Give every family member three coins and a basket or other small container. Explain that before you read the story, you want to show why the town's people hated Zaccheus. Invite your family to help you demonstrate Zaccheus' interactions with the merchants. Ask everyone to hold their baskets and coins.

Explain that the merchants were people who lived in and around the town. The merchants would come to the city where they could sell food and things that they had made. In order to sell their goods they had to get permission from the government. The merchants had to pay a tax, or money, to Zaccheus because he worked for the government. If they paid money then they could sell their goods in the market.

Demonstrate the way that Zaccheus cheated the merchants. As you pretend to be Zaccheus, the rest of your family are to be the merchants. They must line up and pay Zaccheus money in order to enter the city to sell their goods. Your words might sound something like this:

"Good morning, Joshua! What do we have to sell today? Oh, look, fresh fish from the sea. These will bring a good price today. (Zaccheus whispers.) I'll just take a few fish as part of your tax; my wife will fix these beautifully tonight. (Pretend to slip several fish into your basket.) Let's see, that will be only one shekel today. (Take one coin from this family member.) All right, move along! Next!

"Good morning, Lydia! You're looking fine this morning. (In a sarcastic tone.) Were those your brothers and sisters who threw rocks at me this morning? Were they calling out to me as I walked by—minding my own business? Well, in order to sell your baskets that you've made, you will pay three shekels. Yes, three. That is the tax today! You must pay or you cannot sell. What will it be?" (Take three coins from this family member.)

Your family will notice the unfairness of the taxing system. Explain that this is why the townspeople didn't like Zaccheus. He charged some people more money than others. Zaccheus took some of this money himself when it was supposed to go to the government. Zaccheus also stole goods from the merchants.

After your children have a good understanding of the way that Zaccheus cheated the people, begin to read the story out loud. As you read, make the characters come alive. Make your words sharp and cutting as the town's people call Zaccheus names. You might even throw a few rocks as you pretend to yell at Zaccheus. Give the character of Zaccheus a bitter tone as he interacts with the merchants. Stand on your toes as you pretend to look for Jesus. And—as a grand finale—you might even climb a tree as you pretend to have a conversation with Jesus.

Invite your family to act out the Bible Drama with you.

Here are the main points of action in the story.

- Zaccheus walks down the road with his eyes looking only at the ground.
- The town's people call him names and even throw rocks.

- Zaccheus enters the marketplace as the big gate is opened.
- Zaccheus talks with the merchants who are there to sell their goods. Zaccheus looks in their carts and sometimes steals from the merchants.
- Sometimes Zaccheus makes a merchant pay more money than the next—just because he wants more money for himself.
- Zaccheus hears people calling out the name, "Jesus."
- Zaccheus tries to see Jesus. He strains his neck and stands on his toes.
- Zaccheus climbs the sycamore tree in order to see Jesus.
- The crowd begins to laugh at Zaccheus and make fun of him when they notice he's in the tree.
- Jesus walks over to Zaccheus and calls to him. Jesus tells Zaccheus that He would like to be his friend and to have a meal with him.
- Zaccheus gives back all the money that he had ever stolen and even more!

After you have read and acted out the Bible Drama, invite your family to participate in this discussion:
- How do you think the people felt when Zaccheus cheated and stole from them? How would you feel?
- Zaccheus needed a friend. Who asked Zaccheus to be his friend?
- After Jesus and Zaccheus had dinner together, what does the story say Zaccheus told Jesus? What did he do to show the people that he had changed?

As you finish discussing the Bible Drama make these important points. Jesus knew that Zaccheus needed a friend because Jesus asked Zaccheus to spend time with Him. It's important to notice that Jesus asked first. *He* came to Zaccheus, not the other way around. God is like that too. He gives to us first.

Wouldn't it be wonderful if you had a special friend who surprised you with gifts all the time? This friend would give you presents and do good things for you. This friend wouldn't want any presents in return, He would just want to be your friend. Wouldn't it be great to have a friend like that? Well, we do! God is that friend. He likes to give to us. He knows the things that we need, and He likes to "go first" to meet our needs. God knows what we need even before we ask for it.

Gift Grapple

Begin the activity portion of this lesson by playing the game, Gift Grapple. Divide your family into pairs and have them spread out around the room. If you have an odd number in your family, make one group of three. Each group will be competing against the others to see how quickly they can wrap a gift. Supply each group with a box, scissors, tape, wrapping paper, and a bow. Groups must wrap their gift completely and then pick it up and carry it to another group. There is one important challenge to this activity. Each person must only use one hand. While one hand is behind their back, partners must work together to wrap their gift. The first group to "give their gift" wins the game.

As you declare a winner, make these closing comments: God goes first in meeting our needs. He always wants to give to us. God cares about us so much that He's already given us some important gifts even though we didn't ask for them. His most special gift to us is His Son, Jesus. God likes to give to us first.

God's Magnetic Personality

Gather the following materials and conduct a small experiment. You will need a bag of assorted items such as keys, marbles, paper clips, coins, string, cotton balls, etc. There should be an assortment of magnetic and nonmagnetic items in the bag. You will also need a small magnet.

Ask each person to take turns drawing an item out of the bag and predicting whether or not it will stick to the magnet. Will the magnet attract the paper clip? Will the magnet attract the marble?

As you determine the items that are attracted to the magnet and the ones that are not, sort the items into two separate piles. Sort out the magnetic items from the nonmagnetic. Clear away the nonmagnetic items then make this point. The magnet is like us. All of these (magnetic) things are like God's gifts to us. When we have a need (place the magnet on the table), God notices our need, comes to us, and then gives to us (place the paper clip on the table so that it will move toward the magnet). God goes first to meet our needs. Our needs attract God. God knew we would need to eat, so He made the plants and animals for us to have food. God knew that we would need water to drink so He made the streams and rivers. God knew that we would need to rest, so He made the sun to come out during the day and the moon for night. God knew that we would need someone to love us and take care of us, so He made families and friends. God gave to us first. Discuss these ideas as you manipulate each of the magnetic items.

Tell your family that each person will get to demonstrate this idea: God likes to give to us first. Set up an obstacle course on the kitchen table using canned vegetables, spools of thread, and small books for ramps. Open the books and place them print side down on the table. Now by holding a magnet in your hand pull a paper clip around the obstacle course. You can pretend the paper clip is a race car, or if your magnet is strong enough, it will pull real toy cars through the obstacle course. As each person crosses the finish line she says, *I am like the magnet and God's gifts are like the car. My needs attract God. God goes first to meet our needs.*

For the next activity, invite your children to sing this action song with you. Feel free to create your own actions or add new verses.

God Goes First
(sung to the tune of "Twinkle Twinkle Little Star")
God goes first to meet our needs.
(stretch out hands palms up, like you're giving a gift)
He gives to us, He helps, He leads.
(hold hands and walk in a circle)
Food to eat and sun for light.
(pretend to eat with a spoon) (make large circle with hands, high in the air)
Friends to love and moon at night.
(fold arms across chest) (make small circle with hands, high in the air)
God goes first to meet our needs.
(stretch out hands palms up, like you're giving a gift)
He gives to us, He helps, He leads.
(hold hands and walk in a circle)

Closing the Lesson

Close the lesson by talking about how glad you are that God goes first to meet our needs. Emphasize how glad you are that God gives to us even when we don't ask. Then make these statements: Let's see if we can give to others like God gives to us. Let's think of someone who needs our family's help. Let's give to them first—just like God has done for us.

Make sure the project you choose involves a genuine need. Second, make a plan so that each of your family members can participate in the giving. Here are some projects you might want to consider:

- Rake leaves for a senior adult.
- Take food to a family who just had a new baby.
- Take toys or clothes that your children have outgrown to Goodwill or the church nursery.
- Volunteer time at a homeless shelter.
- Write letters of encouragement to missionaries.
- Take a care package to new neighbors in your community. You might include copies of a school calendar, brochure from the YMCA, information about church daycare opportunities, a list of fun places your family likes to visit, and stamps for mailing bills or letters to old friends.

As you make your plans for giving to others, set a specific date when this event will take place. Put it on the family's calendar or parent's daily planner. This will help ensure the activity won't get lost in the flurry of family life.

After you do carry out the plan, talk about how good it feels to give to others first. When we remember that God gives to us first, it helps us want to give to others too.

Great Fun for Grade Schoolers

Materials Needed: Large T-shirt, large pair of shorts, one pair of sneakers, various props for Zaccheus skit, one box for every two family members, gift wrapping supplies for each box, drawing paper and a pencil, cotton balls, paper plates, Vaseline

(Materials for Optional Activities: bowl of water, large glass jar, water plants—pond weed, drinking straw, medicine dropper, and bromothymol blue)

Letting Your Child Know You Tell your family about a childhood experience. Share about a time when a peer said words that hurt your feelings. (Avoid discussions about hurtful words from an adult at this time.) Did a friend call you a name? Did a neighbor or sibling say things that were unkind? Don't give the specific words that were used; instead explain the circumstance and how you felt. Then tell your family how you handled the situation. Did you call him a name as well? Did you go tell an adult? Did you walk away or punch him in the nose? How were your decision-making skills at this time? Was your decision a good one? Do you wish you had done anything differently? Share what was wise and/or unwise in your decision, but don't "preach" to your kids.

Getting to Know Your Child Ask each family member to think of a time when a person *outside* the family said something that hurt her feelings. Did a friend ever call you a name? Has anyone in the neighborhood said words that were mean or ugly? How did those words make you feel? Did you like feeling this way? What are all the possible ways that you could have handled this situation? Brainstorm as many as possible. Give your family the opportunity to think of all the possible responses (no matter how outlandish) and then discuss the consequences of each response. Make this an objective discussion—no lecturing. Finally, ask your family: If the situation occurred again, which response would you choose? Parents will need to be careful not to lecture a child at this point. Let each person tell which response she would choose (even if the consequence would be unpleasant).

Explain that today's story is about a man whose name was Zaccheus. Zaccheus' neighbors didn't like him very much because he stole money from them. Zaccheus probably didn't have many friends in the town where he lived, and the people who knew him must have treated him unkindly. Zaccheus really needed a friend. In this story, Jesus comes to the town of Jericho and selects one person to be His friend. Everyone is surprised because Jesus chooses Zaccheus (of all people) to be His friend!

Becoming Caringly Involved See Preschool section for explanation of the Bible Drama. Grade schoolers will enjoy a more elaborate role play between Zaccheus and the merchants.

Zany Zaccheus

For a hilarious treat that your whole family will enjoy, show your children how to create the character, Zany Zaccheus. We know from the Bible that Zaccheus was a short man. This optical illusion creates a terrifically short character. One person should kneel behind a table and pull a pair of large shorts up around his arms until the shorts reach his elbows. Person #1 also puts his hands inside a pair of tennis shoes and places his arms on top of a table. Person #1 has now created the "legs" for Zany Zaccheus.

A second person pulls a large T-shirt over Person #1's head and pulls the shirt down till it can be tucked inside the shorts. Person #2 then kneels or sits closely behind the first person so she cannot be seen. Person #2 puts her arms through the sleeves of the T-shirt and has now created the "arms" for Zany Zaccheus.

Practice retelling the Bible Drama as the character, Zany Zaccheus. Zaccheus may want to brush his hair or teeth in the morning before he goes to the market. Show the arm and leg movements as Zaccheus walks to town, climbs the tree, and waves to Jesus. Zaccheus may shade his eyes as he looks for Jesus or stroke his beard as he tries to decide the amount of his tax. Allow every family member the chance to be a part of creating Zaccheus and to watch others as well. If you have a Polaroid or video camera you'll want to record this moment. This activity makes a great family memory.

After you have read and acted out the Bible Drama, invite your family to participate in this discussion:

- How do you think the people felt when Zaccheus cheated and stole from them? How would you feel?
- Why didn't Zaccheus have very many friends? Were you surprised to hear that Jesus wanted to be Zaccheus' friend? Why or why not?
- After Jesus and Zaccheus had dinner together, what does the story say about Zaccheus? What did he do to show the people that he had changed?

As you finish discussing the Bible Drama make these points. Jesus knew that Zaccheus needed a friend. We read that Jesus asked Zaccheus to spend time with Him. It's important to notice that Jesus asked first. *He* came to Zaccheus, not the other way around. God is like that too. He gives to us first. God knows what we need even before we ask for it. He "goes first" to meet our needs.

Gift Grapple

See Preschool section.

God's Plan

Begin this activity by involving your family in this discussion. Let's think of all the things that God has given to us even before we asked. What has He given to us first? God knew we would need food so He made fruit, vegetables, and animals so we would have plenty to eat. God knew we would need something to drink so He made streams and rivers where we can get water. God knew that we would need someone to love us, take care of us, and be with us so He created families. God knew ahead of time that we would need these things, and He gave to us first. He knew what we needed, and He made ways to meet those needs.

Let's look at one important need that God has met through His creation. Ask everyone to hold their breath as long as possible. With the second hand on your watch, mark the length of time that everyone can hold their breath. What need does this activity show? We have a need for air, or we need to be able to breathe. Have you ever wondered if we might run out of air to breathe? God thought of a plan when He created this earth that makes certain we will never run out of air to breathe.

Draw a simple illustration as you explain the oxygen-carbon dioxide cycle. God thought of this great plan when He created the earth. He knew that we need air to breathe—we need the oxygen that is in the air. Take a deep breath. When you take a breath you are taking in oxygen. Now let the air out. When you breathe out, you are breathing out a chemical called carbon dioxide or CO_2. We take in oxygen, our bodies exchange some of the oxygen, and we breathe out CO_2.

Now, here's the good part. God also created plants and trees.

Plants need light, water, and soil to grow, but they also need a certain chemical. Plants need carbon dioxide or CO_2 in order to grow. When plants are growing they give off something that we need. Plants give off oxygen. In other words, plants make the oxygen that we need and we make the CO_2 that helps plants grow. God thought of this plan so that we would never run out of oxygen and the plants would be able to grow. This is just one of the ways that God goes first to meet our needs.

Here are two optional experiments that show the release of CO_2 by humans and the release of oxygen by plants.

Optional Experiment #1 In order to demonstrate that plants release oxygen, you will need a bowl of water, a glass jar, and some water plants—such as pond weed. Place the plants in the bowl of water. Fill the glass jar with water by lowering it into the bowl on its side. Turn it upside down so that it covers the plants. Leave the bowl in a sunny place and look at it from time to time. You will notice the streams of oxygen bubbles rising to the surface of the water. Eventually a little pocket of oxygen will collect at the top of the jar. The plant is giving off these pockets of oxygen, just as God intended.

Optional Experiment #2 In order to prove that humans release carbon dioxide, you will need a clear jar of water, a drinking straw, medicine dropper, and bromothymol blue. Bromothymol blue can be purchased from a pet store, drug store, or any store that sells swimming pool supplies. Add a few drops of bromothymol blue to the jar of water. Add enough bromothymol blue so that the water becomes a bright blue color. Put the drinking straw into the water. Blow bubbles in the water with the straw. Be careful not to drink the water! Notice the change in color. Explain that the bromothymol blue has a special reaction to carbon dioxide. Whenever it combines with carbon dioxide, it produces a change in color. Our CO_2 combines with the bromothymol blue to change the color of the water. We give off the CO_2, just as God intended.

Silly Cycle Relay

Play this relay game that illustrates God's plan. If you have enough members in your family divide into two separate teams. Otherwise you can do this activity and compete against the clock. Try to beat your best score. Find a tree outside that has plenty of grass around it. Clear away any rocks or large sticks. Set up these items. Put one paper plate at the base of the tree and put another paper plate about ten yards away. To keep the plates from blowing away, place a rock on each plate. Put a large pile of cotton balls on each plate and put a jar of Vaseline nearby. Explain that the cotton balls represent oxygen and carbon dioxide. The tree gives off the "oxygen cottonballs" and we give off the "CO_2 cotton balls." This game will demonstrate this process.

One-half of the teams stand beneath the tree and the other half of the teams are at the second plate. The first player on each team that is standing near the tree begins the game. Player #1 puts Vaseline on his nose and then puts his nose into the cotton balls. He tries to attach as many cotton balls as possible. Player #1 then crawls to the second plate and deposits his cotton balls. Player #2 begins at the second plate, attaches cotton balls to her nose, crawls back to the first plate and deposits the cotton balls. The other teammates follow the same procedure. If a person loses all his cotton balls before reaching the other plate, he must take his turn again. Each person must deposit a minimum of one cotton ball per turn. This process continues until all team members have completed their turns. The team that finishes first wins the game. If you're playing in just one team, then the object is to complete this process in as little time as possible.

When you've finished the game and have recovered your senses, ask your family these questions. Did we ever run out of cotton balls? Did we ever run out of the things we needed to play the game? No, we had what we needed. The oxygen—carbon dioxide cycle that God designed works well. We never run out of oxygen and the trees never run out of CO_2. God knew we would need oxygen, and He made a special plan to take care of that need. God knows that we need many other things too. He knows when we need a hug. He knows when we need someone to love us. God knows that we need a safe place to live and call our home. God's made a special plan for all these needs too. That special plan is called a family. God went first to meet our needs. He likes to give to us and meet our needs.

Closing the Lesson

Close the lesson by talking about how glad you are that God goes first to meet our needs. Emphasize how glad you are that God gives to us even when we don't ask. Then make these statements: Let's see if we can give to others like God gives to us. Let's think of someone who needs our family's help. Let's give to them first—just like God has done for us.

Make sure the project you choose involves a genuine need and make a plan so that each of your family members can participate in the giving. Here are some projects you might want to consider:

- Visit a senior adult or nursing home.
- Make and give food to a homeless shelter.
- Make get well cards for members of the church who are sick or in the hospital.
- Invite a single adult over for dinner. Play games and experience family time together.
- Host a "Backyard Bible Club" in your neighborhood. Tell your friends about Jesus.
- Write letters of encouragement to church staff members, teachers, or daycare workers.
- Take a care package to new neighbors in your community. You might include copies of a school calendar, brochure from the YMCA, information about church daycare opportunities, a list of fun places your family likes to visit, and stamps for mailing bills or letters to old friends.

As you make plans for giving to others, set a specific date when this event will take place. Put it on the family's calendar or parent's daily planner. This will help ensure the activity won't get lost in the flurry of family life.

After you do carry out the plan, talk about how good it feels to give to others first. When we remember that God gives to us first, it helps us want to give to others too.

Making It Real for Middle Schoolers

Materials Needed: One large pair of shorts, one large T-shirt, one pair of tennis shoes, various props of your choice for Zaccheus skit, index cards, masking tape, paper and pens, letter-size envelopes, balloons, leaves from any green plant, various photographs, and steel nails

Letting Your Child Know You Begin this lesson by thinking about a few of the awkward moments in your own life. Think particularly about the times when you were given a gift and had nothing to give in exchange. Or perhaps a friend remembered your birthday, but you forgot his. Think back to any time when someone did an unexpected favor for you. Try to remember a moment when someone gave to you first. How did you feel? How did you handle the situation? Do you wish you would have done something differently? What would you do the same?

Getting to Know Your Child Ask your family to recount any similar moments. Did they ever receive a gift from someone but have nothing to give in return? Has anyone ever done something nice for you when you weren't even expecting it? How does it feel to have someone give to you first, or give to you unexpectedly? Explain to your family that it is often a humbling experience to receive a gift or favor from another person. We feel humble because the gift reminds us of the "giver's" generosity. The Bible story for this lesson tells about a man who desperately needed a friend. Zaccheus received the gift of a new friend one day. He too felt humble because of the friend's generosity.

Becoming Caringly Involved Read the Bible Drama with your family, then introduce the character of Zany Zaccheus. If there are two adults in the home, the two of you create Zaccheus. You may also enlist the help of one of the children.

Zany Zaccheus
See Grade School section for instructions on assembly.
   As you disassemble the character of Zany Zaccheus, invite your family to participate in this discussion:
   ● Do you see any cause/effect relationships in this story? Zaccheus stole from the community. Did this have any effects? Please explain.

- Who initiated the contact between Zaccheus and Jesus? Who spoke up first? How do you think Zaccheus felt when Jesus first noticed him? How did he feel when this famous Teacher wanted to spend time with him?
- If you had been there that day, would you have been surprised that Jesus wanted to spend time with Zaccheus? Why or why not?

Close the discussion with these important points. Zaccheus had a need—he needed a friend. Because of his stealing and cheating, Zaccheus must have felt very isolated and guilty. Jesus obviously noticed this need. Christ's divine wisdom allowed Him to know exactly what Zaccheus needed and then take the first step in meeting that need. Jesus noticed and took action. God relates to us in the very same way. He notices our needs and takes action. Because of His divine wisdom, God knows exactly what's going on with us. He then takes the first steps in giving to us. God doesn't always give us what we want. He's more concerned about our needs. God may choose to give to us in a different way than we expect or at a different time, but He's always interested in us. God is one of those "generous givers"—He likes to give to us first.

Need Scramble

For the next activity you will need several index cards, masking tape, construction paper, and a pen for everyone. You will need to find a large area outside for this activity. Determine boundaries so players will know the exact size of the playing field.

Ask everyone to stand in a small circle, facing inward. They are not to leave the circle or turn around until you give the direction to do so. Give every person one piece of construction paper and a pen to write with.

While your family is in the circle, write one of the following needs on each index card and tape the index card to a family member's back. Each family member should have one index card with one word taped to his back. Before you start the game ask someone to tape a card to your back as well.

Words for index cards: salvation, relationships, oxygen, food, shelter, clothing, and water.

Finally, give these directions. When I give the signal, everyone is to leave the circle and move around the playing field. The object of the game is to move around so that you can see the words written on other people's backs. At the same time, however, you want to keep people from seeing the word on your back. When you do see a word on a person's back, write it down on your construction paper. If players go more than thirty seconds without movement, count to three and instruct players to move to the opposite side of the playing field. The winner is the first person to have all words written on his construction paper—except the word on his own back. If your family wants to play a second time, just write different needs on the index cards.

Invite your family to return inside and ask each person this question: What do you do when you want to be sure to remember something? What steps do you take to make sure you don't forget? What gets your attention? For example: When I need to remember to get something at the grocery store, I make a list. After everyone has shared, make these comments.

The game we just played illustrates what things get God's attention. The words written on the index cards were some of the needs that we all have. To play the game, we had to notice the needs and then take action. When we have a need for food or clothing or relationships, God notices and gives to us. Our needs get God's attention and then He takes action to meet the needs.

It's important to point out that God isn't like Santa Claus. We don't just make a list of things we *want* and expect God to fulfill the list. It's the things we really need that are important to God—things like food, water, love, forgiveness, and relationships. Second, it is important to remember that God *wants* to give to us, but there is also evil in this world. It is the evil in the world that sometimes steals and destroys the gifts God wants to give to us. That's why there is hunger, suffering, and poverty. These tragedies aren't a reflection on the character of God, they are a reflection on the character of the world we live in.

Gifts from the Generous Giver

Prior to this activity, assemble three gift envelopes for each person in the family. Place all the envelopes on the table so that everyone can see them. One envelope should contain a balloon and several leaves from any green plant. A second envelope should contain a family photo, photos of your child's friends, and photos of other significant people who have been a part of your family's life. A third envelope should contain two steel nails.

Hand the first envelope to each family member and ask them to look inside. Explain that this is God's gift to you and me. This envelope represents our physical needs. God looked down at His creation of man and noted some physical needs. He knew that we would need oxygen in order to breathe. So God designed a foolproof system, an ingenious plan. God designed the oxygen—carbon dioxide cycle. The plant leaves you have in the envelope release the oxygen that we need in order to live. If we were to blow up the balloon that you have in the envelope, we would fill it with carbon dioxide. The CO_2 is what the plants need in order to live. We didn't ask for this gift. We didn't do anything to deserve this gift. God just knew our need and made a plan to meet it. This envelope represents one of the generous gifts of our Father.

Hand the second envelope to each family member and ask them to look inside. Explain that this is another one of God's gifts to you and me. This envelope represents our relational/emotional needs. God knew when He created us that we would need each other. We need other people to love and care for us. God knew that we would need affection. We would need someone to pay attention to us and to support us when things were tough. God knew He could meet some of those needs Himself because He loves us and cares for us. But He also knew we would need someone we could touch and see and talk with. So once again, God had a brilliant plan. He designed relationships like marriage, families, friends, girlfriends, and boyfriends. God saw a need and took initiative to meet the need. We didn't ask for it. We didn't do anything to deserve it. He just wanted to give to us. We have a generous God.

Finally, give out the third envelope. Explain that God saw one final but extremely important need when He created us. God knew that we would need a "bridge." You see, God wants to have a relationship with each person that He creates, but there's a problem. We are separated from God because we sin. We all have this imperfect part in us that wants to do wrong. Because God is holy and perfect, He can't have a relationship with people who have sin in their lives. So once again, God designed a beautiful plan. God built a "bridge" between Himself and us. God allowed His Son Jesus to live on earth and then die for us. It was His death that bridged the gap between God and us. Jesus paid the price for us. There isn't a more generous gift than to give a life. We didn't ask for it. We certainly didn't deserve it, but God gave the gift of His Son for us. The nails you have represent the nails with which Christ was nailed to the cross. His death enables us to have a relationship with God. God saw our need and took initiative because He wanted a relationship with us. God's generosity can save us from eternal separation from Him. A relationship with God can give us a full and meaningful life now.

Close this activity by asking everyone to think back to the beginning of the lesson. We talked about how humbling it was to receive a gift from someone and have nothing to give in return. We talked about how the feelings of humility come because we are reminded of the generosity of the giver. Take a look at your three envelopes and all that they represent—God's gifts of meeting our physical, emotional, and spiritual needs. He gave us these gifts without expecting anything in return. How does that make you feel? What do you think about a God who gives and expects nothing in return? He only hopes for a relationship with us. What thoughts and feelings do you have right now?

Closing the Lesson

Close the lesson by passing out a fourth envelope and a blank sheet of paper to each person. Explain that as we think about how generous and giving God is to us, it makes us feel humble and grateful. Pose this challenge to your family: I wonder what would happen if we adopted the same generosity with each other. For one week, let's give to one another without any expectations. Let's give to someone else first—without conditions or wanting anything in return.

Go around to family members and ask them to share any particular challenges or stresses that they expect in the next week. What school events or pressures will you have this week? What issues at work or home might be of particular concern? Are there any relationships that are difficult right now? After sharing these issues, each family member should finish this sentence: Because of that, I am really going to need _____ (patience, etc.) this week. After each person shares, give the rest of the family an opportunity to write down one way they could give to this person. Write down one way you could meet a need for this person during the week. How could you give to him? For example you might write:

- I will clean my bathroom on Friday. Mom said she's going to be busy getting ready for the shower on Saturday.
- I will make sure my music is turned down low on Tuesday night. Jonathan said he will need to study for his test.
- I will call David at work on Wednesday to give him some encouragement about his project. He said he will need lots of encouragement to get it done on time.
- I will take my shower ten minutes early on Friday morning. Britney said she was going to need our support while she gets ready to leave for choir contest.
- I will make sure I write down any phone messages for Sarah. She will need us to be understanding this week because of the difficulties with Brandon.

By the time everyone finishes, you should have each family member's name written on your paper. Beside his/her name should be one way that you can give to that person this week. Fold the paper and put it in the empty envelope. Put the four envelopes from this lesson where you can see them every day. Let them be a reminder of what God has given you, the gratefulness you feel, and the opportunities you have to give to others.

Now during this next week, look for opportunities to give to each person in your family. You don't have to announce it—just do it. No conditions. No expectations. But, if you do notice that a family member has given to you in some way, be sure to thank her. Try out this experiment for one week.

High School Happenings

Materials Needed: Modeling clay or Play-Doh, index cards, masking tape, paper and pens, letter-size envelopes, balloons, leaves from any green plant, various photographs, and steel nails

Letting Your Child Know You Begin this lesson by thinking about a few of the awkward moments in your own life. Think particularly about the times when you were given a gift and had nothing to give in exchange. Or perhaps a friend remembered your birthday, but you forgot his. Think back to any time when someone did an unexpected favor for you. Try to remember a moment when someone gave to you first. How did you feel? How did you handle the situation? Do you wish you would have done something differently? What would you do the same?

Getting to Know Your Child Ask your family to recount any similar moments. Did they ever receive a gift from someone but have nothing to give in return? Has anyone ever done something nice for you when you weren't even expecting it? How does it feel to have someone give to you first, or give to you unexpectedly? Explain to your family that it is often a humbling experience to receive a gift or favor from another person. We feel humble because the gift reminds us of the "giver's" generosity. The Bible story for this lesson tells about a man who desperately needed a friend. Zaccheus received the gift of a new friend one day. He too felt humble because of the friend's generosity.

Becoming Caringly Involved After you've read the Bible Drama invite your family to participate in this discussion:
- Do you see any cause/effect relationships in this story? Zaccheus stole from the community. Did this have any effects? Please explain.
- Who initiated the contact between Zaccheus and Jesus? Who spoke up first? How do you think Zaccheus felt when Jesus noticed him? How did he feel when this famous teacher named Jesus wanted to spend time with him?
- If you had been there that day, would you have been surprised that Jesus wanted to spend time with Zaccheus? Why or why not?

Close the discussion with these important points. Zaccheus had a need—he needed a friend. Because of his stealing and cheating, Zaccheus must have felt very isolated and guilty. Jesus obviously noticed this need. Christ's divine wisdom allowed Him to know exactly what Zaccheus needed, and then take the first step in meeting that need. Jesus noticed and took action. God relates to us in the very same way. He notices our needs and takes action. Because of His divine wisdom, God knows exactly what's going on with us. He then takes the first steps in giving to us. God doesn't always give us what we want. He's more concerned about our needs. God may choose to give to us in a different way than we expect or at a different time, but He's always interested in us. God's one of those "generous givers"—He likes to give to us first.

Before and After

Begin the activity portion of this lesson by asking everyone to participate in "Before and After." Give each person a section of modeling clay or Play-Doh. Share this explanation: We heard what Zaccheus was like before he met Christ, and what he was like after an encounter with Christ. Think back to the story before Zaccheus meets Jesus. In what way could you relate to Zaccheus? In what way could you identify with his thoughts, feelings, or actions? Then use the modeling clay to represent this thought. For example, you might say:

- I could relate to Zaccheus because I've felt like the whole world is against me.
- I could identify with Zaccheus because I've made some poor choices in my life.

Ask each person to sculpt their idea before they share it verbally. As you work with the clay, discuss what Jesus and Zaccheus might have said to one another. The Bible doesn't tell us what happened during that meal together. We just know that Zaccheus was a changed man. What do you think was said? What topics were not discussed? When sculptures are complete, give everyone an opportunity to tell how they related to Zaccheus. Let each person share how his sculpture represents this idea.

Conclude this activity by stating that Zaccheus was definitely changed by his encounter with Christ. There was a remarkable difference in Zaccheus after Jesus walked into his life. Ask each person to consider this question: Look at your sculpture. If Jesus walked into your life, how would He change what you have sculpted? How would you be different? What would Jesus change? Let individuals think about their answers and then make the changes in their sculptures. Give each family member an opportunity to tell about the changes. Parents will want to share first.

Need Scramble

See Middle School section.

Gifts from the Generous Giver

See Middle School section.

Closing the Lesson

Close the lesson by passing out a fourth envelope and a blank sheet of paper to each person. Explain that as we think about how generous and giving God is to us, it makes us feel humble and grateful. Pose this challenge to your family. I wonder what would happen if we adopted the same generosity with each other. For one week, let's give to one another without any expectations. Let's give to someone else first—without conditions or wanting anything in return.

Go around to each family member and ask for any particular challenges or stresses that they expect in the next week. What school events or pressures will you have this week? What issues at work or home might be of particular concern? Are there any relationships that are difficult right now? After sharing these issues, each family member should finish this sentence: Because of that, I am really going to need _____ (encouragement, support, patience, etc.) this week. After each person shares, give the rest of the family an opportunity to write down one way they could give to this person. Write down one way you could meet a need for this person during the week. How could you give to her? For example, you might write:

- I will ask Mom if she needs me to pick up anything from the store on my way home. She said she would need extra help since Grandma's coming.
- I'll offer to give Christina a ride to the game on Wednesday. I know she's excited about going.
- I will call Wendy on Thursday morning just to give her a

little encouragement. She might be nervous about the speaking engagement.

- I will go with Mom and Dad to Chris' award ceremony. He said that he'd like our support.
- I will offer to watch Haley on Sunday. Mom and Dad both said they will need the rest.

By the time everyone finishes, you should have each family member's name written on your paper. Beside each name should be one way that you can give to that person this week. Fold the paper and put it in the empty envelope. Put the four envelopes from this lesson where you can see them every day. Let them be a reminder of what God has given you, the gratefulness you feel, and the opportunities you have to give to others.

Now during this next week, look for opportunities to give to each person in your family. You don't have to announce it—just do it. No conditions. No expectations. But, if you do notice that a family member has given to you in some way, be sure to thank that one. Try out this experiment for one week. See if it makes any difference in the family climate.

Lesson 8

Humility makes Scripture come alive

Key Scripture Passage *And behold, two of them were going that very day to a village named Emmaus, which was about seven miles from Jerusalem. And they were conversing with each other about all these things which had taken place. And it came about that while they were conversing and discussing, Jesus Himself approached, and began traveling with them. But their eyes were prevented from recognizing Him. And He said to them, "What are these words that you are exchanging with one another as you are walking?" And they stood still, looking sad. And one of them, named Cleopas, answered and said to Him, "Are You the only one visiting Jerusalem and unaware of the things which have happened here in these days?"*
—Luke 24:13-18

And He [Jesus] went in to stay with them. And it came about that when He had reclined at table

with them, He took the bread and blessed it, and breaking it, He began giving it to them. And their eyes were opened and they recognized Him; and He vanished from their sight. And they said to one another, "Were not our hearts burning within us while He was speaking to us on the road, while He was explaining the Scriptures to us?" And they arose that very hour and returned to Jerusalem.
—*Luke 24:29-33*

Bible Drama

Emmaus was not far, only seven miles, and the walk would do them good. The two, Cleopas and Josiah, could no longer stand the confinement of the city. Jesus was dead. And they had lost all hope.

Cleopas had a small farm in Emmaus and was going to begin the spring plowing and planting. After all, with Jesus dead there was no leader to follow, no teacher to learn from. And the Pharisees would now be after every disciple with a vengeance.

His friend, Josiah, was ready for a change of scenery as well. The scene he had witnessed of Jesus suffering on the cross was a nightmare that would not go away.

"I can't get the picture out of my mind," Josiah said as they walked. "It was so horrible, yet I wasn't brave enough to stop it!"

"None of us were," said Cleopas. "Everyone, including Peter, turned and ran away. What else could we do?" Their hearts were like stones within them. Such is the result of guilt-ridden loneliness.

They didn't hear the stranger come up behind them. "Hello!" So lost in thought, the two were startled by the cheery greeting. Sullen faced and suspicious of the stranger, Cleopas and Josiah grumbled a greeting and fell as silent as the dirt they walked on.

"Why so glum on a beautiful day like today, friends? The sun is bright and the air is cool. It's a beautiful day to be alive, don't you think?" The stranger almost chided them with his joy.

His happiness angered the usually soft-spoken Cleopas. "Are you the only one in Jerusalem that hasn't heard what happened? Jesus the Nazarene, a man of God and a prophet, was sentenced to death and crucified! We had hoped that He was the Messiah and had come to deliver Israel. And now on the third day since the terrible murder, some of our women came from the tomb and said they couldn't find His body! The women saw angels, and these angels told them that Jesus was alive. Our friends Peter and John went to the tomb and found it empty, just like the women said. But Peter and John didn't see the angels or Jesus."

The stranger just shook his head. What he said then startled the two sad followers of Jesus. "You are so thick-headed and slow of heart," He began. "Don't you believe all that the prophets say?

They clearly state that the Messiah first must suffer before entering His glory." All the way to Emmaus, the stranger explained the stories of the Bible in a way the two had never heard before. As they listened, their cold and lonely hearts were set on fire with hope. Maybe Jesus is alive! Maybe the women really did see angels!

But then the road came to a fork. Down one way the lights of Emmaus could be seen; in the other direction lay open countryside. "Well, friends," said the stranger, "I have a long way to go. Good-bye."

"Wait!" Cleopas practically grabbed Him to keep Him from leaving. "Nighttime is coming and You have no place to stay. Please come home with us and stay the evening. We have so many questions still to ask. Please don't leave us now!"

Arriving at Cleopas' house the three were again lost in conversation about the Messiah. The two disciples could not believe the wisdom and understanding of the stranger. Never had anyone, except Jesus of course, been able to explain the Scriptures like Him!

Finally, they sat down to eat a little bread together. Cleopas looked at the stranger and said, "Sir, we don't even know your name. But your words have been such an encouragement to us. Would you honor us by saying the blessing over this small meal?"

The stranger smiled and picked up the loaf of bread. Looking up to heaven, he said ever so simply, "Abba, bless this meal." He then turned to the men and said, "My name is Jesus."

It was like blindness was taken from their eyes! Suddenly they recognized their Savior. And just as suddenly, He vanished from their sight! But it was Jesus all right. There was no longer any doubt in their hearts.

Rushing out the door, they practically ran all the way back to Jerusalem to tell the others. How their hearts had been changed the instant they recognized Jesus. Now they could go on forever telling the Good News. He is alive! He is risen! And His name is Jesus!

Goal of Lesson 8: Families will learn this principle: When I ask for help and God helps me, we are making Bible verses come true.

Intimacy Principle: Intimacy is dependent on emotional expression and emotional responding.

Disclosure Goal: Parents will share affirmation and approval by giving a reassuring promise to their children.

Projects with Preschoolers

Materials Needed: A large stack of heavy books, a watch with a second hand, ten to twelve shoe boxes, one box of animal crackers for each family member, three balloons for each person, markers, and a Bible

Letting Your Child Know You Begin this discussion by reflecting on the positive character traits you see in each child. Are they forgiving, kind, helpful, or brave? What positive qualities do you admire? Now think back to your own preschool or grade school years. Which of these qualities did you *not* possess? What character qualities do you see in your child that were not true of you? Share these differences with your child. Your statements might contain these two phrases: "When I was your age, I wasn't good at. . . . But I see that you are good at. . . ." For example, "When I was five years old, I wasn't good at helping my mom. I used to throw a fit any time she asked me to pick up my toys. But I see you helping every day. You help set the table for dinner and you help me by putting your clothes in the hamper." Finally, give each child a reassuring promise. Your promise might sound like: "I see that you are being a good helper. I promise to notice when you're helping and say 'thank you.' " or "You are always such a good sport during your soccer games. I promise to cheer for you during your games."

Getting to Know Your Child Ask each family member to tell about a promise that came true. Did Mom or Dad promise to take you someplace fun? Has Grandma or Grandpa ever promised to bring you a present? Think about the promises that came true. Pick one of your favorites and tell the family about it. What did this person promise? How did you feel when it actually happened?

Explain that the Bible story that we are about to read tells us about one of God's promises. His promises always come true. A very long time ago, God told the men who wrote the Bible to write down these promises. The Bible said that one day Jesus would be born and He would grow up to be an adult. These men also wrote that Jesus would die on a cross, but that three days later He would be raised from the dead. Jesus would live again. Jesus would be the only person in the world who could do this. Our Bible story tells about two friends who knew Jesus. The two friends forgot about the promises of the Bible.

Becoming Caringly Involved Instead of reading this Bible Drama out loud to your children, you might want to retell the story in your own words. As you retell the story, ask your family to pretend that they are looking in a mirror. After you read words from the story, you will stop and show what the characters are feeling or doing. Your family is to mirror your expression or action. Here are some suggestions for retelling the story.

Two men named Cleopas and Josiah are walking down the road toward the city of Emmaus. The two men are friends of Jesus. (pretend to walk in place)

Their friend Jesus has just died. Cleopas and Josiah are sad. (show sad face and pretend to cry) Cleopas and Josiah also feel guilty. They didn't try to help Jesus when He was in trouble. (drop head and look at the floor)

Cleopas and Josiah are so sad that they don't notice a man walking up behind them. The stranger walks up near them and says, "Hello!" (pretend to tap someone on the shoulder and say a big "hello!")

Cleopas and Josiah look over their shoulders and are very surprised. (pretend to look over your shoulder and then jump with a look of surprise)

The stranger is very happy. (show a great big smile) He talks about how beautiful the day is. The sun is shining and the air is cool.

Cleopas looks at the stranger and asks him, "Where have you been? Haven't you heard the bad news? Our friend Jesus is dead and we are sad." (put your hands on your hips and repeat the words above)

The stranger looks at the two men and shakes His head. (shake your head and give a heavy sigh) The stranger says these words, "Don't you remember what the men of the Bible promised? The men of the Bible wrote that Jesus would die, but that three days later (hold up three fingers) He would be raised from the dead and live again."

Cleopas and Josiah walk and talk with the stranger. (walk in place) They feel glad when they are reminded that their friend Jesus might be alive! (give a partner a "high five")

The two men invite the stranger to come to their house and have dinner with them. The three men recline at low tables and get ready to eat. (lay on floor and prop yourself up on one elbow) They are about to say the prayer for the meal. The stranger begins to pray.

The men bow their heads. (bow your head) The stranger prays to God and as the men finish their prayer, they suddenly recognize the stranger. It has been their friend Jesus all along. Jesus isn't dead after all. Jesus is alive! The men are overjoyed! (jump up and down; pretend to cheer)

Jesus disappears right before their eyes. It's all right, though; they know He is alive. Cleopas and Josiah hurry to Jerusalem. (run in place) They want to tell their other friends not to be sad. Jesus is alive! (shake hands with someone and announce "Jesus is alive!")

End the story with these statements: Cleopas and Josiah didn't recognize Jesus at first, but He was there with them. Cleopas and Josiah didn't remember what the men of the Bible had said would happen. The men of the Bible wrote that Jesus would die, but He would be alive again in three days. When Cleopas and Josiah met Jesus on the road, they were a part of making the Bible come true. When they talked and walked with Jesus, they were watching God's promise come true. Jesus was alive. In this lesson we'll find out how *we* can make Bible verses come true.

After you have retold the story, ask your family these questions:
- How did the men feel when they thought Jesus was dead? How did they feel when they finally recognized Jesus?
- What did the men of the Bible say would happen to Jesus?
- Did the promise come true?

Explain to your family that the activities for this lesson help us see that we have an important privilege, just like Cleopas and Josiah. We can be a part of making Bible promises come true. You see, when we ask for help and God helps us, we make Bible verses come true.

Library Load

For the first activity, ask your family to complete an obstacle course. You will race against the clock. Gather several heavy books, like telephone books or encyclopedias, and put them at the starting line. Set up a simple obstacle course around the house. For example, you might start from the kitchen, go around the coffee table twice, touch the front door, and then run back to the kitchen. Give each person two chances to run through the obstacle course. The first chance should be done while carrying a load of books. Give each person a load of books that will make it difficult to complete the obstacle course, but not strain his muscles. The second turn should be done without the load of books. Keep the time for each person's turn. Compare how long it took for the person to complete the course with the books and without.

When everyone has taken their turns, ask these questions: Which time was the easiest—running the course with the books or without? Why? Explain that sometimes we all do things that are wrong. When we do things that are wrong, we feel sorry or guilty. Sorry feelings or guilty feelings are like the heavy books. They make us feel heavy inside or weighed down.

Ask your family to sit down together. Make sure each person is sitting in a chair or flat on the floor. Place a large pile of heavy books near you. Ask each person to listen to the situations you are going to say. After they hear the situations that you describe, you are going to pick up a heavy book and put it in their laps. We are going to pretend that each book is the feeling we have when we've done something wrong.

- Your class is lining up to go outside. You cut in front of someone and step on her toe. That person is hurt. You know this was wrong and you feel guilty. (Place a book on each person's lap.)
- You break one of your mom's dishes, but you lie and tell her that your sister broke the dish. It is wrong to lie. You feel sorry. (Place a book on each person's lap.)
- You want to play with a certain toy, but your brother has

it and you don't want to wait. You grab the toy. You hit him and take the toy away from your brother. This is wrong. You feel sorry. (Place a book on each person's lap.)

- You are playing at the park. A girl who looks different from you comes over to play on the swing set too. You say something mean to the girl. Her feelings are hurt. Your words were wrong. You feel guilty because you said words that were unkind. (Place a book on each person's lap.)

At this point everyone should have at least four heavy books piled in their laps. Make sure that you pile books high enough so that it is difficult for the person to hold them. Each family member should have a load that is too heavy to carry easily. How does this feel? These books are heavy. Do you like the way this feels? When we do things that are wrong, we feel guilty or sorry. These feelings can make us feel heavy inside. Do you like it when you are feeling sorry about the things you have done? Do you like these heavy feelings?

God has given us a Bible verse that tells us what to do about these heavy feelings. When we do what this verse says, we make the verse come true. James 5:16 says to *Confess your sins to one another, and pray for one another, so that you may be healed.* This means that if we confess or tell that we have done something wrong, then we will feel better.

Let's try it. Do you want to make this Bible verse come true? Give every family member an opportunity to answer this question. Then go back to the four situations above. If we cut in front of someone and stepped on her toe, the Bible tells us to say that we are wrong. We should say that we're sorry. Let's say these two sentences when we apologize: "I was wrong for . . ." and "I am sorry." For example, you might say, "I was wrong for cutting in front of you and stepping on your toe. I am sorry." As soon as each person gives this apology, take one book off his/her stack. Ask how that feels. Do you feel better now that you have apologized? You have just made the Bible verse come true. When we say that we were wrong, God makes us feel better. God and I can make the Bible verse come true.

Go through the three other situations above. After a person gives an appropriate apology take one book off his/her lap. Ask how that feels. Do you feel better now that the heavy book is gone? When we confess our wrongs to each other, God makes us feel better. You and God have just made the Bible verse come true.

Pushing Out Fear

Invite your family to join you in making another Bible verse come true. Give each person one shoe box and a marker. Try to find at least ten to twelve shoe boxes for this activity. Ask everyone to open the shoe box and draw a picture inside. They are to draw a picture of something that makes them afraid. Your children might draw a picture of a big dog, a scary monster, or a dark room. Adults might draw pictures of a roller coaster, a tall building, or a slithery snake. Give family members an opportunity to tell what's inside their box.

Explain that God has given us a Bible verse that tells us what to do about the scary things in our lives. In the Book of 1 John, the Bible says that *perfect love casts out fear* (4:18). In other words, love gets rid of fear or love pushes out fear. The Bible verse says that if we are afraid then we need love to push out the fear. Let me show you how this works.

Stack three or four shoe boxes on a tabletop. Stack the boxes on top of each other. Go over these steps with your family. Let's pretend that the shoe boxes are our fears. Look, this is my fear of high places. This box has a picture of the mean dog that lives down the street. I want to get rid of these fears. Does the Bible tell us how? Yes, the Bible says that love gets rid of fear. Where can I find love? Is there anyone here that loves me? (Invite one of the children to stand beside you.) The love you have for me helps me push out fear. Would you hold my hand to show your love for me? Watch what love can do to the things we are afraid of. Use your hand to suddenly knock over the stack of shoe boxes. Push them across the table and onto the floor. This is what love does for us. Love pushes out the fear. Love gets rid of fear.

Before you let others try to push out the fear, ask your family these questions. Would you rather be at home alone when it's dark or with Mom or Dad when it gets dark? Would you be more scared if you found a snake by yourself, or while Mom or Dad were with you? Explain that when we are with someone who loves us, the scary things don't seem so scary. Next, ask your children to name someone who loves them. Brainstorm as many people as possible. Be sure to include God on this list! Then make these statements. God loves us so much that He doesn't want us to be afraid. He's made a plan for us. The Bible verse tells us that love gets rid of fear. God gives us people who love us so that we won't be afraid. God gives us Mom, Dad, Stepmom, Stepdad, older brothers and sisters. When we are with the people that God has given, things don't seem so scary. The love of God that's inside them helps push out our fears.

Let's practice pushing out our fears. Ask one child to sit on the floor. Take all the shoe boxes (ten or twelve) and stack them around the child. Ask the child to name someone in the room who loves her. Then make your comments appropriate to the family member who is chosen. God has given you a mom who loves you. Mom's love helps you push out fears. Would you like for Mom to help you push away all these fears?

Mom joins the preschooler on the floor and together they knock down the shoe boxes. Be creative. Do karate chops and head shots. Try different variations of knocking down the boxes. Try holding hands as you push out the fears, or make a rule that each box must be pushed by both people. After all, it's the love we have for each other that pushes out our fears. Emphasize that we are making Bible verses come true. Make sure every child has an opportunity to knock down the boxes with someone who loves them. We need God's love often shared through others to get rid of fear.

Optional Activity (if shoe boxes are not available)
Invite your family into the kitchen. Let youngsters sit on the countertop or find a comfortable place so they can see. Give everyone a clear glass or jar. On the counter, put a large pitcher of water that has been colored with dark food coloring. Make the water as dark as possible.

Tell your family that the Bible also lets us know what we can do if we are afraid. Let me show you what I mean. Let's say that I get in bed at night. It is dark and it's storming outside. I might be a little scared. This is how scared I would be. Pour a small amount of the dark water into your glass. Point to the water that you have just poured. Now, let's say that I walk outside and find a poisonous snake on the back porch. I would be this scared. Pour more of the dark water into your glass and then point to the water line.

Ask each person if he would be afraid of the dark. Pour dark water into each glass until he tells you to stop. Fill each person's glass again as you ask them about the snake.

Tell your family that you would like to show them what the Bible says about fear. Take your glass that has dark water inside it and hold it over the sink. The Bible says that love pushes out fear. Where can I find love? Is there anyone here who loves me? (Invite a child to stand or sit beside you) The love you have for me helps get rid of my fear. Would you hold my hand to show your love for me?

The Bible says that love gets rid of fear. Let's pretend that my fear is in this glass. My fear is this dark water. God says that love gets rid of fear. Let's pretend the water coming out of the faucet is the love you have for me. Ask the person holding your hand to turn on the faucet. Watch what happens when love is poured in my glass. Hold the glass under the running water. Hold the glass under the faucet until all the colored water is replaced by clear water. Hold your glass up and say, "Look, no more fear. It is all gone. Love got rid of fear."

Before you let others push out their fear, ask these questions: What if you found a snake on the back porch and you were by yourself? Or what if you found a snake on the back porch but you were with Mom or Dad? Which time would be the scariest? When we are with someone who loves us, things don't seem so scary. Would you like to get rid of your fear? Let each person walk to the sink, invite someone who loves them to hold their hand and then turn on the faucet. Each person holds her glass under the faucet until all the colored water is gone.

Repeat these steps of pouring "fear" into the glass and then replacing it with love. Don't single anyone out, but include fears that specifically apply to your children. They may be afraid of bugs, monsters, a big dog, or a scary person. Dramatize the effect of love getting rid of fear. Let the clear water run over the top of the glass and onto their hands. Say, "Look how much love you have. You have so much love that it's spilling over the top. Look, no more fear." We are making Bible verses come true when we push out fear. When we are afraid, God gives us people who love us. The love of God inside them pushes out the fear. This makes the Bible verse come true.

A Reason to Cheer

Invite your family to be a part of making a third Bible verse come true. Ask your children to join you in the dining room. Give each family member a box of animal crackers. Ask everyone to open their animal crackers, take out three crackers, and put them in the middle of the table. Children can eat the rest of the crackers while you talk. Move the animal crackers into a large group at the center of the table. Let's pretend that these animals decided to play a game together. The animals were going to play "Hide and Seek." The group didn't want to play with one of the animals. (Pick up one cracker and set it aside from the others) This animal had to play all by himself. How do you think this animal felt? Talk about how it isn't fun to be lonely. We feel lonely when we don't have anyone to talk with us or play with us. Invite your family to tell about a time when they felt lonely.

Explain that God doesn't want us to feel lonely. He wants us to have others around us who love us and care about us. That's why He's given us family, friends, and teachers. God wants us to have people around us who can be with us during happy times and during sad times. God doesn't want us to be alone, so He had the men of the Bible write to us. The Bible tells us in Romans 12:15 to *Rejoice with those who rejoice and weep with those who weep*. This verse is reminding us to make sure that we pay attention to the people around us. We need to notice when other people are happy and then be happy with them. We need to notice when others are sad and show them that we care. If everyone is careful to notice when others are happy or sad, then we won't be lonely.

Let's make this Bible verse come true. Let's rejoice with those who rejoice. Let's be happy when others around us are happy. Give each person three balloons and a marker. Blow up all the balloons and tie them. Use the markers to write or draw on each balloon. Each person should draw one personal accomplishment or reason they'd like to cheer. Some reasons to cheer might be:

- I can ride a bike.
- I tied my shoes all by myself.
- I got a star at preschool.
- My teacher said I was her best helper.
- I made a goal in my soccer game.
- I can sing in the choir.

After each person has completed his three balloons, have all share their "reasons to cheer" with the rest of the family. Tell your family that you would like for them to go into separate rooms and celebrate. Each person needs to go in a different room and have a party by himself. When you are in the room by yourself, toss the balloons in the air and talk about how proud you are of your accomplishments. Send each person to a different room to have his party.

One adult should stay in the living room or family room. Make sure you laugh and cheer very loudly. Make lots of noise. As you cheer, you will want to say things like, "This is fun, but I sure would like someone to cheer with me. I'd like to have a party with other people too." See if you can draw the other family members out of their rooms. As others join you in the living room, continue to toss the balloons in the air and cheer with one another. Cheer for your accomplishments as you hit your balloons. Try to keep all the balloons off the floor at the same time. Cheer for others' accomplishments as you hit their balloons. It might sound like this: Hooray for Molly! Molly is good at gymnastics! Yea for Dad! I am good at golf!

After a good deal of celebrating, ask your family to sit down together. Which was more fun—celebrating alone or with other people? When we were in different rooms, it wasn't very fun because we were alone. There was no one there to cheer with us. Tell your family that you have just made the Bible verse come true. When we were all celebrating together, we were rejoicing with those who rejoice. We were being happy with people who were happy. We were helping one another not feel lonely. When we follow God's plan, we make Bible verses come true.

Closing the Lesson

Close the lesson by reviewing the three Bible verses. Sit with your family in a circle and place a Bible on your lap. Make these closing comments. We first learned that when we tell that we did something wrong, instead of keeping it inside, we feel better. Pass the Bible to one person in the circle. Ask him to say, "When I say that I'm wrong, instead of keeping it inside, God makes me feel better." Then ask everyone to say these words together, "This makes the Bible verse come true."

Next, we learned that love pushes out fear. Pass the Bible to another person. Have her hold the hand of another family member and say, "Love pushes out fear." Then ask everyone to say these words together, "This makes the Bible verse come true."

In the last verse we learned how good it feels to have others feel happy when we are happy. We need people to care for us when we feel sad. This keeps us from feeling lonely. Pass the Bible to another person. Ask him to say, "When I feel happy, I need others around me who feel happy too. This keeps me from being lonely." Ask everyone to say these words, "This makes the Bible verse come true."

Optional Family Night Activity Invite another family to join you for an Emmaus dinner. Select different kinds of cheeses, fruit, bread, crackers, and grape juice. Sit around the coffee table and prop yourself up with pillows and cushions. Eat by candlelight and retell the Emmaus story. Talk about how happy we are that God keeps His promises. Jesus died on the cross but He lived again after three days. Ask everyone to verbalize thanks to God for one of His promises.

Great Fun for Grade Schoolers

Materials Needed: A large stack of heavy books, various household items for an obstacle course, a watch with a second hand, a set of marbles, a shooter marble, masking tape, three balloons for each person, string, and permanent markers

Letting Your Child Know You Begin this discussion by reflecting on the positive character traits you see in each child. Are they forgiving, kind, helpful, or brave? What positive qualities do you admire? Now think back to your own grade school years. Which of these qualities did you *not* possess? What character qualities do you see in your child that were not true of you? Share these differences with your child. Your statements might contain these two phrases: "When I was your age, I wasn't good at. . . . But I see that you are good at. . . ." For example, "When I was ten years old, I wasn't good at helping my mom. I used to throw a fit any time she asked me to pick up my clothes. But I see you helping every day. You help set the table for dinner and you help me by putting your clothes in the hamper." Finally, give each child a reassuring promise. Your promise might sound like: "I've seen you helping Mom with a good attitude. We promise to notice when you are helping out and say 'thank you.' " or "You are always a good sport at your soccer games, even when things don't go well for your team. I promise to cheer for you at your soccer games."

Getting to Know Your Child Ask each child to tell about a promise that did come true. Did Mom or Dad ever promise to take you someplace fun? Has Grandma or Grandpa promised to bring you a present? Think about these promises that came true. Choose a favorite one to tell your family. What was the promise? How did you feel when the person kept her promise?

Explain that the Bible story that we are about to read tells about a promise that did come true. A very long time ago, God told the men who wrote the Bible to write down these promises. God always keeps His promises. The Bible said that one day Jesus would be born and He would grow up to be an adult. These men also wrote that Jesus would die on a cross, but that three days later He would be raised from the dead. Jesus would live again. Jesus would be the only person in the world who could do this. Our Bible story tells about two friends who knew Jesus. The two friends forgot about the promises of the Bible.

Becoming Caringly Involved Read the Bible Drama out loud to your family. End the story with these statements. Cleopas and Josiah didn't recognize Jesus at first, but He was there with them. Cleopas and Josiah didn't remember what the men of the Bible had said would happen. The Bible said that Jesus would die, but He would be alive again in three days. When Cleopas and Josiah met Jesus on the road to Emmaus, they were a part of making the Bible come true. When they talked and walked with Jesus, God's promise was proven true. Jesus was alive. In this lesson we'll find out how *we* can make Bible verses come true.

Invite your family to participate in this discussion:

- How did the men feel when they thought that Jesus was dead? How did they feel when they finally recognized Jesus?
- What did the men of the Bible write about Jesus? Did the promise come true?
- How were Cleopas and Josiah a part of making the Bible promise come true? (They were witnesses that Jesus died but that He was alive three days later. He talked with them and ate with them.)

Explain to your family that the activities for this lesson help us see that we have an important privilege, just like Cleopas and Josiah. We can be a part of making Bible promises come true. You see, when we ask for help and God gives us help, we make Bible verses come true.

Library Load

For the first activity, ask your family to participate in an obstacle course. You will race against the clock. Gather several heavy books, like telephone books or encyclopedias, and put them at the starting line. Set up an obstacle course outside your house. For example, you might set up trash cans and have family members weave in and out of them. Jump ropes can be tied between two chairs and everyone must crawl underneath. A garden hose can be formed into pairs of circles on the ground. Participants must step into each circle as they run. Use your imagination and household supplies to set up a military-like obstacle course. Let your children be involved in creating and setting up the ideas for the course.

Give each person two chances to run through the obstacle course. The first turn should be done while carrying a load of books. Give each person a load of books that will make it difficult to complete the obstacle course, but not strain their muscles. The second turn should be done without the load of books. Keep the time for each person's turn. Compare how long it took for the person to complete the course with the books and without.

When everyone has taken their turns, ask these questions: Which time was the easiest—running the course with the books or without? Why? Explain that sometimes we all do things that are wrong. The Bible calls the things we do wrong, "sin." One of the consequences for our sin is guilt. Sorry feelings or guilty feelings are like the heavy books. They make us feel heavy inside or weighed down.

Return inside the house and make sure everyone is sitting in a chair or flat on the floor. Place a large pile of heavy books near you. Ask each person to listen to the situations you are going to say. After they hear the situations that you describe, you will pick up a heavy book and put it in his lap. We are going to pretend that each book is the guilty feeling we have when we do something wrong.

- Your class in lining up to go outside. You cut in front of someone and jab her in the stomach with your elbow. She is hurt. You know this was wrong and you feel guilty. (Place a book on each person's lap.)
- You break one of your mom's dishes, but you lie and tell her that your sister broke the dish. It is wrong to lie. You feel guilty. (Place a book on each person's lap.)
- You want to play a certain video game, but your brother is watching television and you don't want to wait. You grab the remote control. You hit your brother and take control of the television. This is wrong. You feel guilty. (Place a book on each person's lap.)
- You are taking a test in spelling. The person next to you gets up from her seat. You look on her paper to get answers. It is wrong to cheat. You feel guilty. (Place a book on each person's lap.)

At this point everyone should have at least four heavy books piled in their lap. Make sure that you pile books high enough so that it is difficult for each person to hold them. Each person should have a load that is too heavy for them to carry easily. How does this feel? These books are heavy. Do you like the way this feels? When we do things that are wrong, we feel sorry or guilty. These feelings can make us feel heavy inside. Do you like feeling guilty about the things you have done? Do you like these heavy feelings you have?

God has given us a Bible verse that tells us what to do about these heavy feelings. When we do what this verse says, we make the verse come true. James 5:16 says, *Confess your sins to one another and pray for one another that you may be healed.* The verse means that if we admit that we have done something wrong, instead of keeping it inside, then we will feel better.

Let's try it. Do you want to make this Bible verse come true? Do you want to get rid of these heavy feelings? Do you want to feel better? Give every family member an opportunity to answer these questions. Then go back to the four situations above. If you cut in front of someone and elbow her in the stomach, this is wrong. You need to apologize. When we admit that we are wrong, God helps us feel better. Let's say these two parts in our apology: "I was wrong for. . . ." and "I am sorry." For example, you might say, "I was wrong for cutting in front of you and hitting you in the stomach. I am sorry." As soon as each person gives an apology, take one book off his stack. Ask him how that feels. Do you feel better now that you have apologized? You have just made the Bible verse come true. When we admit that we were wrong, instead of keeping it inside, God helps us feel better. God and I can make Bible verses come true.

Go through the three other situations above. After a person gives an appropriate apology, take one book off his lap. Ask how that feels. Do you feel better now that the heavy book is gone?

When all of the books have been removed, ask your family to tell what makes it hard to apologize. Discuss why admitting that we did something wrong is difficult. Finally, end with this encouragement. God wants us to admit when we are wrong, because God wants us to feel better. He doesn't want us to feel guilty. When we confess our wrongs to each other, instead of keeping them inside, God makes us feel better. You have just been a part of making the Bible verse come true. God and I together make James 5:16 come true.

Pushing Out Fear

Prior to this activity you will need to find a set of marbles, a large shooter marble, and a smooth playing surface (concrete, tile, or wood). Make a circle on the playing surface with string or masking tape. Adjust the size of the circle so that your children will have success in shooting their marbles outside of the circle. You may also want to practice your own shooting technique!

Ask your family if they would like to join you in making another Bible verse come true. Give each family member three marbles. Ask them to hold up each marble and let each marble stand for something that they are afraid of. One marble might stand for being afraid of snakes, another marble might represent being afraid when someone yells. The last marble might stand for being afraid of getting lost.

After each person has had a chance to explain what their marbles stand for, make these comments: I would like to show you what the Bible says about fear. First John 4:18 says that *love casts out fear* or that love gets rid of fear. The verse says that it is love that pushes out fear. Demonstrate this verse in the following way. Take three marbles and put them in the playing circle. As you toss each marble into the circle, identify the fear. "That marble stands for my fear of snakes, that marble stands for my fear of roller coasters, etc."

The Bible says that love pushes out fear. Where can I find love? Discuss the relationships where love might be found. Is there anyone in this room who has love in their heart for me? (Ask one of the children to come and sit next to you.) Hold up the shooter marble. Let's pretend that this large marble is the love you have for me. Here's what the Bible says about love. The Bible says that love pushes out fear. Hold the shooter marble in your hand by cupping it in your index finger. Your index finger should be curled around the marble with your palm facing up. Shoot the marble with your thumb by flicking your thumb against the marble. Aim the shooter marble at one of the smaller ones. Try to push the smaller marble out of the circle. Then make these remarks: See, that's what love does with fear. Love pushes out fear and then stays in its place.

Let everyone practice shooting their marbles and pushing out their fears. You'll need to take turns if you only have one shooter marble, or you can designate one regular marble as your shooter. Be sure to have the person who is shooting, ask for someone who loves them to sit nearby. Emphasize that it is God's love inside of us that pushes out fear.

After everyone has improved their shooting skills, ask your family three questions. Would you rather find a snake when you are by yourself or with Mom or Dad? Would you rather be in the house alone at night, or with Mom or Dad? Would you want to ride a roller coaster by yourself or with your older sister? Give children a chance to respond and explain their answers. Emphasize that things are less scary when we're with someone who loves us. When we are scared and we say that we need God's help, God gives us people who love us. Their love makes us feel safe. When love pushes out our fear, we make the Bible verse come true.

Ask each person to name someone in their life who loves them. They might name Mom, Dad, Stepmom, sister, or God. When these people are around us, things seem less scary. When we remember that God is always with us, things seem less frightening. God's love pushes out our fears. Let's show how God's love can push out fears. Divide your family into groups of two or three. Make additional playing circles for the marbles if necessary. Tell everyone to toss their fears into the playing circle. Name your fears as you throw each marble. Each person must hold out one marble as a shooter. Now by working together, push out all the fears. Shoot all the marbles out of the playing circle. As you play, point out how much easier it is when two of you are shooting. We can push out the fears much better when both of us are playing. The love of God that is inside of us is pushing out these fears. We are making the Bible verse come true. Our love is casting out fear. When we tell God that we are afraid, He gives us people who love us. The love of God inside them casts out our fear. This makes 1 John 4:18 come true.

A Reason to Cheer

Invite your family to be a part of making a third Bible verse come true. Ask your children to join you in this discussion. Describe this scene as you begin the discussion: Your class is in the gymnasium for P.E. one day. Your teacher tells the class that the boys can have half the gym and the girls can have the other half. The two groups are free to play anything they choose. You walk to your side of the gym. The rest of the group has already decided on an activity. No one notices you and they begin a game without you. How would you feel? Talk about how it isn't fun to be lonely. We feel lonely when we don't have anyone to talk with us or play with us. Invite each family member to tell about a time when he felt lonely.

Explain that God doesn't want us to feel lonely. He wants us to have other people who love us and care for us. God gave us family, friends, and teachers. God wants us to have people around us who can be there during happy times and during sad times. God doesn't want us to be alone, so He had the men of the Bible write to us. The Bible tells us in Romans 12:15 to *Rejoice with those who rejoice and weep with those who weep.* This verse is reminding us to make sure that we pay attention to the people around us. We need to notice when others are happy and then be happy with them. We need to notice when other people are sad and show them that we care. If everyone is careful to notice when others are happy or sad, then we won't be lonely.

Let's make this Bible verse come true. Let's rejoice with those who rejoice. Let's be happy when others are happy. Give each person three balloons and a marker. Blow up all the balloons and tie them. Use the markers to write or draw on each balloon. Family members should draw one reason they'd like to cheer onto each balloon. Some reasons to cheer might be:

- I can do wheelies on my bike.
- I got an "A" in spelling.
- I made two new friends at church.
- I learned my multiplication tables.
- I made a goal in my last soccer game.
- Megan invited me to her birthday party.

After each person has completed their three balloons, have them share their "reasons to cheer" with the rest of the family. Tell your family that you would like for them to go into separate rooms and celebrate. Each person needs to go in a different room and have a party by him/herself. Toss the balloons in the air and talk about how happy you are. Send each person to a different room to have a party.

One adult should stay in the living room or family room. Make sure you laugh and cheer very loudly. Make lots of noise. As you cheer, you will want to say things like, "This is fun, but I sure would like someone to cheer with me. I'd like to have a party with other people too." See if you can draw the other family members out of their rooms. As others join you in the living room, continue to toss the balloons in the air and cheer with one another. Cheer for your accomplishments as you hit your balloons. Try to keep all the balloons off the ground at the same time. Cheer for others' accomplishments as you hit their balloons. It might sound like this: Hooray for Molly! Molly is good at gymnastics! Yea for Dad! I am good at golf!

Complete the celebration by tying one balloon to each person's ankle. Tie string to the balloon and then tie the other end of the string loosely to your ankle. When everyone's balloon is ready, take the family outside. Let's really celebrate with one another. Let's jump up and down and try to pop each other's balloons. Race around the yard, stepping on the balloons.

After a good deal of celebrating, ask your family to sit down together. Which was more fun—celebrating alone or with other people? When we were in different rooms, it wasn't much fun because we were alone. There was no one there to cheer with us. Tell your family that you have just made the Bible verse come true. When we were all celebrating together, we were rejoicing with those who rejoice. We were being happy with people who were happy. We were helping one another not feel lonely. When we feel happy while others are feeling happy, this is God's plan to keep us from being lonely. When we follow God's plan, we make Bible verses come true.

Closing the Lesson

Close the lesson by praying together. Thank God for giving you a way to feel better when you do things that are wrong. Thank God for showing you what gets rid of fear. Finally, thank God for giving people who can feel happy when you are happy and care for you when you're sad. Close the prayer by asking everyone to say these words together, "When I ask for help, God helps me. Together we can make Bible verses come true."

Optional Family Night Activity See Preschool section.

Making It Real for Middle Schoolers

Materials Needed: Plastic grocery sacks, a bag of potatoes or similarly weighted items, newspaper, markers, and a deck of playing cards

Letting Your Child Know You Think back to your middle school years. What made you a unique individual? What sports, interests, or hobbies were uniquely you? What were you really "into" at this age? Share these remembrances with your family. Think also about the interests of your teen that might be different from your own. What are they "into" at this age? What differences can you appreciate or admire? Based on these differences, share affirmation and a reassuring promise with your teen. For example, "Kelly, I really admire your interest in the environment. When I was in middle school, that was the farthest thing from my mind. I promise to support your efforts in recycling." Another example might be: "I appreciate your interest in mechanics, Michael. I never seemed to quite get the hang of mechanical things. I promise to help you clean out the garage so that you'll have a place to work."

Getting to Know Your Child Ask your child to think about two times in his life. Think about a time when a promise was made to you and then broken. Second, think about a time when a promise was kept. What were the circumstances? How did you feel when the promise was broken? How did you feel when the promise was kept? Please share both times with your family.

Parents will want to provide an open atmosphere for sharing. Give plenty of eye contact and communicate a readiness to listen. Listen with your ears and with your heart. Your young person's words may reveal the areas that are most important to him.

The Bible Drama for this lesson tells about a promise that was written in the Bible. The Bible tells about a Savior who would come to this earth as a little child. This Savior would be named

Jesus. He would live for only thirty-three years and then He would be crucified on a cross. But the Bible doesn't stop there. God promised that Jesus would die on the cross, but three days later would be raised from the dead.

God's promises are never broken. Our story tells us about two men who forgot about God's promises. They saw Jesus die, but they forgot the rest of the story!

Becoming Caringly Involved Invite your adolescent to read the Bible Drama out loud for your family. When she has finished reading, begin this discussion:

- In your own words, tell what you think was going on inside Cleopas' and Josiah's heads as they first met "the stranger." What were they thinking when He began to talk about Scripture?
- The two men had forgotten the promises of the Bible. Why was it so hard for them to believe that these promises might really come true?
- How do you think they felt when they realized that they were actually part of making Scripture come true? (Cleopas and Josiah could testify that Jesus was alive. They walked, talked, and ate with Him.)

As you finish the discussion, make these final comments. Cleopas and Josiah were involved in making biblical promises come true. They were two of the witnesses who were able to say, "We know He's alive! We walked, talked, and ate with Him!" Their personal interactions with Jesus made the promises of the Bible come to life. In this lesson, we are going to see how our interactions with one another can make Scripture come true. *We* can make the Bible come to life as we relate to each other.

Guilty Potatoes

Invite your family to join you at the kitchen table. Place a plastic, three-liter soda bottle in the middle of the table. Fill the soda bottle with a small amount of water, just to provide a little weight. Give everyone a plastic grocery sack and ask them to carefully stretch the handles of the sack. Stretch the handles so that they will fit over the head and hang around the neck. Be careful not to tear the sack completely. When the sacks are stretched appropriately, ask everyone to put the handles over their heads so that the sacks hang loosely around their necks. Next, place a large bag of potatoes on the floor next to you. (Small cans of vegetables or other items may be substituted for the potatoes. Use any items that are approximately the same weight as the potatoes.)

Tell your family that this game is called, "Guilty Potatoes." The bottle that you see in the middle of the table is going to help us determine the outcome of several situations. The sentences we are about to read will describe a time when we have done something wrong. In each situation the person has the opportunity to admit their wrongdoing or keep it to themselves. Every one of us does things that are wrong—the Bible calls that sin. When we do things that are wrong, there can be different consequences. One consequence of sin is a feeling of guilt. When we sin, we feel guilty. The Bible has a remedy for these guilty feelings. James 5:16 says we need to, *Confess [our] sins to one another and pray for one another so that [we] may be healed.* In other words, God knew that one result of our sin is the feeling of guilt. God doesn't want us to feel guilty, so He provided a way for us to be free from guilt. He tells us to admit our sins to each other.

In this game, we are going to pretend that the potatoes are the feelings of guilt. We may not always acknowledge our guilt, but it's there. Any time we do something wrong, we feel some amount of guilt. These feelings of guilt make us feel heavy inside. Each time that you receive a potato during the game, this represents the guilt you feel because of sin.

You will read one situation at a time and then give the bottle a spin. When the bottle stops, the family will identify the two people the bottle is pointing toward. The cap of the bottle should be pointing to person #1 and the bottom of the bottle should be pointing toward person #2.

The rules of the game are as follows. When person #1 is identified, that person must put two potatoes inside the sack that is hung around her neck. Person #1 always chooses *not* to admit their wrong. Person #2 does not have to put potatoes into his sack, because he does admit he's wrong. However, Person #2 must verbalize an appropriate apology or admit the wrong for each situation. If the bottle does not point to anyone specifically, then all players get one potato. No one admits their wrong.

Read the first situation:

- You borrow your sister's favorite shirt without asking. While you are wearing it, you spill something on it that stains it permanently. (Person #1 stuffs the shirt in the dirty clothes and never admits her wrongdoing—two potatoes) (Person #2 tells her sister about the shirt and offers to replace it.—no potatoes)

- Your mom asks you to help with yardwork after school. You don't want to do the yardwork, so you lie and tell her that you have a major test the next day. (Person #1 goes to his room and doesn't admit the lie.—two potatoes) (Person #2 admits that she really doesn't have a test, but is very tired. She apologizes for not telling the truth in the first place. She schedules another time to work in the yard.—no potatoes)

- You pull a practical joke in one of your classes. The joke goes bad and someone gets hurt. (Person #1 never admits his involvement.—two potatoes) (Person #2 admits to the practical joke and apologizes to the person who was hurt.—no potatoes)

- Your mom asks you to walk to the grocery store for her. She sends you with a list and enough money to purchase the items. When you return, your mom thanks you and asks you to put the change on the counter. You choose to ignore her request and keep the money. You are hoping to buy a CD you've seen at the music store. (Person #1 never admits to stealing the money.—two potatoes) (Person #2 admits to her mom that she kept the money. Person #2 also returns the money. She apologizes for not asking for the money to buy a CD, instead of just taking it.—no potatoes)

- You are walking down the hall on your way to class. Your day started off terribly and has steadily gotten worse. A group of friends is standing by the lockers talking about their weekend. One of the group accidentally turns around too quickly. She knocks your books and belongings all over the hallway. As you pick up your things, you call your friend several unpleasant names and yell at her for being so stupid. (Person #1 never admits that he was unkind.—two potatoes) (Person #2 apologizes to his friend at lunch.—no potatoes)

- Your best friend invites you to a concert. You are afraid your parents will not allow you to go to the concert. You ask to go out with this friend, but lie about your plans. (Person #1 never admits to the lie.—two potatoes) (Person #2 admits to the lie and apologizes for not being truthful.—no potatoes)

Play this game until everyone has at least three or four potatoes. Repeat the situations if necessary or have family members create their own situations from "real life." Ask everyone how it feels to have these guilty potatoes around their necks. In all the situations we just described, we had an opportunity to admit our wrong. But because we didn't admit our sin, the result is a feeling of guilt. We all have guilty potatoes.

Save the rest of this discussion until later in the lesson. Instruct your family members to leave the sacks of potatoes around their necks while they participate in the next activity.

Pushing Out Fear

For the next activity pass out plenty of newspaper and markers. Distribute at least ten pages of newspaper for every person. Give these instructions: Take one sheet of newspaper at a time. On this paper draw or write something that you are afraid of. You may choose from this list of fears or come up with your own. Think of at least ten things that scare you or make you feel anxious.

I am sometimes afraid of . . .

- spiders, roller coasters, heights, public speaking, driving at night, closed-in spaces, loud noises
- our country going to war, getting AIDS, failing a class, death, financial difficulties, being robbed
- being alone, losing my friends, being embarrassed in front of my friends, being rejected

Model vulnerability as you draw or write about your fears. Parents will not want to share information that would cause their children more concern. Share general fears that were present for you at the age of twelve or thirteen.

Give each person a chance to explain their newspaper drawings. Allow for differences in opinion and perspective. Things that may seem frightening to others may not scare you at all. These type of comments would not be appropriate: "Oh, that's silly. You shouldn't be afraid of that." As each person shares, remind the family that although we may be fearful of different things, we have all felt afraid. The feeling of being afraid is something we have in common. Fear just feels like fear, no matter what the source. This means that we can empathize and show understanding for one another. After everyone has shared, explain that God has given us a way to get rid of our fears. He's written a remedy for the things that frighten us. Let's demonstrate the way we get rid of fear.

Clear away some furniture so that you have plenty of room for this game. Using masking tape, divide the room into two equal playing fields. Ask everyone to bring their newspaper drawings, crumple them up, and leave them on one side of the room. Family members then move to the opposite side of the playing field. Ask one person to leave the rest of the group and stand with the crumpled newspaper. Crumple up twenty extra pages of newspaper and put them on the field with the "Single Player" as well. Explain that the crumpled newspaper represents our fears. Many times we try to handle our fears alone. This usually doesn't work too well, as this game is going to illustrate.

Each round of this game will last two minutes. When the game is started, the Single Player tries to get rid of all their "fears" or wads of newspaper by pushing them across the taped line. The rest of the players try to push the newspaper back across the line. At the end of two minutes, the Single Player wants to have as much of the newspaper across the line as possible. The other players want to have as little of the newspaper on their side as possible.

Begin a new round after each two-minute period. Designate a new Single Player and start with all the newspaper on her side. The Single Player who has the least amount of newspaper on her side wins the game.

When you've finished all the rounds, make these comments: When we try to handle our fears alone we find ourselves in a situation much like the game we just played. We can't ever seem to get ahead. We can't get rid of our fear alone, just like we couldn't get rid of the newspaper alone. In fact, our fears can seem pretty overwhelming. God doesn't want us to be afraid or overwhelmed by the fear. He certainly doesn't want us to be alone when we're afraid.

Ask your teens these questions. If you had to go into the hospital for surgery, would you want to go alone or have someone with you? If you had to confront a store manager about merchandise that was faulty, would you want to go alone or have someone with you? If you were going to a youth meeting for the first time, would it be easier to go with someone or go alone? As teens answer these questions, make these statements: Things don't seem as scary when we have someone with us. The things that frighten us aren't quite so bad if we know that someone who loves us is nearby. This is all part of God's plan. He tells us in 1 John 4:18 that *love casts out fear.* When we are afraid, God gives us people who love us. It is God's love inside them that helps push out our fear. Love gets rid of fear.

Let's demonstrate God's plan. Go back to the playing field. Ask one of your teens to be the Single Player. Move all the newspaper to her side. Ask the Single Player to pick up three of the pieces of crumpled newspaper. The Single Player holds up each of the pieces of paper and tells the fear it represents. Now ask the Single Player these questions. Do you want to get rid of all these fears? (Point to the newspaper on the ground.) The Bible says that love gets rid of fear. There are several people in this room who love and care about you. Is there anyone here that you would like to help you get rid of your fear?

The Single Player selects one or two people and invites them to move to her side of the playing field. The same two-minute game begins. But this time the Single Player is joined by one or two other family members. At the end of two minutes, look at the amount of newspaper left on each side. How much newspaper does the Single Player have now? How does this compare to when she was working alone?

End the game with these comments. There are things and events that happen in our lives that make us afraid. But God's given us a way to get rid of the fear. He's given us a way to push out the fear so that it won't seem so overwhelming. First John tells us that love casts out fear. It's the love of God inside us that gets rid of fear. We can't tackle the fear on our own. We need each other and we need God.

Guilty Potatoes Discussion

Before you begin the last activity, ask your family about their sacks of potatoes. How did it feel to have the sacks around your necks all this time? The extra weight we've carried around has made it more difficult to move. The sacks have been uncomfortable and unpleasant. They might have made us irritable or tired. Explain that the guilt we carry around can be just as unpleasant. Guilt can make us irritable and even depressed at times. Feelings of guilt can also make it difficult to get along with one another. God doesn't want us to feel any of these things. He has told us the way to get rid of guilt and feel better. James 5:16 says, *Confess your sins to one another, and pray for one another, that you may be healed.* This verse tells us that if we admit our wrongs to each other we will feel better. When we admit mistakes or confess sins we unload the guilt. When the heavy load of guilt is gone, we feel better.

Ask each person to say these words as he removes his sack of potatoes: "When I admit to the wrong, I unload the guilt. God gives the healing." Through our confessions and God's provision we make Scripture come true.

Joy and Pain

Invite your family to join you in making a third and final Bible verse come true. You will need one sheet of paper, a pen, and a deck of playing cards. On a sheet of paper, write the following card values. This will become your "Values Sheet": Ace—You win $10 million from Publisher's Clearing House; King—You get selected to be on the front cover of your favorite magazine; Queen—Your friends pitch in money to send you to Hawaii for the summer; Jack—You get a promotion and a raise at work; Ten—You're going to your favorite concert with the guy/girl that you've liked since kindergarten; Eight—You break out with a severe case of acne right before the date with the guy/girl you've liked since kindergarten; Six—You fail two courses in school and have to go to summer school; Four—Someone close to you dies; Three—You become pregnant or get someone pregnant; Two—You are severely injured in a gang-related shooting.

Gather your family around a table and distribute four cards (facedown) to each person. Place the rest of the cards in a pile facedown near the dealer. Tell your family to keep their hands a secret at all times. It is important not to give away the value of your hand, whether it be good or bad. Give these instructions: Your goal is to come up with a hand that has the fewest bad events. Tell your family to look at their cards and evaluate them based on the written values. Players then may discard up to three of their cards. The dealer distributes to each player up to three new cards and replaces any cards that are discarded on the bottom of the deck. This concludes one round of the game. Cards are shuffled and a new dealer is chosen for each round. Cards that do not appear on the Values Sheet have no positive or negative values and should be discarded. If a player discards one to three cards and receives a nonvalued card as a replacement, it may be discarded and replaced. Players should have only valued cards in their final hand.

After family members have their final hands, ask them two questions: How would you feel if these events really happened? Would you prefer to keep the news to yourself or talk with someone else? Each person should give a simple, "Keep it to myself" or "Talk with someone else." Do not explain your answer at this point. After everyone has given a brief answer, ask each person to reveal their cards. Look for the person who has the most positive events. Look for the person who has the most negative events. Ask everyone to explain why they would like to keep this information to themselves or share it with someone else. Play several rounds. Make a point to celebrate when individuals have a good hand and console those who drew a bad hand.

Explain that we want to tell others when good things happen to us because we want people to celebrate with us. We tell others when the bad things happen because we need to know that someone cares when we hurt. When we talk with other people we don't feel so alone. God knew that we would need others in our lives to share the good times and the bad times. He reminds us in Romans 12:15 to, *Rejoice with those who rejoice, and weep with those who weep.* God doesn't want us to feel alone so He gave us this reminder. He wants us to notice when people are happy and celebrate with them. God wants us to notice when others are sad and show them that we care. If we all follow this reminder then none of us have to feel lonely.

Closing the Lesson

Close the lesson by asking everyone to find a piece of newspaper, a potato, and a playing card from this lesson's activities. Ask one person to explain what the potato represented. What does the Bible tell us to do about the guilt we feel as a result of sin? Ask another family member to tell what the newspaper represented. What does the Bible say gets rid of fear? And finally, ask someone to explain what the playing cards represented. What is God's plan for helping us prevent loneliness? Ask each person to also share which activity meant the most to them. Which Bible verse is the most important to you and why?

High School Happenings

Materials Needed: Plastic grocery sacks, one bag of potatoes or similarly weighted items, newspaper, markers, a camera, film, and a deck of playing cards

Letting Your Child Know You Think back to your high school years. What made you a unique individual? What sports, interests, or hobbies were uniquely you? What were you really "into" at this age? Share these remembrances with your family. Think also about the interests of your teen that might be different from your own. What are they "into" at this age? What differences can you appreciate or admire? Based on these differences, share affirmation and a reassuring promise with your teen. For example, "Kelly, I really admire your interest in the environment. When I was in high school, that was the farthest thing from my mind. I promise to support your efforts in recycling." Another example might be: "I appreciate your interest in mechanics, Michael. I never seemed to quite get the hang of mechanical things. I promise to help you clean out the garage so that you'll have a place to work."

Getting to Know Your Child Ask your child to think about two times in her life. Think about a time when a promise was made to you and then broken. Second, think about a time when a promise was kept. What were the circumstances? How did you feel when the promise was broken? How did you feel when the promise was kept? Please share both times with your family.

Parents will want to provide an open atmosphere for sharing. Give plenty of eye contact and communicate a readiness to listen. Listen with your ears and with your heart. Your teen's words may reveal the areas that are most important to him/her.

The Bible Drama for this lesson tells about a promise that was written in the Bible. The Bible tells about a Savior who would come to this earth as a little child. This Savior would be named Jesus. He would live for only thirty-three years and then He would be crucified on a cross.

But the Bible doesn't stop there. God promised that Jesus would die on the cross, but three days later would be raised from the dead. God's promises are never broken. Our story tells us about two men who forgot about God's promises. They saw Jesus die, but they forgot the rest of the story!

Becoming Caringly Involved Invite your adolescent to read the Bible Drama out loud for your family. When she has finished reading, begin this discussion:

- In your own words, tell what you think was going on inside Cleopas' and Josiah's heads as they first met "the stranger." What were they thinking when He began to talk about Scripture?
- The two men had forgotten the promises of the Bible. Why was it so hard for them to believe that these promises might really come true? Why do you think it is so hard for us to believe that God keeps His promises?
- How do you think they felt when they realized that they were actually part of making Scripture come true? (Cleopas and Josiah could testify that Jesus was alive.)

As you finish the discussion, make these final comments. Cleopas and Josiah were involved in making biblical promises come true. They were two of the witnesses who were able to say, "We know He's alive! We walked, talked, and ate with Him!" Their personal interactions with Jesus made the promises of the Bible come to life. In this lesson, we are going to see how our interactions with one another can make Scripture come true. *We* can make the Bible come to life as we relate to each other.

Guilty Potatoes

See Middle School section for explanation of this activity. Life situations for this activity are as follows:

- You have planned to meet a friend after school. The two of you are supposed to work on a chemistry project together. You decide to go to the mall instead, but never tell your friend. (Person #1 doesn't call the friend that night and never apologizes.—two potatoes) (Person #2 calls his friend from the mall and apologizes. They agree to a later meeting time.—no potatoes)

- You are in the cafeteria during lunch one day. You tell a joke that has a racial slur and don't see a friend sitting a few seats down from you. This person is obviously offended by your prejudicial remarks. (Person #1 goes on telling jokes and pretends not to notice. No apology is given later.—two potatoes) (Person #2 stops the jokes and apologizes privately.—no potatoes)

- One of your friends is now dating your former boyfriend/girlfriend. All three of you have just arrived at the same party. While in conversations with other people, you "accidentally" let private information slip about your friend. Your friend confronts you about this information. (Person #1 never admits to telling the information but says the friend deserves the embarrassment.—two potatoes) (Person #2 admits that he/she was wrong to share the information.—no potatoes)

- You take your parent's car out for the evening. You let one of your friends borrow the car while you go to a movie. Your parents have given explicit rules against this. Your friend dents the car door. (Person #1 lies to her parents and says that someone must have hit the car in the parking lot of the theater.—two potatoes) (Person #2 admits to lending the car and offers to pay for repairs.—no potatoes)

- You are busy talking to one of your friends while you are at work. Because you are distracted, several customers leave the store discontent. Your manager notices and asks you about it. (Person #1 pretends to know nothing about it. No apology is given.—two potatoes) (Person #2 admits to their manager that he was distracted. He apologizes and reassures the manager that this won't happen again.—no potatoes)

- You told your younger brother that you would take him to the arcade on Saturday. He's been looking forward to this all week long. You sleep late on Saturday and then your friends invite you to go out. You leave the house and break the promise you've made. (Person #1 decides that the younger brother doesn't need an apology because he's too young. You give no apology—just a lot of excuses.—two potatoes) (Person #2 apologizes that evening and changes plans for the next week in order to take brother to the arcade.—no potatoes)

Pushing Out Fear

See Middle School section.

Guilty Potatoes Discussion

Before you begin the last activity, ask your family about their sacks of potatoes. (Bring additional potatoes for this discussion. How did it feel to have the sacks around your neck all this time? The extra weight we've carried around has made it more difficult to move. The sacks have been uncomfortable and unpleasant. They might have made us irritable or tired. Explain that the guilt we carry around can be just as unpleasant. Guilt can make us irritable and even depressed at times. Feelings of guilt can also make it difficult to get along with one another. God doesn't want us to feel any of these things. He has told us the way to get rid of guilt and feel better. James 5:16 says, *Confess your sins to one another and pray for one another that you may be healed.* This verse tells us that if we admit our wrongs to each other we will feel better. When we admit mistakes or confess sins we unload the guilt.

Ask your family to think about these questions: Why is it so difficult for us to admit that we are wrong? Why do we hesitate to tell others that we blew it? We may feel **ashamed or embarrassed** by our actions. We may feel **afraid** to face the consequences of our sin or we may be just too **proud** to apologize or say that we are wrong.

Most of your family's ideas should fit under these three headings: shame, fear, and pride. Explain that when we are reluctant to admit and confess our sins then we increase our load. We compound the problem. Hand each person three potatoes. Ask your family to put the potatoes inside their sacks one at a time. As they drop each potato into the sack, they should name it as "shame," "fear," or "pride." Shame, fear, and pride don't make us feel better. The only way to lighten our load of guilt is through confession. Before removing your sacks, take a family photograph. This will provide an important reminder of the James 5:16 principle. Ask each person to say these words as they remove their sack of potatoes: "When I admit to the wrong, I unload the guilt. God makes me feel better." Through our confessions and God's provision we make Scripture come true.

Joy and Pain

Invite your family to join you in making a third and final Bible verse come true. You will need one sheet of paper, a pen, and a deck of playing cards. On a sheet of paper, write the following card values. This will become your "Values Sheet": Ace—You win 10 million dollars from Publisher's Clearing House; King—You are voted as "Best Looking" and "Most Likely to Succeed" in your class; Queen—Your parents buy you the car you've always dreamed about for your sixteenth birthday; Jack—You get tickets and backstage passes to your favorite concert; Ten—You make a "B" in algebra; Eight—The guy/girl you've dated for three years breaks up with you the week before the prom; Six—Your family moves to another state the summer before your senior year; Four—Someone close to you commits suicide; Three—You become pregnant or get someone pregnant; Two—You are severely injured in a gang-related shooting.

See Middle School section for explanation of this activity.

Closing the Lesson

Close the lesson by asking everyone to find a piece of newspaper, a potato, and a playing card from this lesson's activities. Ask one person to explain what the potato represented. What does the Bible tell us to do about the guilt we feel as a result of sin? Ask another family member to tell what the newspaper represented. What does the Bible say gets rid of fear? And finally, ask someone to explain what the playing cards represented. What is God's plan for helping us prevent loneliness? Ask each person to also share which activity meant the most to him. Which Bible verse is the most important to you and why?

Unit Three

A Lesson in Decision-Making

Unit Outline

I DON'T REMEMBER what the decision was about. It was something to do with spending his Christmas money, along with what he had saved from his allowance. Whether it was a new bike or a skateboard was really insignificant to me.

What I do remember was the question. After we were home and after the bike or the skateboard was admired and used, he asked this question. My young son James caught me totally off guard with his childlike sincerity.

"Dad." His face filled with gathering seriousness. "Do *you* think I made a good decision?" At first I didn't know what he was talking about. But then I realized that my son had just made the biggest purchase of his young life. He had saved and saved. Now all the time and effort was embodied in his new possession. And what he needed from me was the assurance that he had made the best decision.

The purchase he made has gone the way of all the toys of his youth. Now his "major purchases" are new car speakers and slalom skis and other "big boy" toys. But those early years taught me something very important about my son. No matter what his age, James wants to make good decisions. And my approval or disapproval has a lot to do with how he ultimately feels about his choice.

What would have happened if I had not taken that first questioning look with the same seriousness with which it had been offered? Most likely, he would have stopped asking. He probably would have figured that I was not the one to teach him about decision-making. Most likely, he wouldn't be seeking my advice now about the really important issues of life. Issues such as: "What values will I base my life on?"

Kids are like that, you know. They tend to take us at our word. And if our words or lack of words reflect that we're not interested, they will believe exactly that.

Oh, and by the way, it doesn't take long for kids to find someone who will give them what they seek. The world, after all, is filled with people who want to tell our kids how to think.

This is why you need to teach your children the skills of good decision-making. So start with the most important decision of their life. Don't think for a moment that their childlike choice to follow Jesus is not significant. Show them by your words and actions that it is the greatest decision they will ever make. Teach your children that you are to be trusted when it comes to helping them with good choices.

And I can guarantee, they'll continue to come back for more.

Lesson 9

The excitement of following Jesus

Key Scripture Passage *Now it came about that while the multitude were pressing around Him and listening to the word of God, He was standing by the lake of Gennesaret; and He saw two boats lying at the edge of the lake; but the fishermen had gotten out of them, and were washing their nets. And He got into one of the boats, which was Simon's, and asked him to put out a little way from the land. And He sat down and began teaching the multitudes from the boat.*

And when He had finished speaking, He said to Simon, "Put out into the deep water and let down your nets for a catch." And Simon answered and said, "Master, we worked hard all night and caught nothing, but at Your bidding I will let down the nets."

And when they had done this, they enclosed a great quantity of fish; and their nets began to break; and they signaled to their partners in the other boat, for them to come and help them. And they came, and filled both of the boats, so that they began to sink. But when Simon Peter saw that, he fell down at Jesus' feet, saying, "Depart from me, for I am a sinful man, O Lord!" For amazement had seized him and all his companions because of the catch of fish which they had taken. . . . And Jesus said to Simon, "Do not fear, from now on you will be catching men." And when they had brought their boats to land, they left everything and followed Him.—Luke 5:1-9, 11

Leader Preparation

What's the traffic like in your city? What do these items bring to mind: traffic lights, speed limits, yellow stripes, and one-way streets? These simple words probably conjure up hazardous road-way images. Just the thought of them may make your blood pressure rise. But think about what traveling would be like without them. There would be no way to determine who drives where or when. There would be no limit to the number of accidents and fender benders. Some of us hate to admit it, but traffic lights and speed limit signs are necessary. They provide the guidelines that increase our safety and protection. The yellow stripes and one-way streets are needed. They caution our movements and point the way.

In this challenging world of ours, we need guidelines to help us maneuver through life. We need some kind of standard on which to base decisions. Rules or guidelines help us know what decisions to make and when to make them. Fortunately, God's Word shares with us both content and timing as He gives direction to our lives. As we look in on Peter and one particular fishing trip, we'll see these valuable lessons:

It's exciting to follow Jesus! There's nothing more exciting to a fisherman than catching fish. Peter had done the best he could and had nothing to show for his labor. But in deciding to heed Christ's words, "Let down the net for a catch," Peter's day got exciting. Deciding to follow Christ isn't boring. He's not looking to spoil our fun or ruin our chances for joy. On the contrary, Christ wants to provide for us abundantly, just as He did for Peter. Anytime Jesus does tell us no it's because He loves us and doesn't want us to get hurt. He intends the best for us. His best is rewarding, fulfilling, and exciting. We don't have the privilege of hearing Jesus' words firsthand, so it's important for us to know what's in His book. Decision-making gets much easier the more we know about God's Word. In it, we'll find the eternal guidelines that increase our safety and protection. The Bible is life's necessity. It cautions our steps and points the way.

Second, we see that having **a relationship with Jesus brings daily miracles.** Peter began his day tired from the night of fishing, but ended his day thrilled by a boatload of fish. He started the morning kneeling to clean nets and ended the day kneeling before the Messiah. Peter's day turned into a miracle because of Christ's provision and His very presence. We have these same "miracle workers" available to us. When we have decisions to face, we can look for God's provision. Many times He provides direction Himself; at other times He provides the wisdom and counsel of others. We also have the resource of Christ's presence. We move through decisions more easily after we've spent time with God in prayer. As we talk with Christ and spend time in His presence, we develop a sense of peace. The peace of Christ is present when our decisions are in line with His will.

Through Peter's fishing adventure we learn another important lesson. Following Jesus means that our **selfish living can be replaced with a divine perspective.** Before his encounter with Christ, Peter was most concerned about his priorities and his agenda. But when Peter spends a few moments with Jesus his entire focus changes. He is willing to leave behind his nets and his boat and follow Christ on behalf of other people. It's important to learn that our first reaction to decision-making is often a selfish one. We have our interests and agenda as top priority. As followers of Christ, it is important to resist giving quick answers or making quick decisions. We need to allow time to consider the question: What would Jesus do?

Peter's experience on the Sea of Galilee shows us one final lesson. Following Jesus means that our **temporal concerns can be replaced with eternal.** Peter changed from worrying about his nets to wondering about the condition of his heart. He went from working for fish to fishing for men. Therefore our own decision-making must reflect these priorities. No matter how confusing and demanding our life gets, we need to continue to measure our decisions by this standard: People are more important than things. As we prioritize people, we prioritize ones who are dear to God. God wants our focus on those things that are eternal—God, His Word, and people.

Bible Drama

What a night. It was wet, windy, and just plain miserable.

Peter, Andrew, and the boat crew were the worse for it. Foul tempers, matched only by their foul smell, were the only signs they had worked all night. They had no fish to show for their toil.

"That's why they call it 'fishing,' Peter," said Andrew. "You see, if we always caught fish it would be called 'catching' because . . ."

"Oh, just shut up! It's bad enough that we couldn't even catch our breakfast. We don't need you going on and on, Andrew! Go over there and get to work!" Peter was in no mood for philosophical discussions. He was in no mood for discussions about any subject for that matter. With a family to feed and bills to pay, Peter didn't have time to sit and chat about life.

Work was what Peter knew. And work was what he really believed in. No one else was going to provide for him or his family. It was all up to him and, to tell the truth, Peter liked it that way. He made his own decisions and stuck by them. No one was man enough to tell Peter what to do.

Peter was lost in thought about bills and food and the new sandals that his little boy needed. He didn't notice the crowd of people walking across his nets that were spread out to dry on the beach. Now looking up, he exploded in a fit of angry words. "Hey, all of you get off my nets or you'll answer to my fist! What's the matter with you! Get out of here!" Peter held up his clenched rock of a fist and grabbed the shoulder of the closest intruder. Peter spun the man around in order to confront him face-to-face.

"Peter! It is so nice to see you! It's been a while since you and I have talked." Peter just stood there. The person who he had threatened was the new rabbi in town. It was Jesus! How could the day get any worse?

"It's OK, Peter. We should have been more careful not to step on your nets," said Jesus. "But since I've got you here, would you mind if I used one of your boats for a pulpit? There are so many people coming that they are liable to drive us into the sea. Your fishing boat would be the perfect place for Me to speak from. Everyone will be able to hear, and I won't get wet!" Jesus laughed at His own joke, but Peter just politely smiled and nodded his head. He really liked this new Teacher because He was so different from all the others. But Peter was still unsure of anyone who "talked" instead of "worked" for a living.

Dutifully, Peter anchored the boat a few feet from shore and went back to work. The crowd was gathering quickly now. The crew of fishermen moved down the beach to scrub the nets and hang them to dry. As they worked, Jesus talked about God's love.

How could anyone care so much for people? Peter thought to himself. *This Jesus has a way about Him like no other man I have ever met.*

Jesus talked on and on throughout the morning hours. Now the sun was high and burned on the backs of the fishermen who neatly stacked their nets and prepared for the night's work. Ready to go home, they patiently waited for Jesus to finish speaking so that they could pull the boat up onto the beach. Finally, Peter and Andrew waded out to the boat where Jesus was resting after the long morning of teaching.

"I've always been fascinated by fishing," said Jesus. "Why don't you give Me a quick lesson? Throw your nets out one more time." The brothers just looked at one another and tried hard not to laugh! "Well, Jesus. This is not exactly the best time to fish. You see, the sun is hot and the nets are already dry and . . ."

"Go out into deep water and let your nets out one more time." The request of the simple Teacher suddenly changed to a command of Someone in high authority. Andrew looked at his brother. Peter did not take instruction well. In fact, he didn't take instruction at all! It seemed like an eternity as Jesus and Peter just stared at one another. But the power that seemed to be wrapped with great love overwhelmed the silence. Peter knew that Jesus was a man that he couldn't say no to.

"Master, we've been fishing hard all night and haven't caught a thing," Peter said as he lifted himself into the boat. "But if You say so, I'll let out the nets." Andrew scrambled onto the boat and stared with amazement at his brother. Never before had he seen him bend to another man's order!

The short trip out to the deep water was spent in silence. The brothers lifted the net over the side and watched it slip beneath the dark water. And in the time it took for the net to sink, the little boat began to pull over on its side. Peter feared that the net had hung on a rock, but as he began to pull the net back up to the boat the water suddenly began to churn with fish! In all their years of fishing, Peter and Andrew had never seen anything like this. It couldn't be . . . but what else? It was a miracle!

Pulling in the great haul of fish took two boats and a great deal of time. By now the beach was full of people. Jesus stood and watched with a big smile on His face.

But Peter was not smiling. The whole time he worked to get the fish into the boat, he thought of all the judgmental and angry words that he'd said throughout his life. His lack of trust in God's provision churned up in his heart like the fish caught in the net. He was caught and felt as if there was no escape from the guilt. He didn't deserve this miracle. And he certainly didn't deserve the special friendship with Jesus.

Now on the shore with the other fishermen, Peter fell on his knees before Jesus. The poor man couldn't even look Jesus in the eye, so great was his shame.

"Master, please leave. I'm a no-good sinner and can't handle Your goodness. Please leave me here alone." Peter knew that Jesus was holier than anyone he had ever met. He knew that he didn't deserve God's help at all. He knew that his sin was so great and Jesus was so holy. Jesus had left His world of teaching and talking and entered into Peter's world of fishing. He entered Peter's world in order to meet Peter's need! No one had ever done that for Peter before.

Jesus lifted Peter up from his knees. Looking straight into his tear-filled eyes, the Master said, "Don't be afraid, Peter. From now on I'll teach you how to fish for men and women." Peter and the others knew that their days of fishing for trout and bass were over. From now on they would learn a new trade from a new Teacher. They would become "fishers of souls."

Pulling their boats up on the beach, the crew took one last look at the nets that had been their livelihood. They had all decided to follow Jesus. And even though none of them knew what lay ahead, one thing was for sure. If the great haul of fish was the result of following the Master's orders, the days ahead were sure to be full of excitement.

Goal of Lesson 9: Families will discover that the Bible helps us make right choices. God gives us rules to protect us and help us get along with each other.

Intimacy Principle: Intimacy is based on our need to experience biblical truth.

Disclosure Goal: Adults will tell about a time when they deliberately disobeyed their own parent(s).

Projects with Preschoolers

Materials Needed: Contac paper, construction paper, scissors, chalk, one blindfold, goldfish crackers, decorated boxes or bags for the goldfish crackers

Letting Your Child Know You Begin this lesson by telling your family about a time when you deliberately disobeyed your parent(s). How old were you? Where did you live? What were you thinking at this time? What made you decide to disobey? What were the consequences of your actions? What did you learn from this event?

Getting to Know Your Child Ask your family to tell about one rule they think is hard to follow. Which rule is hard for you to remember? Which rule is tough for you to follow? Some rules that may be difficult for preschoolers to follow are: "No running around the pool," "Use quiet voices in the library," and "Footballs are only used outdoors." Give each person a chance to share one rule and the reason she thinks it is hard to follow. Be sure to allow family members to share openly. At this point, resist the temptation to explain why these rules are in place.

Explain that today's lesson is about a fisherman named Peter. Peter has an important decision to make. Jesus tells Peter to do something, and Peter has to decide whether or not he will obey. Listen for the instructions that Jesus gives to Peter. Jesus gives instructions that are hard for Peter to follow.

Becoming Caringly Involved Read the story once for your family. Then invite them to help you retell the story using "water tiles." You will need the following supplies: Clear, plastic Contac paper, brightly colored construction paper, and scissors. Trace and cut shapes out of the colored construction paper. Patterns for this activity are on page 246. You will need to cut out two boats, four people-shapes, and eight fish.

> Cut the shapes from the construction paper.
> Cut a large sheet of Contac paper and lay it on a flat surface, paper side up.
> Peel off the paper backing from the Contac paper.

Place the cut-out shapes on top of the Contac paper.

Cut a second sheet of Contac paper and remove the paper backing.

Lay the second sheet of Contac paper (sticky-side down) on top of the cut-out shapes.

Smooth out any wrinkles or bubbles, then cut around the colored shapes.

Press around the edges in order to make sure the shapes are waterproof.

These water tiles will stick onto bathroom tile or glass when wet. Invite your children to join you at the window. Bring a small bowl of water and the water tiles you have just made. Work with your children to retell the Bible Drama using the water tiles. Dip them into the bowl of water and stick the tiles to the window. The window becomes the background for each scene of the Bible Drama. You will want to include these points of action as you retell the story:

- Peter and Andrew are in the boat. They've been fishing all night, but haven't caught anything.
- Peter and Andrew row their boat to shore. They get out of the boat and begin to wash their nets.
- Jesus meets Peter. Jesus asks if He can use Peter's boat.
- Jesus begins teaching from the boat. A crowd of people are listening to Him on the shore.
- After the lesson, Peter goes out to the boat to talk with Jesus.
- Jesus tells Peter to put his nets out in the deep water.
- Peter explains that they have been fishing all night long, but he decides to follow Christ's instructions.
- Peter lets down his nets and catches a huge amount of fish. It takes two boats to haul the fish to shore.
- When Peter gets to shore he kneels in front of Jesus. He is very surprised by the miracle of the fish. Peter knows that Jesus is someone special. Jesus wants the best for Peter.
- Peter and his friends leave their boats and decide to follow Jesus.

After you have finished retelling the story, invite your family to participate in this discussion:

- What did Jesus tell Peter to do? Did Peter follow Jesus' instructions?
- Do you think it was hard for Peter to do what Jesus asked? Why or why not?
- What happened after Peter obeyed Jesus? Do you think Peter was glad that he had done what Jesus asked? Why or why not?

Road Map

Ask your family to help you create a giant road map outside your home. Use sidewalk chalk to make roads on your driveway or back porch. Create city blocks and major intersections. As an alternative, you may want to use masking tape and create the road map inside.

After the road map is complete, divide your family into groups of one, two, or three. A single person will represent a car. A two-person team will represent a truck and a three-person team will represent a large bus. Each single person or group will start from a different point on the map, but everyone will travel the roads at the same time. Family members must stay on the roads at all times. They may travel as fast, but as safely as possible. Groups of two or three people must travel together. They must hang onto their leader's waist or belt loops at all times.

While making your best "vehicle noises" and using your invisible steering wheels, maneuver your way through the road map. Collisions and traffic jams are sure to occur, but they will serve as an important discussion tool later. Continue playing on the road map until family members have all experienced a few traffic accidents.

As you sit down together, ask your family these questions. Can you think of anything that might be missing from our roads? Did we need something to keep us from crashing into each other? Your children will eventually identify the need for traffic lights or stop signs. Explain that the stop signs are on the roads to protect us. When we are riding in real cars we need the stop signs. They keep us from getting hurt in a car accident. We need the traffic lights because they help us take turns with other drivers.

God's rules are like the stop signs. His rules keep us from getting hurt. God has written down some rules that will protect us. God's rules are also like the traffic lights. His rules help us get along with each other. God has written down some rules in the Bible because He wants the best for us. When we decide to do what God says, we choose what's best. (Activity adapted from *Lively Bible Lessons for Kindergarten,* 1992, Group Publishing)

Follow the Rules

This activity is a variation on the game, "Red Light, Green Light." Designate one adult to be the Caller for the first round of the game. Find a large play area outside. Decide on a starting line and a finish line that are approximately thirty yards apart. Ask all family members, except the Caller, to stand behind the starting line. The Caller stands at the finish line.

The goal of the players is to reach the finish line. The first player to reach the finish line wins the game. The game begins with the Caller turning his back toward the rest of the players. The Caller gives the signal, "Follow the rules." When players hear this signal they may move toward the finish line. Players want to move toward the finish line without the Caller seeing their movements. To make the game most interesting, the Caller can specify that family members take bunny hops, hop on one foot, walk backward, etc. Players must stop moving before the Caller turns around. The Caller waits a few seconds and then quickly turns around to face the players. At the same time, the Caller gives the signal to stop, "Don't break the rules." If the Caller sees a player move after the signal to stop, that player must go back to the starting line. The player has been seen "breaking the rules."

The same signals and movements are repeated until one player finally reaches the finish line. This player wins the game and becomes the Caller for the next round.

After several rounds of play, make these points about the game: As we played the game, we gave two different signals. When we heard the words, "don't break the rules" and were seen moving, then we had to go back to the starting line. If we broke the rules, it was harder to win the game.

When we heard the words, "Follow the rules," we could move toward the finish line. If we were careful to follow the rules, then we won the game. The same is true when we follow God's rules. Good things happen when we follow His rules. He wants the best for us. God has given rules so that we can be safe and get along with others. God's rules are written in the Bible.

Go for the Goldfish

For the final activity, return to the road map that you created earlier. This time you will need a blindfold and a package of goldfish crackers (or some other snack that your children will enjoy). Put the crackers into boxes or bags that have been decorated. These bags are the prizes for the game. You will need one prize for each family member. Place the crackers at a specific point on the edge of your road map. Make these statements: God has written the Bible to help us make decisions. The Bible helps us make good choices. Let's see how the Bible can help us.

Ask for a volunteer. Give these instructions: We are going to see if you can make your way through this road map and reach the prize. You will have to do this task while you are blindfolded. I will give you instructions about how many steps to take and when to stop. You may have someone hold your hand as you walk. At certain points along the way I am going to tell you to stop. I will ask you a question. If you make good choices you will reach the prize.

Ask the player to start on the map opposite from the prize. Guide the player through the map with your directions and questions. Your dialogue might sound something like this:

Parent:	Take two steps forward. Stop. Let me ask you a question. Sara took something from the store without paying for it. Does the Bible say this is right or wrong?
Child:	*Wrong.*
Parent:	That's correct. The Bible helps you make good choices. Now turn right. (Parents may need to help distinguish between right and left) Take four steps forward. Stop. Let me ask you a question. Jonathan told his mom the truth. Does the Bible say this is right or wrong?
Child:	*Right.*

Parent: That's exactly right. The Bible helps you make good choices. Now turn left. Take three steps forward. Stop. Take off your blindfold. You have reached the prize! Pick up your prize and enjoy it!

Allow each family member the opportunity to complete the activity. If a child gives a wrong response, emphasize the right choice and move on. Lead each one to the prize successfully. Here are some additional "Right or Wrong Situations":

- Nathan picked up his toys when his dad asked him to.
- Jessica hit her little sister.
- Andrew called the boy an ugly name.
- Eric shared his cake with a friend.
- Christina helped her friend when she fell down.
- Ryan rode out into the street when his mom told him not to.
- Erin let her friend go first on the slide.
- Holly grabbed a toy away from her friend. Holly wouldn't share.

When everyone has had a chance to participate, close the activity with these comments. The Bible helps us make good choices. We all took turns playing the game. We had to decide if the situation was right or wrong. The Bible helped us make the right choices. We all reached the prize because of our good choices. We make God happy when we make right choices. God wants the best for us. He's given us the Bible to help us.

Closing the Lesson

Close the lesson by going inside, serving something to drink, and enjoying your goldfish snack. Before all your goldfish are eaten, ask everyone to arrange their goldfish into the shape of a boat. The boat is a reminder of our Bible Drama. The boat in the Bible Drama belonged to Peter. Peter had an important decision in our story. He had to decide whether to obey Jesus' words. It was hard for Peter to follow Jesus' words, just like it is hard for us sometimes. But Peter knew that Jesus loved him and wanted the best for him. Peter was glad that he obeyed Jesus' words. God loves us and wants the best for us. When we follow God's words we can be happy too.

Great Fun for Grade Schoolers

Materials Needed: Sidewalk chalk, blindfolds, goldfish crackers, sacks or boxes that have been decorated, red and green construction paper, dark-colored marker, scissors, pens and pencils

Letting Your Child Know You Begin this lesson by telling your family about a time when you deliberately disobeyed your parent(s). How old were you? Where did you live? What were you thinking at this time? What made you decide to disobey? What were the consequences of your actions? What did you learn from this event?

Getting to Know Your Child Ask your family to tell about one rule they think is hard to follow. Which rule is hard for you to remember? Which rule is tough for you to follow? Some rules that may be difficult for grade schoolers to follow are: "No running around the pool," "Use quiet voices in the library," or "Footballs are only used outdoors." Give each person a chance to share one rule and the reason he thinks it is hard to follow. Be sure to allow family members to share openly. At this point, resist the temptation to explain why these rules are in place.

Explain that this lesson is about a man who did what Jesus told him to do. It was a hard decision, but Peter followed Christ's instructions. And when it was all said and done, Peter was really glad he did.

Becoming Caringly Involved Read the Bible Drama out loud to your family. As you finish reading invite your family to join you in this discussion:

- What did Jesus tell Peter to do? Did Peter follow Jesus' instructions?
- Do you think it was hard for Peter to do what Jesus asked? Why or why not?

- What happened after Peter obeyed Jesus? Do you think Peter was glad that he had done what Jesus asked? Why or why not?

Road Map

See Preschool section. Parents may want to play this game using blindfolds. Blindfold the leader of each pair or trio; single players are not blindfolded. This will make the activity more challenging for grade schoolers.

As you sit down together, ask your family these questions. Which game did you like the best? Did you like playing with the blindfolds or without? Can you think of anything that might be missing from our roads? Did we need something to keep us from crashing into each other? Your children will eventually identify the need for traffic lights or stop signs. Explain that the stop signs are on the roads to protect us. When we are riding in real cars we need the stop signs. They keep us from getting hurt in a car accident. We need the traffic lights because they help us take turns with other drivers.

God's rules are like the stop signs. His rules keep us from getting hurt. God has written down some rules that will protect us. God's rules are also like the traffic lights. His rules help us get along with each other. God has written down some rules in the Bible because He wants the best for us. When we decide to do what God says, we choose what's best.

If we try to make decisions without knowing God's rules, we are like the blindfolded players. If we don't know God's rules then we don't know which way is right or wrong. We don't know the best choices to make. If we try to get along with people and try to please God without knowing what the Bible says, then we don't have very much success. We need to know God's rules for us and be able to understand them clearly. Let's learn some of the important rules of the Bible.

Red Lights and Green Lights

For the next activity you will need to cut out six large construction-paper circles. You will need four green circles and two red ones. Using the Bible verses below, scramble the letters in each word and write them on the construction paper circles.

One of your red circles might look like this:

oD ton lsate

Exodus 20:15

This circle would represent the Bible verse from Exodus that says, *Do not steal.*

Red Lights
Do not steal.
Exodus 20:15
Do not lie.
Exodus 20:16

Green Lights
Do what your parents ask you to do.
Colossians 3:20
Only say words that are kind and helpful. Ephesians 4:29
Be thankful for everything. Colossians 3:17
Treat others the way you want to be treated. Matthew 7:12

Explain to your family that the city traffic officials have made a big mistake. They made these lights for us, but scrambled the letters. We will have to unscramble the words in order to find out what the lighted signs are meant to say. Give one circle to each family member or divide into teams and work together. After all verses have been unscrambled, make these comments:

These red and green signs show us the two kinds of rules that God has written in the Bible. He has written down certain things that we are *not* to do. These are on the red circles. God has also written down things that He *does* want us to do. These are on the green circles. Let's find out why God has given the two kinds of rules.

Let's pretend that I have asked you to watch your baby sister for a moment. Your sister reaches for a sharp knife. She wants to play with it. What would you tell her? Why?

What if you and your baby brother were playing outside. Your brother starts to run after a ball that has gone into the street. You see that a car is coming. What would you tell him? Why? In both of these situations, you wouldn't want your sister or brother to get hurt. That's why you tell them no. This is the reason that God has given us the "Red Lights." These are the times when God says no. Anytime God tells us no it is because He doesn't want us to get hurt.

Now, let's pretend that I have asked you to watch your baby sister again. She is on the floor playing with one of her two-year-old friends. Your sister grabs a toy away from her friend. The friend begins to cry. What would you tell your sister? Why?

You know that sharing the toys is the right thing to do. Your baby sister doesn't know that yet. You want her to get along with her friend. God gives us the "Green Lights" because these are the things that He does want us to do. He wants us to follow these rules because He wants us to get along with each other. If we follow these rules, we not only have good friendships and family relationships, we also make God very happy.

End this activity by dividing into pairs. Assign each pair two of the Red or Green Lights. Ask each pair to think about a time when knowing God's rules helped them make the right choices. Has there been a time when you chose to tell the truth because you knew that lying was wrong? Have you ever been tempted to say something mean, but you kept quiet instead?

Ask each pair to share their experiences. Emphasize the help that the Bible gives us. The Bible helps us know what is right and wrong. God has given us the Bible to help us make good choices. Let's practice making good choices.

Go for the Goldfish

See Preschool section for an explanation of this game. Your dialogue might sound something like this:

Parent:	Take two steps forward. Stop. You and your friends are riding your bikes home from school. You pass by a man who is handicapped. He has trouble walking and has to use some special crutches. Your friends start making fun of the man. They say the comments so loudly that you are certain the man can hear them. Your friends ask you to join in. God says that we are to only say words that are kind and helpful. What are you going to do?
Child:	I would just ignore my friends and keep riding.
Parent:	Great! The Bible helps you know how to treat other people. Now, turn to your left. Take four small steps forward. Stop. Two of your friends have invited you to go to the mall. The adults give permission for the three of you to go into a store alone. While you are looking around, a woman next to you drops a $5 bill. Your friend dares you to steal the money. The Bible tells us not to steal. What are you going to do?
Child:	I would tell my friend, "No. Forget it. That's her money."
Parent:	Good choice. The Bible helps us know right from wrong. Take two giant steps forward. Turn to your right. Take off your blindfold and receive your prize. Congratulations!

Allow every family member the opportunity to go through the road map blindfolded. Parents will want to participate as well. This will give you an opportunity to model appropriate verbal responses for your children. For example, when you are going through the road map yourself, you might say, "I would tell my friends to leave the guy alone. I'm not going to make fun of anybody, because I don't like it when people make fun of me."

Here are additional "Right and Wrong Situations":

- You invite a few friends over to spend the night. Your parents go to bed early. You are playing too rough in the living room and accidentally break one of the lamps. Your friend says, "Just tell your mom that we broke it when you were out of the room. Then you won't get in trouble." (Ex. 20:16)

- Your grandmother has come for a visit. She brings an early birthday present for you. You are saving your money for a particular brand of sneakers. Your grandmother gives you money for your birthday, but it is not as much as you had hoped. What do you say to your grandmother? (Col. 3:17)
- Your team has just won an important soccer game. You and some of your friends go out for pizza after the game. Several members of the opposing team are at the same restaurant. Your friends make rude faces and begin to mimic the other team. What do you do? (Matt. 7:12)
- You have ridden your bike over to a friend's house and your mom has asked that you be home by 2 o'clock. Your friend has just purchased the most popular video game. He starts it up at 1:45. At 2 o'clock you look at your watch. What do you do? (Col. 3:20)

After everyone has had a chance to complete this activity, close with these comments: We all took turns playing the game. We had to decide what to do in each situation. The Bible helped us make the right choices. We all reached the prize because of our good choices. We make God happy when we listen to His words. God wants the best for us. That's why He's given us the Bible to help us.

Closing the Lesson

Invite your family to return inside. Serve something to drink and enjoy your goldfish snack. As you eat together, remind your family of the Bible Drama. Peter had a difficult decision to make in the Bible story. He had fished all night long and hadn't caught anything. Peter was an "expert" fisherman, but Jesus told him to let down his nets anyway.

Peter chose to follow Christ's words and good things happened. He made the right choice and Christ performed a miracle. When we choose to follow God's words, we are in a position for God to bring good things into our lives as well.

Close by saying a prayer of thanks to God for His Word. Thank God for giving the Bible to help us make good choices.

Making It Real for Middle Schoolers

Materials Needed: Several sheets of paper, newspaper, two small trash cans, envelopes, a small gift for each teen—such as a movie pass or gift certificate

Letting Your Child Know You Begin this lesson by telling your family about a time when you deliberately disobeyed your parent(s). Choose an example from your own middle school or high school years. Where did you live? What were you thinking at this time? What made you decide to disobey? What were the consequences of your actions? What did you learn from this event? Parents will need to be careful not to turn this into a chance to preach to your kids. Share about your own experience, don't lecture.

Getting to Know Your Child Invite your family to answer these questions. Be sure to point out that there are no right or wrong answers. Any answer is acceptable.

Describe the qualities of your best friend. What do you like about him? Describe his personality. Now, if Jesus walked into this room, what would He be like? Would you try to talk with Him? Why or why not? Describe His personality.

Second, let's pretend that you had a telephone conversation with God last night. What was He like? How did He act on the phone? Describe His personality. What did the two of you talk about?

As family members give their answers, write them on a sheet of paper so that everyone can see. Summarize your answers as you finish each section of questions. How do we see Christ? How do we see God?

Explain that this lesson is about a man who has a personal encounter with Jesus. Peter has met Jesus before this occasion. But after this particular fishing trip, Peter looks at Jesus a little differently than before.

Becoming Caringly Involved Ask one of your family members to read the Bible Drama. As she finishes, invite your family to participate in this discussion:

- Do you think it was difficult for Peter to follow Jesus' instructions? Why or why not?

- If you had been in Peter's position, how do you think you would have responded to Jesus' command?
- Why did Peter's view of Jesus change? What was different after the catch of fish?

For and Against

Ask your family to decide whether they are "for" or "against" these regulations. Each person sits an equal distance from two trash cans. Designate one trash can as "for" and the other trash can as "against." To show whether you are "for" or "against" a regulation, you must shoot crumpled newspaper into the appropriate trash can. Pass out plenty of newspaper for each person.

After each question, participants show their decision by shooting into one of the two trash cans. Then give everyone a chance to *briefly* explain their choice. Parents should deliberately take an opposing position on a few of the regulations. Your responses should reflect the common attitudes we often have about God and His "regulations." Give responses such as these: "I don't think metal detectors are necessary in airports. I think the federal government just likes to tell us what to do." Or "I don't think any airline should prohibit smoking on their flights. That's just their way of spoiling people's fun." Ask for your family to respond to these regulations. Are you "for" or "against":
- mandatory use of football pads and helmets?
- making cafeteria helpers wear those funny little nets on their heads?
- "No smoking" regulations on airplanes?
- metal detectors in schools?
- metal detectors in airports?
- seat belt laws?
- making employees of restaurants wash their hands before returning to work?
- mandatory school attendance?

As you conclude this activity, explain that all of these regulations are in place for our safety or well-being. The people who came up with these regulations have our best interest in mind. These regulations are not there to spoil our fun or cause us inconvenience.

Many times, though, we have this attitude about God and His Word. We mistakenly think that God has this long list of rules and regulations that we have to follow. We may wonder if He's up in heaven thinking of rules just to spoil our fun. Many of us have the idea that all God wants to do is make sure we "keep it in line." But the truth is just the opposite. God gives us guidelines to protect us. The only time He tells us no is for our own safety. He doesn't want us to get hurt. And, in fact, God wants the best for us so He's written a "guidebook." This guidebook is the Bible. The Bible gives us the guidelines for living the best life possible. The words in the Bible are there because God cares about us. He has our best interest in mind.

If God has written this guidebook for us, then we need to find out what it says. The Bible can help us make good choices. You'll need the Bible for the next activity.

Bible Scavenger Hunt

Invite your family to join you in this Bible Scavenger Hunt. The following scavenger hunt can be completed by consulting your Bible. Family members follow the clues in order to find the "treasure." Explain that God has given us the Bible to help us make good choices. Many times we try to live our life without the help of His Word. When we try to make decisions without the Bible's help we often make poor choices.

Give your teens this challenge. They may try this scavenger hunt with or without the help of the Bible. You will need to work together as a group to complete this activity. Let the group decide if they would like to use the Bible or not. They need to remember, though, that knowing God's Word helps us make decisions. Knowing what the Bible says will also help them in this game. If the teens choose not to use the Bible at first, they may change their decision at any point.

Prior to this activity you will need to have written each of the clues below on a separate sheet of paper. Put each clue in an envelope and then hide them in the appropriate location. You will also need some kind of reward for the end of the hunt. Purchase something that you know will motivate your teens and can be hidden easily. You might purchase a movie coupon or small gift certificate from a music store. Give your teens a hint about the prize, but don't give it away. Let them know just enough to peak their interest.

Try to give as little help as possible as your teens solve the clues. Give them help only if they begin to get frustrated. However, if teens decide not to use the Bible, they do not receive hints from Mom or Dad either.

When family members are ready, give out the first clue.

Clue #1 (shown to each person)
   The first of your clues will be found in a pouch. It'll be in the living room underneath the _____.

Clue #2 (hidden underneath the couch)
   The first two letters of the next hiding place,
   Can be found in 15, that's just the case.
   Do not (S T)__ __ __, says Exodus twenty.
   This clue is hidden where the heat is plenty.

Clue #3 (hidden on the stove)
   The next location has a special line.
   You'll find your clue in Ephesians 4:29.
   This verse gives us caution, "Don't let these come out."
   But we use these items to sing and shout.
   The clue is hidden where we use these the most.
   Ears are perched and messages we post.

Clue #4 (hidden under the telephone)
   (Parents may need to explain some translations of this verse.
      This verse means, "Do not lie.")
   Exodus twenty gives us another fine rule.
   Verse 16 is the necessary tool.
   "Do not __ __ __," says the Bible true.
   This hiding place starts with that letter too.
   You'll find the clue under a certain fixture.
   The word ends with a "p," the rest is a mixture.

Clue #5 (hidden under a lamp)
   Congratulations! It's going to be just like heaven,

The last verse you need will be in Matthew seven.
Find the verse that tells us how to act toward others.
You will need this number, my dear brothers!
There's a six opposite this number, you see.
Your prize is hidden with the nine and three.

Hide the prize underneath or behind a clock. As you return to the living room, make these comments. God gave us the Bible to help us make decisions. We found out that when we are faced with a choice to lie or tell the truth, the Bible tells us that the truth is best.

We don't have to wonder if stealing is wrong. The Bible tells us that taking something that doesn't belong to us is wrong.

When we are faced with decisions about relationships, these verses can also help. God's Word tells us to say things that are helpful or "wholesome." Scripture tells us to treat other people the way we want to be treated. This kind of policy covers a wide range of decisions.

The Bible helped you make the right choices in this activity. It can also help you make good daily decisions. Let's think of some real situations where the Bible can help.

Application Conversations

In order to get help from the Bible, we've got to know what it says. Print these five verses on a piece of paper so that everyone can see them.

- However you want people to treat you, so treat them . . . Matthew 7:12 (addresses kindness and respect; in actions and in words)
- Let no unwholesome (unhelpful, inappropriate) word proceed from your mouth . . . Ephesians 4:29
- Do not look out for your own personal interests, but also for the interests of others. Philippians 2:4 (addresses selfishness)
- You shall not steal. Exodus 20:15 (applies to cheating)
- You shall not bear false witness against your neighbor. Exodus 20:16 (Don't lie.) (applies to stretching the truth or not telling the whole truth)

Divide your family into groups of two or three. Ask each group to select two different verses. If you only have two or three people in your family, you will need to select at least three verses from the list. You will decide on and perform a skit that shows this verse in action. Think of a situation in which a person could be faced with a decision, and this Bible verse gives the answer. You will perform a telephone skit that depicts this situation. A telephone skit requires that two people sit back to back and pretend to have a telephone conversation.

For example, you might act out this telephone conversation. Stacey is faced with this decision: Will I treat others the way I want to be treated?

Stacey: Katrina is such a witch! I cannot believe that she embarrassed me like that today at lunch. I wanted to die!

Julie: She said she was sorry, Stacey. She didn't know that your little brother is in a wheelchair. She's new to the school, remember? She wouldn't have asked that question if she had known.

Stacey: I don't care. She shouldn't have said what she did. I'm having a party after the game on Friday. I haven't decided if I want to invite her after what she said. What do you think?

Pause at this point in the telephone conversation. Read Matthew 7:12. Talk about how this verse might apply to the situation. Discuss how difficult this decision might be for Stacey. What would make it hard for her to invite Katrina? Remember that God is the expert on living life at its best. Anything He's written in the Bible is guaranteed to work. All He wants us to do is follow the Guidebook. Jesus would look at Stacey and say, "Will you act kindly? Will you treat her the way you would like to be treated?"

Give time for the groups to prepare their skits and then perform for one another. Pause after each skit and discuss the difficulties of the situation. Emphasize that God's reason for telling us these things is because He wants the best for us. He knows that we are faced with tough choices, but these verses give us the wisdom we need to handle the choices. He knows what He's doing. God knows what He's saying. He wants us to trust Him and "let down our nets." He wants us to follow His words.

Closing the Lesson

Close this lesson by asking everyone to close their eyes. Ask each person to visualize Jesus walking into his bedroom tonight. He walks into your bedroom and sits down on the bed to talk. His opening comments are, "I love you and want what's best for you." Then He asks you one question. "Will you . . ."

In your mind, fill in that blank. What would Jesus want you to do? What decision would He want you to make? Would He ask you to tell the truth? Would He ask you to be honest or kind? Would He ask you to think about others?

Close in prayer and ask God for the strength to say yes to whatever Jesus might ask. Thank Him for having a heart that cares for us and only wants the best.

High School Happenings

Materials Needed: Several sheets of white paper, red and green markers or crayons, two bed sheets, one large container of water, and one loaf of bread

Letting Your Child Know You Begin this lesson by telling your family about a time when you deliberately disobeyed your parent(s). Choose an example from your own middle school or high school years. Where did you live? What were you thinking at this time? What made you decide to disobey? What were the consequences of your actions? What did you learn from this event? Parents will need to be careful not to turn this into a chance to preach to your kids. Share about your own experience, don't lecture.

Getting to Know Your Child Invite your family to join you in this opening activity. Give each person one sheet of white paper. Each person will also need one red and one green marker. Ask everyone to make two lists. Using the red marker, write down decisions that you regret from the last two weeks. For example, "I regret that I waited so long to get gas last week. My choice to wait meant that I walked to the gas station." With the green marker, write down choices that you are glad you made in the last two weeks. For example, "I am proud of my choice to stay calm, even when the washing machine flooded the kitchen."

Parents will want to share their responses first and model vulnerability for their children. Make this a pleasant but sincere time of sharing. When everyone has had a chance to explain their lists, make these comments. This lesson tells us what happened when Peter made a difficult decision. This decision was difficult because it challenged his ability, self-centeredness, and common sense. As you'll see in the story, Peter didn't regret this decision.

Becoming Caringly Involved Ask one of your family members to read the Bible Drama. As she finishes, invite your family to participate in this discussion:

- Do you think it was difficult for Peter to follow Jesus' instructions? Why or why not?
- If you had been in Peter's position, how do you think you would have responded to Jesus' command?
- Why did Peter's view of Jesus change? What was different after the catch of fish?
- What would have happened to Peter's life if he hadn't let down his nets? What do you think would have been different?

Perspectives

For the first activity, give every family member another sheet of white paper. Make sure each person still has a green and red marker or crayon. Ask your family to make two lists again. Using the red marker, write down all the things that the Bible tells us *not* to do. Write down all the ones that come to mind. Using the green marker, write all the things that the Bible tells us that we *should* do. Write down all the ones that you remember.

On the back of the paper, write down adjectives or phrases that describe God. Pretend that you had a telephone conversation with

God last night. What was He like? How would you describe Him to your friends? What did the two of you talk about?

Allow five or six minutes for your family to write. Then ask everyone to read their red and green lists. Compare the length of the two lists. Which list has the most responses, red or green? Most teenagers and adults think of the Bible as a book of "Do not's." You might see this reflected in the number of items on your red list. Is the red list longer?

Second, ask everyone to share their lists of adjectives about God. What do you think He's like? Let everyone tell their answers and explain them if necessary.

Close the activity with these comments: Many of us think of the Bible as being a list of no-no's. This perspective also carries into our perspective of God. We may think that God is a giant meanie, wanting to keep us in line. The truth is that God loves us more than we can imagine. He only wants the best for us. But God knows that we face many tough choices. He's well aware of how complicated the world can get. So because He loves us, He's given us a Guidebook for life. The Bible is like a guidebook. It is designed to make the process of maneuvering through life easier. God gave us the Bible so that we could make good choices. Let's practice making some good choices. Invite your family to join you in the next activity.

Australian Survival

For this activity you will need the following supplies: one pitcher or gallon jug of water, one loaf of bread, and two large bed sheets. Spread the sheets on the floor and then ask your family to sit on the floor with you. Every person needs to be sitting on one of the sheets. Place the other supplies on the sheets with you. Set up this scenario:

Select one of your teens to be the leader of the group. Choose the family member who would take this role most seriously. It will be important for adults to help facilitate the discussion during this activity. You will need to set up this scenario and then "stay in character" for the activity to be most effective.

Explain that John (teenager that is selected) is to be our leader for this activity. John, you have graduated from high school and college. Through several successful business ventures you have become independently wealthy. One of your hobbies is hosting tours along the coast of Australia. You have taken our group out on your boat, but there's been a terrible storm. Our boat was destroyed in the storm. Our group has been stranded on this small island in the middle of the ocean. You alone have the skills and expertise that will help our group survive.

Before the ship sank, we were able to get this one container of water and these slices of bread. You are fairly certain that a fishing boat passes through these islands every two days. So all you have to do is help our group survive for two days.

There are several dangers on this island. First, a small group of natives lives on this island. This particular group of natives are some of the only survivors of a tribe of cannibals that inhabited these islands many years ago. Second, the island is full of traps and cages that these natives have set. The traps are cleverly disguised, and it takes a trained eye to be able to spot them. Last, there are many types of poisonous fruit on this island. They look delicious but the consequences of eating them can be fatal.

Because you are the host of our group and you know the important survival skills, it will be necessary for you to come up with guidelines that will keep us safe until help arrives. What guidelines do you think are appropriate? How will you handle the food supplies? What about the natives and their traps? How will you make sure no one eats the poisonous fruit?

Parents will now want to give plenty of time to identify the survival guidelines. Allow the leader to come up with several guidelines for survival. Allow some group input, but as long as the leader gives guidelines that are appropriate they should be accepted. Write down the final version of the guidelines and post them so that everyone can see them.

Parents will need to role play at this point. Prior to this activity, designate one adult to play the role of "troublemaker." The troublemaker tries to ignore or go against each guideline that has been set. If the leader protests, then the troublemaker's position is always: You're just trying to spoil my fun. This adult will make statements such as:

- It's only going to be two days until the fishing boat arrives. Would you mind if I used a little of this water to wash my hair? (When leader objects): That's not fair. You're just trying to ruin my fun.

- I've never actually met a headhunter. Let's invite them over for a cookout! (When leader objects): Do you just like spoiling everything?
- Any berries that look this delicious are sure to be OK. Besides, I'm starving. (When leader objects): All you do is say, "No." I don't like people telling me what to do.

The other parent should try to encourage the leader to stick to his guidelines. Remind the leader that he/she is responsible for the group's safety and well-being. The leader wants the group to survive and only has their best interest in mind. The guidelines are for our protection.

Involve the whole family in this discussion regarding the rules and survival. Is the leader making these rules because he/she wants to spoil our fun? Does he/she just like saying no? Does this leader even care about us at all?

When you have arrived at the clear understanding that the leader has given the guidelines because he/she really does care about the safety of the group, make these comments.

God is very much like the leader in this situation. He is the expert in skills for survival. He is the expert on life. He's given us some guidelines. These guidelines are given because He cares about our safety and well-being. He isn't trying to spoil our fun. God doesn't just like to tell us no. Anytime he tells us no it is for our protection. God just wants the best for us.

Application Conversations

See Middle School section.

Closing the Lesson

Close the lesson by asking everyone to consider this the time when Jesus looks at each one of us and says, "Let down your nets." Jesus looked at Peter and proposed a difficult decision. What decision do you think Jesus has for you? If Jesus stepped into this room right now, what would He say to you? What decision would He put before you? Consider God's words:

- However you want people to treat you, so treat them. Matthew 7:12
- Let no unwholesome [unhelpful, inappropriate] word proceed from your mouth. Ephesians 4:32
- Do not look out for your own personal interests, but also for the interests of others. Philippians 2:4
- You shall not steal. Exodus 20:15
- You shall not bear false witness against your neighbor. Exodus 20:16

Close by asking everyone to write down the point of decision that Christ might propose to them. It can be one of the verses above or they may choose their own. Invite family members to share, but allow privacy of these thoughts as well. You may want to share the verse or the thought that Christ would say to you. Then write your decision on the paper. Will you choose to follow these words of Jesus? Are you willing to "let down your nets"?

Lesson 10

Daily routine includes the miraculous

Key Scripture Passage *There came a woman of Samaria to draw water. Jesus said to her, "Give Me a drink." For His disciples had gone away into the city to buy food. The Samaritan woman therefore said to Him, "How is it that You, being a Jew, ask me for a drink since I am a Samaritan woman?" (For Jews have no dealings with Samaritans.) Jesus answered and said to her, "If you knew the gift of God, and who it is who says to you, 'Give Me a drink,' you would have asked Him, and He would have given you living water."*

She said to Him, "Sir, You have nothing to draw with and the well is deep; where then do You get that living water?"—John 4:7-11

Jesus answered and said to her, "Everyone who drinks of this water shall thirst again; but whoever drinks of the water that I shall give him shall never thirst; but the water that I shall give him shall become in him a well of water springing up to eternal life."—John 4:13-14

So the woman left her waterpot, and went into the city, and said to the men, "Come, see a man who told me all the things that I have done; this is not the Christ, is it? They went out of the city, and were coming to Him.—John 4:28-30

And from that city many of the Samaritans believed in Him because of the word of the woman who testified.—John 4:39

Bible Drama

It was just another day. The dusty road that led from the village to Jacob's Well was so familiar she could almost walk the distance without opening her eyes. Every day at noon she padded down the path to fetch the water needed at the little shack where she stayed. It was just another day in the hard and bitter life of this woman of Samaria.

Her name was Joanna. She made the best of her life in the little village of Sychar. Her home was near the well that Jacob had given to his son Joseph. She had been married many times, and yet was considered evil because she was never able to have children. Now too old to bear children at all, she had taken up with a man in the village, even though they were not married. The whole village rejected her. They called her awful names and looked the other way when they saw her on the street. But she didn't care anymore. She was just trying to survive.

Coming to the well every day was one of the few things that she really enjoyed. She would daydream about how she and her sisters would race to this spot as children. She would think of her mother, now dead and gone, who would tell stories to her as they walked along. But that was many years ago. Alone now, she would draw her water from the deep well, place the clay pitcher on her head, and walk slowly home. Today was no different, just another long and lonely day.

But what's this? There is a man at the well today. And He is not dressed like the other men of the village. In fact, He is dressed like a Jew. What could He possibly be doing at the well?

Jews, you see, had nothing to do with Samaritans. Centuries before, there had been an argument between neighbors. Now the two groups would not even talk to one another. So keeping her eyes cast downward, Joanna approached the well. She was determined to get her water and go home. The Jew would hear nothing from her, nothing at all. That was for sure!

"Give Me a drink of water." Her ears flushed red with the words she heard. How dare He speak to her!

"Excuse Me, Madam. Would you please give Me a drink of water?"

Joanna never looked up. Hurrying to pull the bucket from the well, she threw her words at the stranger like a fiery arrow. "How come You, a Jew, are asking me for a drink? What do You really want?"

She expected a good cursing. But the stranger spoke with the soft and gentle voice of a shepherd herding his sheep.

"Woman, if you knew the kindness of God and who I am, you would be asking Me for a drink. I would give you fresh, living water. Everyone who drinks of Jacob's Well will get thirsty again and again. Anyone who drinks the water that I give will never thirst. The water I give will be a free-flowing spring that gushes with abundant life."

An ordinary day had just turned into an encounter with God. The simple task of drawing water from the well had turned into a marvelous discovery of a life-giving spring!

Jesus talked more about the gift of God to Joanna. She finally ran to the village to announce that she had met the Messiah and He had forgiven her sins. The whole village came to see and hear the words of Jesus.

The long shadows of evening came. All the villagers had gone home. Only Joanna lingered behind at the well. This day had changed her life forever. Never before had she felt so clean, so whole and complete. She was afraid that she would wake up and it would be all over. Peering over the edge of the deep well, she searched the dark water for the answer to her fear.

"Joanna." Startled, she looked up to find Jesus standing next to her. "I just want you to know that what I told you today is true. Your life will never be the same as a result of meeting Me. Remember that 'well of living water' that I promised you? It's inside your heart right now. And it will never stop flowing!"

Joanna just cried. The day had started just like every other day, but turned into a day like no other.

Goal for Lesson 10: Families will discover that God gives us two "everyday" gifts that will help us make good choices. He gives us people and prayer.

Intimacy Principle: Intimacy is enhanced through receiving of God's manifold grace.

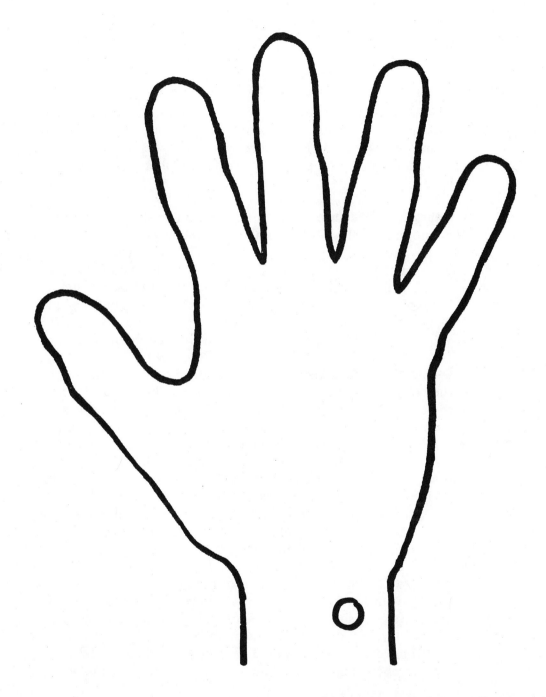

Disclosure Goal: Parents will tell about the first purchase they made with money they had saved.

Projects with Preschoolers

Materials Needed: One pitcher of water, bath towel, a scarf, small cup for each person, ten to twenty unsharpened pencils, poster board, scissors, glue, hole punch, yarn, markers or crayons, Helping Hand pattern on page 251, old family photos, and playground ball

Letting Your Child Know You Begin this lesson by sharing a positive remembrance. Tell your family about a time when you saved up your money and made a special purchase. What were you saving for? How much did it cost? Describe the anticipation you felt as you saved. Tell about the day you finally got to purchase the item. What were you feeling? What were you thinking? Did someone help you make the decision or did you decide all on your own? What were you feeling as you brought the item home?

Getting to Know Your Child Ask your children to think of an item that they would like to save for. What would you like to buy? Describe the color, style, size, etc. What do you plan to do with this item? How might you go about saving money to buy it? How long do you think it will take to save this money? Pretend that you are going into the store to buy this item. How would you feel? Think about how good it would feel to know that you have saved your money and then made a good choice.

Explain that this lesson tells us about a woman who has made some bad choices in her life. She meets Jesus one day at the well. Jesus tells her how she can make good choices.

Becoming Caringly Involved Instead of reading the Bible Drama out loud to your family, you might want to retell it in your own words. Tell the story using these props: one towel, a scarf, one large pitcher of water, and one cup for each family member. Drape the unfolded towel over your head. The towel should come down over your forehead and then drape over your head and shoulders.

Using either a large rubber band or a scarf, secure the towel in place. The rubber band or scarf should fit over the towel and around your forehead. You've now created the headdress for many Middle Eastern men. Also show your children how the women of the Middle East used to wear their veils across their face. Hold the large pitcher on your head as you begin the story and then move it to your lap. Fill the pitcher with only a small amount of water. All the water will be poured out into the individual cups.

Your summary of the Bible Drama might sound like:

"The Bible tells us about a woman who walked to the well to fetch water. Each day she would carry her waterpot to Jacob's Well. (Let each child try to hold the pitcher of water on her head while seated. Adults may need to give assistance.) We don't know her real name, but we'll call her Joanna. Joanna couldn't walk to the well when the other ladies did. They made fun of her and called her ugly names. Joanna had made some poor choices early in her life. Because of those choices, the town's people treated her badly.

Joanna walked to the well on this one particular day and met a Man there. This Man was a Jew and Joanna was a Samaritan. These two groups of people didn't like each other because of an argument that had happened years before. The Jews and Samaritans wouldn't even talk to one another. (Ask half of your family to be the Jews and the other half to be Samaritans. Turn your backs toward one another and refuse to look at each other.)

But this Man surprised Joanna, because He talked to her anyway. He asked her for a drink of water. Joanna was again surprised because He continued to talk with her about her life and her choices. He told her about God's love for her. He told her that the water that she got from the well would soon be gone, but that God's love will never run out. (Pour water into each person's cup. Show your children the empty pitcher. Emphasize this point: We ran out of the water from the pitcher, but we will never run out of God's love.)

Joanna suddenly realized that the man she was talking to was Jesus. Jesus was the man that the Bible had promised would come to save the world. Joanna was so excited. Her dull, boring day had turned out to be very exciting. She actually got to meet with Jesus.

She got to talk with Him. Joanna was so excited that she called all the town's people out to meet Jesus. Many people believed in Jesus because of the words of Joanna.

After retelling the Bible Drama invite your family to participate in this discussion:

- What did Jesus say would never run out? What will never be empty? (God's love.)
- Jesus made friends with Joanna even though the Jews and Samaritans were not supposed to like each other. Who would Jesus want us to make friends with?

Explain to your children that Jesus helped Joanna by telling her about God's love. He said that God's love would always be with her. Jesus helps us in *two* different ways each day. He gives us other people to show us God's love; these people help us make good choices. Second, Jesus helps us because He is ready to hear us any time we want to pray. When we pray to God, He also helps us make good choices.

Pick-up Sticks

Begin the activity section of this lesson by playing "Pick-up Sticks" or "Jenga." Each of these games requires players to choose which playing piece to move. Pick-up Sticks can also be played with un-sharpened pencils. Using pencils may be more appropriate for pre-school hands.

These are the basic rules for Pick-up Sticks: Gather ten to twenty unsharpened pencils and hold them upright, six inches above the floor. Let go of the pencils and let them drop to the floor. The object of the game is to pick up one pencil at a time and remove it from the playing area. As you pick up each pencil, you cannot move any of the others. If any other pencil moves, you lose your turn. If you successfully pick up a pencil without moving any others, then you may go again. Each player takes turns until the last pencil is removed from the playing area. The player with the most pencils wins the game.

Play the game as indicated above. Then as you play the game a second time, incorporate this one additional rule. Divide your family into pairs. If possible, pair one adult or older sibling with each preschooler. Before a player can make a move he must consult with his partner. Before he tries to move a pencil, he must ask his partner, "Which pencil should I choose?" Then play the game as before.

As you end the game, make these closing comments: Which game did you like better? Children may say, "I liked the first one better because I could do it myself" or "I liked the second game better because we won!" Point out that we made better choices when we had help from our partners. When we were playing with our partners, they helped us decide which pencils to move.

God gives us moms and dads, teachers and coaches to help us make other decisions. God gives us these people to be our partners when we have hard choices to make. God knows that sometimes we need help deciding what to do or how to act. We can go to these people and they will help us make good choices. Let's think of all the people that God has given to help us.

My Helping Hands

For this activity you will need to trace and cut several hands from the pattern on page 251. Each person will need two cut-out hands. Parents will want to make this craft along with their children. We suggest that you use poster board or some other heavy paper. Punch a hole in the "wrist" of each hand. Place markers and crayons on the table. You will also need several family pictures that you do not mind cutting up.

Explain to your children that we are going to make a special book today. This book will show the people who help us make good choices. Let's each name five people who can help us make good choices. As you name each person, touch one of the fingers on your left hand. For example, Mom can help me make good choices (touch your thumb). Dad can help me make good choices (touch your first finger). My Sunday School teacher can help me make good choices (touch your middle finger). My stepdad can help me make good choices (touch your ring finger). Our pastor can help me make good choices (touch little finger).

Keep brainstorming until everyone has named five people. Next, look for photos of each of these people. Then paste a picture of each "helper" onto each finger of one cut-out hand. Use only one cut-out hand at this point. If no picture is available, draw a picture and/or write the name of this person onto one finger of the cut-out hand.

To complete the second cut-out hand, use a marker or crayon to make the cover of this book. Write the words, "My Helping Hands" in the middle of the second cut-out hand. Cut a piece of yarn approximately six inches long. Lay the cover (second hand) on top of the first hand and then pull the yarn through both holes. Tie the yarn into a bow. You've just made a book of helping hands! Hang the book of Helping Hands in your room after this lesson.

Helping Hands Discussion

Let's use our book of Helping Hands for this next activity. I am going to read a situation to you. Pretend that these things are happening to you and that you want to make a good choice. I want you to open your book and point to the person who could help you make a good choice.

Read these situations. Then ask each family member who they would choose to ask for help. Who could help you make a good choice? Who could help you decide what to do? *Point to that person on your Helping Hand.* Parents will want to be sure to participate in this activity too. Your children need to see that even adults ask for others' help.

- A boy in your preschool class has been picking on you. He is always careful not to get caught by the teacher, but he calls you names and takes your snacks. You don't know what to do. Show us who could help.
- Your teacher makes you sit in "Time Out" two days in a row. She thinks that you are making noises and disrupting the class, but it's not you. It's the person who sits next to you. You don't know what to do. Show us who could help.
- You want to buy some gum with the money that Grandma gave you. You also know that you need to save some money to buy your dad a birthday present. You don't know what to do. Show us who could help.

(Adapted from *I Always, Always Have Choices*, Revell Company, Tarrytown, New York, 1992)

Helper Action Rhyme

Invite your family to join you in this action rhyme. Explain to your children that some children are born into this world without their hearing. They can't hear sounds or talk in the same way that we can. They must use their hands to communicate. This action rhyme incorporates sign language to represent several of the words.

God gives us **family**	(show sign for "family")
Mom and **Dad**	(show signs for "Mom" and "Dad")
To **help** us make good choices	(show sign for "help")
Know **good** from **bad**	(show signs for "good" and "bad")
God gives us **friends**	(show sign for "friend")
And teachers **come along**	(wave arm; motion for someone to come)
To **help** us make good choices	(show sign for help)
Know **right** from **wrong**	(show signs for "right" and "wrong")

Choices Discussion

Take your family outside and play a game of catch or kickball. After your children have expended some energy, sit down and ask this question: Let's pretend that we were playing ball just now, and our ball accidentally hit the neighbor's window and broke it. What could we do? Let's name all the ideas we can think of. Allow your family to give several options. Some options might be:

We could do nothing and hope that nobody finds out.
We could say that the people next door must have done it.
We could tell our neighbors that we're sorry and ask to pay for it.

How do we know which choice is right? Well, we know that it is wrong to lie, so we can't say that the people next door did it. But what about the other two choices? Which do you think is the best choice? Allow children to give their responses and then confirm that apologizing would be the best.

Or

FATHER

FAMILY

FRIEND

HELP

COME

MOTHER

Or

GOOD

RIGHT

BAD

WRONG

Explain that God wants us to pray when we have hard choices to make. He wants us to tell Him about our choices. When we pray, God can let us know that we are making good choices. If a choice feels wrong, then it probably isn't what God wants us to do. God helps us know the best choice by giving us good feelings. We have these good feelings when we share with a friend, help a teacher erase the blackboard, or pick up trash that doesn't belong to us. We feel good when we obey God's rules.

Closing the Lesson

Close the lesson as you put each child to bed that evening. Talk with each child about any decision or choice that she might need to make. Then invite her to pray with you about that choice. Tell God about the decision. Ask Him to tell you and your child what He thinks would be best. For example: "Taylor, let's ask God what He would want you to do when Andrew picks on you in class." or "Rebecca, let's ask God what He wants us to do when you and Elizabeth have a hard time playing together. I will ask God how He wants me to talk to you girls. Let's ask God how He wants you to talk to Elizabeth."

Parents will want to continue to pray about choices throughout the week. You might even want to make it a habit. Pray together about which job Daddy should take. Pray together about how to care for Grandma as she gets older. Pray at any time and at any place. Let your children see that God is concerned about us and wants to be intimately involved in our daily lives.

Great Fun for Grade Schoolers

Materials Needed: One bath towel, one large rubber band or scarf, one pitcher of water, one cup for each person, a ball for kickball or bat and ball for baseball, colored poster board, hole punch, colored yarn, scissors, old family photos, markers or crayons

Letting Your Child Know You Begin this lesson by sharing a positive remembrance. Tell your family about a time when you saved up your money and made a special purchase. What were you saving for? How much did it cost? Describe the anticipation you felt as you saved. Tell about the day you finally got to purchase the item. What were you feeling? What were you thinking? Did someone help you make the decision or did you decide all on your own? What were you feeling as you brought the item home?

Getting to Know Your Child Ask your children to think of an item that they would like to save for. What would you like to buy? Describe the color, style, size, etc. What do you plan to do with this item? How might you go about saving money to buy it? How long do you think it will take to save this money? Pretend that you are going into the store to buy this item; how would you feel? Think about how good it would feel to know that you have saved your money and then made a good choice.

Explain that this lesson tells us about a woman who has made some bad choices in her life. She meets Jesus one day at the well. Jesus tells her how she can make good choices.

Becoming Caringly Involved Prepare this Middle Eastern costume before you read the story to your family. You will need one large bath towel and a large rubber band or scarf. Drape the unfolded towel over your head. The towel should come down over your forehead and then drape over your head and shoulders. Using either a large rubber band or a scarf, secure the towel in place. The rubber band or scarf should fit over the towel and around your forehead. You've now created the headdress of many Middle Eastern men.

Now practice carrying water as the Middle Eastern women did. Fill a large pitcher half full of water. Go outside and let each person practice walking with the pitcher on top of their heads.

Return inside and begin reading the Bible Drama. As you read the words of Joanna, draw one side of your towel across your face. Show your children how the Middle Eastern women wore their veils. The veils covered the women's nose and chin, only their eyes could be seen.

As you read the words of Jesus that describe the "living water" show your children the pitcher of water once again. Give each child a small cup. Pour water from the pitcher into each cup, emptying the pitcher. Ask each person to drink their water. Explain that Jesus told Joanna about God's love. He said that God's love is not like this water. We ran out of this water. Look, the pitcher is empty. But we can never run out of God's love. He just keeps on loving and loving.

When you have finished reading the story, ask your family to participate in this discussion:

- What did Jesus say would never run out? What will never be empty? (God's love.)
- Jesus made friends with Joanna even though the Jews and Samaritans were not supposed to like each other. Who would Jesus want us to make friends with?

Difficult Choices

Ask your family to join you outside. Play a game of kickball, baseball, or just a game of catch. After you've had a chance to play for twenty or thirty minutes, go inside to ask this question: What would we have done today if the ball had hit and broken the neighbor's window? What if you kicked the ball just hard enough to go over the fence and into the window? What if you curved the ball just enough to knock out that window? Let's name all the things we *could* do. Allow your family members to brainstorm several possibilities. Some ideas might include:

- We could pretend that it didn't happen and hope that nobody found out it was us.
- We could say that it was some other kids in the neighborhood.
- We could go tell the neighbors that we saw it happen, but not say that it was us.
- We could tell the neighbors that it was an accident and offer to pay for the broken window.

As your family gives their ideas, write them down so that everyone can see them. Discuss the advantages and disadvantages of each choice. For instance: "If we decided not to tell and the neighbors did find out, they would be even more upset with us." or "If we say that someone else did it, then they might get in trouble. They might find out that we blamed them and get mad at us."

When you have discussed all the options, let each person choose which way they would respond. Let every person choose for him-self. Don't give any pressure or criticism if you do not agree with a person's choice. Ask your family if they think it would be easy to make this decision. Would it be easy or hard to make the right choice in this situation?

Explain that God knows that we have tough decisions to make. He has given us family and friends to help us with these decisions. When we have hard decisions to make, we can get help from the special adults that God has given.

Helping Hands Directory
See Preschool section for explanation of this activity. You may also want to include phone numbers in your Helping Hands Directory.

Helping Hands Discussion
Let's practice identifying the people who can help us make tough decisions. Listen to the situations that I am about to read. Pretend that you are in this situation. Then look at your directory and choose the person whom you would ask for help.

- Your friend tells you a secret and makes you promise not to tell anyone. Your friend could get hurt if you keep this secret, but you don't want to break your promise either. Who would you go to for help? Point to that person on your directory.
- One of your classmates has not studied for her spelling test. She asks you to let her copy off your paper during the test. Who would you go to for help? Point to that person on your directory.
- Every time that you go over to your friend's house, he wants to play in an abandoned building. You know the building isn't safe, but you don't want to look like a wimp in front of your friend. Who do you ask for help? Point to that person on your directory.
- Your little brother has gone into your room and de-stroyed the art project that took you weeks to make. You are so angry that you feel like hitting him. Who could you talk to about this? Point to that person on your direc-tory.

- You have just had a terrible fight with your best friend; both of you said some mean things. It has been five days since the two of you have talked. You told your friend that you would never say you were sorry, but now you're feeling guilty. Who do you ask for help? Point to that person on your directory.

End this activity with these comments: God doesn't want us to have to make tough decisions alone. He's given us good friends and family members so that we can go to them for help. God has given us adults to help us make good choices.
(Adapted from *I Always, Always Have Choices,* Revell Company, Tarrytown, New York, 1992)

Choices: Field Trip

For the final activity, ask your family to go on a field trip with you. Explain that you are going to take a trip to the toy store together. On this trip you will help each other make good decisions. Tell your children that each of them will get five dollars. They will be free to spend this five dollars in any way that they choose. You want them to make a good decision, so they will be pleased with their purchase. Ask these questions on your way to the toy store:
- Do you want to buy something that you play with by yourself or with other people?
- Do you want something that will last a long time or will be used up quickly? (For instance, a Nerf football will last a long time. A paint-by-number kit will be used up quickly.)
- Do you want something that you can play with right away? (Some toys you have to put together before they are ready for play. Others have batteries that have to be recharged.)
- Do you want an inside toy or an outside toy?
- Do you want something that you can take in the car or that we leave at home?

Let each child answer these questions for himself. Through this discussion, you will want to help your children define their preferences. Make sure that you give them the freedom to choose, even if you don't agree with their choices. The only stipulation should be that the toy they choose must fall within their dollar amount. If some children want to save their money and not spend it on this trip, they are free to choose that option.

Before you reach the toy store, you should have a preliminary idea about each child's preferences. Summarize what you think each child has said. This will give them an opportunity to clarify or adjust their answers. For example:

"So, Christina, you want a toy for inside. You want it to be something that you and Sarah can play with together and you want it to last a long time. Is that right?"

When you do get to the toy store, give each child plenty of time to look. Patiently guide them through the questions again. Help your children narrow their options and find the possible alternatives. Don't hesitate to ask the salesperson if a particular toy will need batteries or assembly. Show your children how to get accurate information so that they will be better equipped to make a decision. Avoid giving your own opinions and avoid criticizing their choices. This will encourage your children to clarify their own opinions. Avoid the "why" questions: "Why do you like this color?" or "Why do you want this particular model?" These questions only undermine your child's ability to make his own decisions. Remember, you want to help your child meet his objectives, not yours.

Let each child go to the counter and pay for the merchandise herself. Let her carry the bag and receive any change that is left. When you get home, let each person play with her new toy and enjoy her purchase. Ask each child if she thinks she made a good choice. Are you happy with the toy that you chose? How does it feel to make good choices? Emphasize that when we work together and talk with each other, we can make good choices. God gives us adults to help us make good decisions. That help is available every day.

Optional Activity

If no money is available to actually purchase toys, parents may want to do this same activity with a catalog. Find a toy store or department store catalog and let your children do their "shopping" at home.

Closing the Lesson

Close the lesson by telling your family about the second way that Jesus helps us every day. He gives us the privilege to talk with Him in prayer. Explain that prayer is like talking on the telephone.

Let each child call a friend or a relative and talk for two minutes. Then ask these questions: Were you able to talk to your friend or family member? Were you able to see them? Talking on the phone is like talking to God. We can't see Him but we can still talk to Him. He hears us any time and any place. He wants us to talk to Him about our choices. He wants to hear how we feel. As you put each child to bed that evening talk with each child about any decision or choice that he might need to make. Then invite him to pray with you about that choice. Tell God about the decision. Ask God to tell you and your child what He thinks would be best. For example: "Taylor, let's ask God what He wants you to do when boys from the other soccer team are not good sports." or "Shelby, let's ask God what He wants you to do when Hannah says mean things to you."

Parents will want to continue to pray about choices throughout the week. You might even want to make it a habit. Pray together about which job Daddy should take. Pray together about how to care for Grandma as she gets older. Pray at any time and at any place. Let your children see that God is concerned about us and wants to be intimately involved in our daily lives.

Making It Real for Middle Schoolers

Materials Needed: A book of matches, several sheets of paper, two or three coins, a favorite food item that will serve as a prize, one-inch wooden blocks with holes or one-inch wooden toy wheels, paint, fine-tip black permanent marker

Letting Your Child Know You Begin this lesson by sharing a positive remembrance. Tell your family about a time when you saved up your money and made a special purchase. What were you saving for? Was it a car stereo, a bike, or a dress for a special occasion? How much did it cost? How long did you have to save? Describe the anticipation you felt as you saved. Tell about the day you finally got to purchase the item. What were you feeling? What were you thinking? Did someone help you make the decision or did you decide all on your own? What were you feeling as you brought the item home?

Getting to Know Your Child Ask your teen to name something that she would like to save for. What item would you like to buy? How much does it cost and how do you plan to save? Parents will want to encourage teens to think and plan, but don't lecture. Ask thought-provoking questions in a gentle way.

Second, ask your teens to help you by giving their input on a particular problem. Each adult should share a decision that they face, then ask for each child's input. Choose a topic that is outside the realm of family relationships. Adults may want to discuss ministry decisions, work dilemmas, or upcoming purchases. Then summarize the topic in a way that teens will understand. For example: "I would like your input on this situation. One of my coworkers has had some poor interactions with customers. Several of these customers have called and complained to me about my coworker. I don't know whether to talk to him directly or take it up with my boss. What do you think?"

When an adult asks for a teen's opinion it communicates approval and respect. Listen to each person's input. Give credibility to what they say. Teens can pick up on insincerity, so make sure you hear their ideas with a receptive heart. They will be much more open to hearing your input if you take the time to hear from them. Be sure to keep your family members updated about your decision. Tell your teens how you decided to handle the situation, how it turns out, and then thank them for their input.

Explain that this lesson is about a woman who meets Christ. She has lived her whole life making poor choices. These choices have had severe consequences. Listen to how Jesus deals with this woman. You might be surprised at what He says and what He doesn't say.

Becoming Caringly Involved Read the Bible Drama along with your family. You might also emphasize these points as you read: Joanna had chosen to go to the well during the middle of the afternoon.

This was the hottest part of the day. All of the other ladies came to the well each morning when it was cool. But Joanna chose to come when the others did not. She didn't want to endure the looks and comments of the other women.

Second, the story gives a little information about the relationship between Jews and the Samaritans. The hatred between these two groups of people was intense. Most Jews, in fact, would travel many miles out of their way in order to avoid going through Samaria. To call someone a Samaritan meant a great insult.

In this Middle Eastern culture, women were treated as property. The average man showed little respect or honor to any woman. Women were considered just above slaves in the ranking system of the day. Showing interest in a woman's well-being was almost unheard of.

Jesus' interaction with this woman was extremely unusual for this time in history. He looked past her reputation, her race, and gender and cared about her. He didn't hound her about her mistakes or scold her for her choice of living. He simply gave her hope. Christ held out the hope that life could be different after meeting Him. He made a miraculous difference in her daily life.

As you finish reading the story, ask these questions:

- Think about the woman's circumstances. How do you think she was feeling when she first met Christ? How do you think she was feeling after the conversation with Jesus?
- Were you surprised to find out that Jesus didn't scold the woman for her mistakes? How did you expect Him to respond to her?
- If Jesus didn't scold the woman at the well for her mistakes, maybe He doesn't operate this way with us either. How do you feel when you think about this possibility?

Burn Out

Gather one book of matches and choose one person to record all the answers given during this activity. Each person will hear a situation in which he must make a decision. They are to imagine themselves in this situation. Each person will light a match and then think of as many choices of action as possible before the match burns out. The object is to think of as many choices as possible; they don't necessarily have to be choices that you would actually make. The recorder writes down each answer as it is given. Someone else assumes the job of writing down answers when it is the recorder's turn to light the match. As a safety precaution, adults will want to remain present during all portions of this activity. Here are six possible situations:

- Your best friend has not studied for his history test. He wants you to sit next to him so that he can cheat off your paper. He'll probably fail the course if he doesn't pass this test. What do you do?
- You have just graduated from high school. The future is yours for the asking. You have saved $3,000. What do you do with the money?
- Your friends are going to a party where you know there will be alcohol served. One of them calls on Friday afternoon and invites you to go. What do you do?
- One of your friends has dared you to perform a certain task. He/she has offered $100 if you take the dare. What *wouldn't* you do for $100?
- You are shopping with your friend at the mall. Your friend asks you to stand next to her and watch for employees of the store. She's planning to steal merchandise. What could you do?
- Your English teacher has assigned a five-paragraph essay. Your essay must be a persuasive essay on the "Reasons to Avoid Nose-Rings." What reasons can you think of?

When you have finished this activity, go back over each situation and ask the recorder to read the responses that were given. Then as a group, brainstorm other possibilities for the situation. Ask these questions: How did you feel when you had to come up with choices while the match was lit? Did you like having to make choices under pressure? Was it easy or difficult to think of choices and make decisions alone? How does this compare to brainstorming as a group?

Explain that God doesn't want us to have to make difficult decisions alone. We can decide which clothes to wear or what food to eat without too much stress. But there are some decisions that come our way that require more thought and more input. We may need to talk to someone about a decision because we feel nervous or pressured. We may need to talk with someone because the decision is just too big to handle alone. We may also need to talk with another person just to get a new perspective or different alternatives that we haven't seen before. This is one of the ways that God helps us make decisions on a daily basis. He has given us relationships to help make decision-making easier. We have a "divine decision-making resource" in our relationships with other people.

Coin Toss

For this activity divide your family into pairs. One person is the "tosser" and the other person is the "crosser." Instruct each team to stand behind the starting line. An object or prize is placed in a closet or pantry. The starting line should be approximately thirty feet from the closet.

The goal is to reach the prize first. When the game begins, the tosser stands behind the crosser and flips a coin. If heads come up, the crosser takes two steps forward. If tails come up, the crosser must take one step back. Steps are taken heel-to-toe only. Be prepared; things may get a little crowded as you approach the closet.

After you have declared the winner, ask these questions: How did you feel when the coin came up heads? How did you feel when it came up tails? Were these feelings especially true as you got closer to the closet?

Make these closing comments: It was pretty frustrating when our actions were dictated by the toss of a coin. We weren't making the decisions ourselves, we were playing the odds. Sometimes we try to live life like the toss of a coin. We make decisions without careful planning or thinking it through. Sometimes we decide to take action without asking for help. When we make tough decisions without thinking it through or asking for help, we're playing the odds. Things may turn out well or sometimes things may not turn out well at all. God has given us several gifts that help us make good decisions. These gifts keep us from having to play the odds. He's given us the Bible, other people, and prayer.

Cabinet Officials

Ask your teens to explain the function of the President's Cabinet. The President of the United States appoints a group of people known as his Cabinet. What do they do? Allow your family time to give their answers, then emphasize that the Cabinet exists to support the President. The Secretary of Education, the Secretary of State, and the other Cabinet officials have the specific job of advising the President.

These Cabinet members are selected because of their knowledge and skillful handling of difficult situations. Any time the President needs information about the area of education, he consults the Secretary. If the President needs to make a decision related to foreign policy, he gets input from the Secretary of State.

There are times when we also need a "cabinet of advisers." We need people around us who can give input and information. We need people around us who share their knowledge and are able to handle difficult situations. Let's spend some time thinking of who you might want to be on your "cabinet of advisers." Who would you go to if you faced a difficult decision? Who would you go to if you just needed to talk? Write down five names and telephone numbers if you know them.

Ask each person to share the names he has listed. Parents will want to make their own lists as well. Invite your family to join you in making a tangible reminder of the people you've chosen to be on your cabinet.

Prior to this activity you will want to make one of these key rings as an example. You will need: one-inch wooden toy wheels or one-inch wooden cubes with holes already drilled, strips of leather or ball chains found in the jewelry section of most craft stores, several colors of paint, one fine-tip black permanent marker. The wooden toy wheels and wooden cubes can be found at craft stores as well.

Paint two of the wooden cubes with any color that you wish. You may also want to decorate the cubes with designs or pictures. Just make sure that you leave five sides of the cubes undecorated. When the paint has dried, use the black permanent marker to write the initials or names of all five of your chosen cabinet members. Write the names on the undecorated faces of the cubes.

Connect two ball chains together to form one long chain. Slip the chain through the two painted cubes and your key ring is ready. You can put your house key on this key ring or hang it in your room. It will serve as a reminder of the five people who are available to help you make decisions.

Cabinet Officials Discussion

Ask your family to use their lists of cabinet officials in the following discussion. We are going to practice identifying the people who can help us make good choices.

I will read a situation. I want you to pretend that you are in this situation and you must decide how to handle it. Think about your list of advisers. Who would you go to for advice or support? Here are the situations:

- The girl whose locker is next to yours is a friend from kindergarten. The two of you don't hang out together much any more, but you do have a long-standing friendship. She comes to school one day with a black eye. She says that she slipped and fell, but you know that's not true. Who do you ask for help? Which cabinet member could help with this difficult situation?

- One of your friends is very rude and disrespectful to his mother. He yells at her so much that you become uncomfortable any time the two of you are at his house. Your friend always wants to hang out at his house. Who could you talk with about this issue? Which cabinet member might be able to give some good input?

- You broke up with your boyfriend/girlfriend about a month ago. This person has begun to spread rumors about you that are not true. You've asked this person to stop talking about you, but the rumors continue. Who could you go to for help? Which cabinet member might be able to give you some new ideas?

Close this activity by encouraging your family members to use the gifts that God has given them. Explain that it is not a sign of weakness to ask for help in difficult situations. In fact, it is a sign of maturity to realize that you are not able to handle every situation alone and could benefit from involving other people.

Closing the Lesson

Close the lesson by making some easy decisions. Invite your family to make homemade pizza. Buy ready-made pizza crust and sauce. Then purchase a variety of toppings such as: pepperoni, hamburger, several kinds of cheese, mushrooms, olives, or anchovies. Designate one-half of a pizza for each person. They may put any toppings they wish onto their half of the pizza. Bake the pizzas and enjoy!

As you are eating, ask each person to fill her drinking glass according to how much wisdom she thinks she has. If the glass is full this means they are wise 100 percent of the time. If the glass is half full then they are wise 50 percent of the time. Give everyone a chance to explain their percentages and then make these final comments: In order to make good decisions, we need wisdom. God tells us in James 1:5 that if anyone lacks wisdom he should ask God for it. God gives generous amounts of wisdom if we ask for it. God will give us generous amounts of wisdom when we pray to Him and talk with Him. God wants us to make good decisions because He wants the best for us. He's given us people in our lives to help us and He's given us the privilege of prayer.

Close the time by praying about any decisions that family members are currently facing. Be very specific to ask God for His wisdom in each situation. Thank Him in advance for the generous wisdom He will give.

High School Happenings

Materials Needed: A book of matches, several sheets of paper, one-inch wooden blocks with holes or one-inch wooden toy wheels, paint, fine-tip permanent black marker

Letting Your Child Know You Begin this lesson by sharing a positive remembrance. Tell your family about a time when you saved up your money and made a special purchase. What were you saving for? Was it a car stereo, a bike, or a dress for a special occasion? How much did it cost? How long did you have to save? Describe the anticipation you felt as you saved. Tell about the day you finally got to purchase the item. What were you feeling? What were you thinking? Did someone help you make the decision or did you decide all on your own? What were you feeling as you brought the item home?

Getting to Know Your Child Ask your teens to name something that they would like to save for. What item would you like to buy? How much does it cost and how do you plan to save? Parents will want to encourage teens to think and plan, but don't lecture. Ask thought-provoking questions in a gentle way.

Second, ask your teens to help you by giving their input on a particular problem. Each adult should share a decision that they face, then ask for each child's input. Choose a topic that is outside the realm of family relationships. Adults may want to discuss ministry opportunities, work dilemmas, or upcoming purchases. Then summarize the topic in a way that teens will understand. For example: "I would like your input on this situation. One of my coworkers has had some poor interactions with customers. Several of these customers have called and complained to me about my coworker. I don't know whether to talk to him directly or take it up with my boss. What do you think?"

When an adult asks for a teen's opinion it communicates approval and respect. Listen to each person's input. Give credibility to what they say. Teens can pick up on insincerity, so make sure you hear their ideas with a receptive heart. They will be much more open to hearing your input, if you take the time to hear from them. Be sure to update your family members about your situation. Tell your family how you decide to handle the situation, how it turns out, and then thank them for their input.

Explain that this lesson is about a woman who meets Christ. She has lived her whole life making poor choices. These choices have had severe consequences. Listen to how Jesus deals with this woman. You might be surprised at what He says and what He doesn't say.

Becoming Caringly Involved Read the Bible Drama along with your family. You might also emphasize these points as you read: Joanna had chosen to go to the well during the middle of the afternoon. This was the hottest part of the day. All of the other ladies came to the well each morning when it was cool. But Joanna chose to come when the others did not. She didn't want to endure the looks and comments of the other women.

Second, the story gives a little information about the relationship between Jews and the Samaritans. The hatred between these two groups of people was intense. Most Jews, in fact, would travel many miles out of their way in order to avoid going through Samaria. To call someone a Samaritan meant a great insult.

In this Middle Eastern culture, women were treated as property. The average man showed little respect or honor to any woman. Women were considered just above slaves in the ranking system of the day. Showing interest in a woman's well-being was almost unheard of.

Jesus' interaction with this woman was extremely unusual for this time in history. He looked past her reputation, her race, and gender and cared about her. He didn't hound her about her mistakes or scold her for her choice of living, He simply gave her hope. Christ held out the hope that life could be different after meeting Him. He made a miraculous difference in her daily life.

As you finish reading the story, ask these questions:

- Think about the woman's circumstances. How do you think she was feeling when she first met Christ? How do you think she was feeling after the conversation with Jesus?
- Were you surprised to find out that Jesus didn't scold the woman for her mistakes? How did you expect Him to respond to her?
- If Jesus didn't scold the woman at the well for her mistakes, maybe He doesn't operate this way with us either. How do you feel when you think about this possibility?

Burn Out

See Middle School section for the explanation of this activity. The six situations for this activity are:

- You meet a college recruiter who is friends with your parents. He tells you that one way to increase your chance for selection to a college is by demonstrating community involvement. What are the possibilities?
- One of your friends has dared you to perform a certain

task. He/she has offered you $100 if you accept the dare. What *wouldn't* you for $100?

- You've ridden with a friend of yours to a party. The party is just about over and your friend is drunk. He/she has the car keys. What could you do?
- You have just graduated from high school. The future is yours for the asking. You have saved $3,000. What do you do with the money?
- Your best friend never studies for exams. He has asked you to sit across from him so that he can copy off your paper during the test. How might you respond?
- Your English teacher has assigned a five-paragraph essay. Your essay must be a persuasive paper that gives "Reasons to Avoid Working in a Nudist Camp." What reasons will you give?

Cabinet Officials

See Middle School section.

Cabinet Officials Discussion

See Middle School section for explanation of this activity. Ask your family to use their list of Cabinet officials in the following discussion. We are going to practice identifying the people who can help us make good choices. I will read a situation. I want you to pretend that you are in this situation and you must decide how to handle it. Think about your list of advisers. Who would you go to for advice or support? Here are the situations:

- One of your good friends has been deliberately omitted from a party on Friday night. You know he's been left out because of the color of his skin. The person who is throwing the party calls to make sure you're coming. The friend who was not invited calls and wants you to go to a movie on Friday. Who would you go to for input? Which Cabinet member would you tell about this situation?
- The girl whose locker is next to yours has been a friend since kindergarten. She comes to school one morning and looks very upset. Your friend hints about suicide, but makes you promise not to tell anyone. Who would you

go to for help? Which Cabinet member could help you handle this difficult situation?

- Your boss has accused you of stealing money from the register. You haven't taken the money, but you may know the person who did. Your boss has threatened to fire you if the money is not returned or the person who stole it identified. Who would you ask for help? Which Cabinet member could assist you?

Close this activity by encouraging your family members to use the gifts that God has given them. Explain that it is not a sign of weakness to ask for help in difficult situations. In fact, it is a sign of maturity to realize that you are not able to handle every situation alone and could benefit from involving other people.

C-H-O-I-C-E

One of the most vital skills of living is how to make sound decisions. Use the following steps to teach your family a practical decision-making process. You will want to use an actual decision that your family members are facing. If no decision is currently pending, then you may want to use the topic we have chosen for this exercise.

Good decision-making involves a process. Let's pretend that Jacob has decided that he wants to find a job this summer, but he doesn't know what kind of job. We can use this process of decision-making to help Jacob with his job search. The process includes these six steps:

C—Call it! This means that you need to write down or name the specific decision. For example, Jacob might write down, "I must choose which jobs I would like to apply for this summer." Notice that the description is specific. Also notice that Jacob is stating that his choice lies in which jobs to apply for, not which job he is going to get. He realizes that the potential employers' decision will affect the final outcome.

H—Hammer out the objectives. In other words, what issues are important to you? What conditions have to be met? What objectives do you want to be met? In Jacob's situation, he would need to consider the answers to these questions: Do you have transportation available or will you have to find employment within walking distance? Do you have any scheduling conflicts like family vacations or summer band practice? Do you want to work full time or part time, days or evenings? Do you want to work outside or inside? Do you want to work primarily with people your own age or with adults? After Jacob defines what issues must be met and what his preferences are, he's ready to move to the next step.

O—Order your objectives. Jacob needs to rank the objectives by order of priority. Some objectives will be "absolutes" and others will be optional. Assign each objective a number. The top 1–3 objectives should be the "absolutes." The bottom objectives should be the objectives that reflect your preferences. For example, Jacob's top five objectives might look like this:
1. Location within walking distance, in case I don't have a ride every day.
2. Primarily afternoon or evening hours so that I can still go to football practice.
3. Opportunity to work with people my own age.
4. Pays slightly above minimum wage.
5. Something sports oriented.

I—Identify alternatives. Brainstorm all the possibilities given your objectives. Jacob will want to ask friends, family, and coaches about job opportunities. He will want to look in the newspaper and check other printed resources. Jacob will want to find as many creative alternatives as possible. He may need to make some changes in his objectives at this point. After brainstorming all the possibilities, Jacob may determine that there are only two job possibilities within walking distance from his home. He may choose to alter his list of objectives, perhaps it is too narrow (i.e., he may need to look for a job that is not necessarily sports related). Jacob may also choose to keep his list of objectives the same and pursue the two job possibilities.

C—Choose from the alternatives. Look at the alternatives and choose the one(s) that best meet your objectives. Jacob may prefer to apply to only one of these two job possibilities because it meets all his priorities and preferences. He may also want to apply to both jobs, since his options are so few.

E—Evaluate your choice. Does your decision meet your objectives? Will you be pleased with this choice? If Jacob answers no to these questions then he needs to modify some point in the process. Perhaps Jacob has not truly defined his objectives. Jacob may have a strong preference against retail jobs, but has not identified this preference before. As pointed out earlier, Jacob's list of objectives may be too narrow or he may need to do additional brainstorming to identify other alternatives.

As you take your family through this process, adults will need to remember that you are training your children in the decision-making process. You're not training if you are deciding for them. Guide your teens through the process and direct them in the process, but not on which decision to make. Your teens' priorities and objectives will probably be quite different from yours. Just remember, you want to teach them to make decisions that they can live with and are pleased with. You will be called on to give your children opportunities to decide, but the freedom to fail. The lessons they learn from the process and even from the failures will be invaluable.

Closing the Lesson

Close the lesson by making some easy decisions. Invite your family to make homemade pizza. Buy ready-made pizza crust and sauce. Then purchase a variety of toppings such as: pepperoni, hamburger, several kinds of cheese, mushrooms, olives, or anchovies. Designate one-half a pizza for each person. They may put any toppings they wish onto their half of the pizza. Bake the pizzas and enjoy!

As you are eating, ask each person to fill a drinking glass according to how much wisdom they think they have. If the glass is full this means they are wise 100 percent of the time. If the glass is half full then they are wise 50 percent of the time. Give everyone a chance to explain their percentages and then make these final comments: In order to make good decisions, we need wisdom. God tells us in James 1:5 that if anyone lacks wisdom he should ask God for it. God gives generous amounts of wisdom if we ask for it. God will give us generous amounts of wisdom when we pray to Him and talk with Him. God wants us to make good decisions because He wants the best for us. He's given us people in our lives to help us and He's given us the privilege of prayer.

Close the time by praying about any decisions that family members are currently facing. Be very specific to ask God for His wisdom in each situation. Thank Him in advance for the generous wisdom He will give.

Lesson 11

Selfish view gives way to the divine

Key Scripture Passage *And there arose also a dispute among them as to which one of them was regarded to be greatest. And He said to them. . . . "But let him who is the greatest among you become as the youngest, and the leader as the servant."*
—Luke 22:24-26

Then He poured water into the basin, and began to wash the disciples' feet, and to wipe them with the towel with which He was girded. . . . "If I then, the Lord and the Teacher, washed your feet, you also ought to wash one another's feet. For I gave you an example that you also should do as I did to you."—John 13:5, 14-15

Bible Drama

"That's my place, Peter. Don't you dare sit there." John seldom spoke to his friend with such stern seriousness.

All of the other disciples were rushing to the best places at the dinner table too. It was Passover, the most important meal of the year. The 12 Apostles were dining with Jesus in the upper room of a friend's home. But instead of acting like adults, they were pushing and shoving to get the best places at the table. They were acting like a bunch of schoolboys instead of the future leaders of the church!

Jesus, you see, would certainly be seated at the head of the table. Those to His left and right would be considered next in importance to Him. So every one of the disciples was fussing and arguing about which of them should sit next to Jesus.

The room grew louder and the arguing more intense, so intense that no one noticed when Jesus entered the room. In the glow of the oil lamps, He simply stood there taking in the scene of grown men acting like little boys. By the look on His face you could tell that this was not the first time they had argued about who was the greatest!

"Excuse Me, but where do I sit?" The disciples froze when they heard Jesus' voice. Now scurrying to make room at the table for Him, their loud arguing became silent shoving as they seated themselves around the low table. Everyone wanted to sit next to Him, but for all the wrong reasons. They just wanted to feel more important than the others.

Jesus began to speak. "It is so good to be here with you all! We just haven't had enough of these times together lately, have we?" Everyone nodded their agreement, thankful that they had been invited to share Passover with Jesus. My, weren't they important? They felt more important than His other friends, that's for sure!

"So tell Me, men. Just what were you discussing so angrily when I first came into the room? It must have been something of great significance." The room fell silent. Every man knew that Jesus had overheard their prideful talk. But no one said a word. All were too embarrassed to even try to explain their selfish pushing and shoving.

"Men, let Me tell you something. A bully always tries to prove that he is more important than anyone else. He is always concerned about who is bigger, better, or stronger. But it's not going to be that way among you, not if you are determined to be like Me. I have come as a servant, not as a master. My kind of leadership is the kind that leads by serving."

The disciples had never heard Jesus describe Himself that way. But as they thought about it, that was exactly what He had always done. He was always giving to people and never expected anything in return.

They were humbled by His words. Every eye was cast downward as they considered how selfish and rude they had been to one another. All the talk about who was best seemed so silly now!

Jesus got up from the table. Hanging by the door was the apron worn by the servant who cleaned the feet of the houseguests as they arrived. Wrapping the apron around His waist, He picked up the pitcher of water and knelt at the dirty feet of one of the disciples. Not a sound could be heard except the cool water splashing over dirty feet. One by one, the Servant Master washed the feet of the now humbled apostles. One by one their hearts broke as they realized the pride that kept them from serving one another. The most important person in the room was now serving them.

The act of kindness completed, Jesus sat again at the table. "Do you know what I have done for you? I have given you an example, that you should do as I have done. Do this for one another and you shall be blessed! Now, let's have something to eat."

The apostles passed the food around the table, amazed and humbled at what had taken place. This night would be one they would never forget. In the midst of their selfish behavior and harsh words, Jesus had shown them a better way to live. He was certainly the greatest servant of all!

Goal of Lesson 11: Families will learn that Jesus wants us to treat other people in the way we would like to be treated.

Intimacy Principle: Intimacy is hindered by selfishness, but encouraged through serving others.

Disclosure Goal: Parents of younger children will share their remembrances of holiday traditions. Parents of teens will share about their early dreams and aspirations.

Projects with Preschoolers

Materials Needed: Plates and glasses for Bible Drama reenactment, Froot Loops, Cheerios, long strands of licorice, saltine crackers, peanut butter, two apples, toothpicks

Letting Your Child Know You Begin this lesson by telling your family about your favorite holiday as a child. When you were in preschool or grade school what holiday did you like best? Did you like Thanksgiving, Christmas, July 4th, or one of the other holidays best? What traditions went along with this holiday? Did you like seeing certain relatives at this time of year? What foods were served? What activities took place? What did the kids do? What did the adults do? What other positive memories are attached to this holiday?

Getting to Know Your Child Give each child an opportunity to tell about his favorite holiday. Which one does he like best? Talk about your current holiday traditions. Which of the traditions does each child especially enjoy? Ask questions such as: What's your favorite food at Christmas? What is fun about getting to pick the Christmas tree? Which decorations do you like the best? Do you like singing Christmas carols or making cookies the best? Let each family member tell about his favorite holiday tradition; this reinforces a sense of belonging and security.

Explain that today's Bible Drama takes place during a holiday. The disciples are celebrating a holiday called the Passover. During the Passover celebration the disciples and Jesus were to sit down together for a special meal. Listen to the story. See if this holiday scene sounds like ours.

Becoming Caringly Involved Read the Bible Drama to your family and then invite them to join you in acting it out. Prepare a place setting for each person in the family. Set these items on a coffee table or other low table. Designate one special plate for "Jesus." Make His place somehow different from the rest. Jesus' plate might have a special place mat or flower beside it.

Designate one person to be Jesus and the rest of your family are the disciples. Your reenactment might look like this:

- The disciples are alone in the room.
- They start to sit down at the table but are pushing and shoving one another.
- Everyone wants to sit at the place next to Jesus.
- The disciples might be saying things like, "I want to sit there!" "Hey, I was here first!"
- Jesus comes into the room and sits down at His special place.
- The disciples get quiet and sit still immediately.
- Jesus welcomes the disciples and they start to eat.
- Jesus gets up and starts to wash the disciples' feet.
- Jesus tells the disciples that they should serve or help others.

You may want to use a wet washcloth instead of a basin of water for this dramatization. Give each family member the chance to play the part of Jesus. When you have finished acting out the Bible

Drama ask these questions:

- How were the disciples acting when Jesus first came in? Do we ever act this way?
- How does Jesus want the disciples to act? How does He want them to treat one another?

Candy Faces

Ask everyone to sit around the table. Give each person a handful of Cheerios and Froot Loops and several long strands of licorice. Give these instructions: Let's make faces with our licorice and cereal. We can place several pieces of licorice in a big circle to make the face. We can use the cereal for two eyes, and use small pieces of licorice for eyebrows. We can put one Froot Loop here for a nose and we can use a piece of licorice for a nice smile. Now, we can use these faces to show feelings.

Let's practice identifying feelings together. Make your candy face look happy. Let children manipulate their candy so that it shows "happy." Describe the happy face together. Look, we can tell this is a happy face because we see a smile. Tell me about a time when you were happy. Give each person a chance to tell about a time when she felt happy.

Next, ask your children to make the candy face show "sad" and "mad." Let children manipulate their candy to demonstrate these feelings. Again, describe the faces together and then ask each person to tell about a time when he felt sad and mad. Tell your family that you are going to use the candy faces for one more activity.

The Bible tells us the important things that God wants us to remember. God tells us to *Do unto others as we would have them do unto us* (Matt. 7:12). In other words, God wants us to treat other people the way we would want to be treated.

Explain the following activity to your family: I am going to read some short stories. I want you to think about how the person in the story would feel. If the person would feel sad, then make a sad face with your licorice mouth. If the person would feel happy, then make a happy face with your candy face. If the person would feel mad, then make a mad face with the licorice. Read the situations.

- Your preschool class is outside on the playground. You

and your friends are playing a game of "Freeze Tag." One of your classmates is playing too rough. He pushes Sarah so hard that she falls on the ground and hurts her knee. How would Sarah feel? Use the licorice to make the face. God says that we should treat others the way we want to be treated. Would you want to be treated the way Sarah was treated?

- Zachary is making a tall tower with his Legos, but he can't fit two pieces together without some help. David comes into the room and notices that Zach is having trouble. David offers to help Zachary with the tower. How do you think Zachary feels? Use the candy to make the face. God tells us to treat other people the way we want to be treated. Would you want someone to help you if you were having trouble?

- You and your friend are painting at the kitchen table. Your little sister comes to the table to get her bottle of juice. She is too little to reach the juice and can't climb up in the chair. She needs some help. Your friend picks up the bottle and starts to tease your little sister. Your friend holds the bottle in front of her but won't let her have it. How do you think your little sister is feeling? Use the candy to make the face. God says that we should treat others the way we want to be treated. Would you want to be teased like that?

- Bradley and Lisa are playing at the park. Both of them run to the swing set. They see that there is only one swing left. Bradley lets Lisa swing first. How do you think Lisa feels? Use the candy to show the feeling. God says that we should treat people the way we want to be treated. Would you like for someone to let you go first sometimes?

- You and your friends are playing in a sandbox. You are building a castle. You work very hard to make the walls and the doors of the castle. You stand up to admire your work but Elizabeth accidentally falls and smashes the castle. Andrew calls her stupid and says that she can't play there anymore. How do you think Elizabeth feels? Use the candy to show the feeling. God says that we should treat others the way we want to be treated. Would you want to be called names?

Close the activity by reminding children of Jesus' example. Jesus wants us to treat others the way we want to be treated. Invite your children to use the cereal and candy for one last activity. Make edible jewelry by stringing the Froot Loops and Cheerios onto the licorice. You can make necklaces or bracelets with the candy. As you string the cereal, tell about a time when someone treated you kindly. Tell about a time when someone helped you or let you go first. Tell about a time when someone was kind to you. Let the jewelry be a reminder of good deeds.

Can Anyone Help?

While your children are still at the table, tell everyone that you would like to fix them a snack. Pass out five saltine crackers to all family members except one. One person should be without any saltine crackers. Ask them not to eat the crackers until everyone has been served. As you come to the last person, say: Oh, no! I don't have any more crackers. Can anyone think of a way to help? Let your children think of ideas. As they give ideas, try to encourage children to share one of their crackers. Tell your kids that you think their idea to share crackers is great.

Next, place a jar of peanut butter in front of one person at the table. Make these comments: Oh, dear. We only have one jar of peanut butter. We don't have a jar for everyone. I wonder how we can all put peanut butter on our crackers? Can anyone think of a way to help? Again, let children give their ideas. Try to encourage children to take turns putting peanut butter on their crackers.

Last, set plastic or paper glasses in the middle of the table. Tell your children to leave the glasses in the middle of the table. The glasses should be half filled with juice or milk. Say these words: Let's think of the best way to give everyone a glass of milk. I know some people who might think it would be best to grab the glass that you want. What do you think? Would that be the best? Why or why not? Can anyone think of another way to give everyone a glass of milk? Let children make suggestions. Encourage responses that indicate passing the glasses around the table or asking politely for a glass of milk.

As children are enjoying their snack make these comments: You gave three great ideas just now. You saw that one person didn't have any crackers and you shared with her. You saw that there was only one jar of peanut butter and you suggested that we take turns. You knew that grabbing things from others is not the best. You said that passing to others or asking politely is a better choice. We have just made God very happy. Remember that God says that we should treat other people the way we want to be treated. (Ask this question of one family member who did receive crackers.) What if you had been the one who didn't get crackers? Would you have wanted us to share with you? (Ask this question of all family members except the one who got the peanut butter first.) What if we hadn't decided to take turns? What if Jonathan (family member) had hogged all the peanut butter and not let us take turns?

When we think about other people and not just ourselves, this makes God very happy. When we share and take turns we get along with each other. When we treat other people the way we want to be treated we all feel happy.

Sticks and Stones

For this activity you will need two apples and several toothpicks. One of the ways we can treat other people kindly is by watching the words that we say. Explain that we are going to pass this apple around. I want you to say something mean to the apple and then drop it onto the floor like a rock. After everyone has had a chance to complete this step, pass the apple around the circle again. This time I want you to call the apple a mean name and put a toothpick into the apple.

After these two steps, remove the toothpicks from the apple. Cut the apple in half. The apple should be quite bruised by now. Show your family the inside and outside of the apple. What do you notice about the outside of this apple? What do you notice about the inside of this apple? Explain that sometimes we might hear the words, "Sticks and stones may break my bones but words will never hurt me." The words we say may not hurt the outside of a person, but words can hurt on the inside. Look at the apple. When we dropped the apple like a rock and said the mean things, it hurt the apple on the inside. It is bruised and brown. When we say mean things to people they may not be hurt on the outside, but they hurt on the inside. The mean words hurt people's feelings; kind words make others feel happy.

Let's pass another apple around the circle. This time I want you to say words that are nice and kind. You might say the words, "please and thank you." You might tell the apple, "You sure look nice today." Or you might tell the apple, "I love you." These are all kind words that make others feel happy. Pass the apple around the circle twice.

You may need to help children give different responses. When you have finished passing around the apple, cut it in half. Show the apple to your family. Look, no bruises on the inside. We said kind words this time, and kind words make people feel good. When we are kind to others we feel good too.

Closing the Lesson

God wants to remind us to touch others the way we want to be touched. Let's name touches that we don't like. Some responses might be: "I don't like to be hit." "I don't like to be pushed." or "I don't like to be pinched." God wants us to remember that other people don't like these touches either. Now, ask everyone to name a touch that they do like. Some responses might be: "I like hand-shakes." "I like kisses on the forehead." or "I like to be tickled." Let's practice giving one kind of touch that we do like. Let's give a special hug, called a "Jellyroll." Ask everyone to join hands while standing in a straight line. Instruct one of the people on the end to stand still; he is Person #1. Now ask the person on the opposite end to begin walking around Person #1. The entire group follows. Continue walking in a circle until you have fairly tight concentric circles. Instruct everyone to give one giant squeeze. You've just given a Jellyroll hug!

Great Fun for Grade Schoolers

Materials Needed: String, balloons, butcher paper, marker, Scotch Tape, several sheets of paper, pen or pencil for each person

Letting Your Child Know You Begin this lesson by telling your family about your favorite holiday as a child. When you were in preschool or grade school what holiday did you like best? Did you like Thanksgiving, Christmas, July 4th, or one of the other holidays best? What traditions went along with this holiday? Did you like seeing certain relatives at this time of year? What foods were served? What activities took place? What did the kids do? What did the adults do? What other positive memories are attached to this holiday?

Getting to Know Your Child Give each child an opportunity to tell about his favorite holiday. Which one does he like best? Talk about your current holiday traditions. Which traditions does each child especially enjoy? Ask questions such as: What's your favorite food at Christmas? What is fun about getting to pick the Christmas tree? Which decorations do you like the best? Do you like singing Christmas carols or making cookies the best? Let each family member tell about her favorite holiday traditions; this reinforces a sense of belonging and security.

Explain that today's Bible Drama takes place during a holiday. The disciples are celebrating a holiday called the Passover. During the Passover celebration the disciples and Jesus were to sit down together for a special meal. Listen to the story. See if this holiday scene sounds like ours.

Becoming Caringly Involved Read the Bible Drama with your family and then invite them to join you in acting it out. Prepare a simple snack of bread, cheese, and fruit. Set these items on a coffee table or other low table. Set places for each person. Designate one special plate for "Jesus." Make His place somehow different from the rest. Jesus' plate might have a special place mat or flower beside it.

Designate one person to be Jesus and the rest of your family are the disciples. Your reenactment might look like this:
- The disciples are alone in the room.
- They start to sit down at the table but are pushing and shoving one another.
- Everyone wants to sit at the place next to Jesus.
- The disciples might be saying things like "I want to sit there!" "Hey, I was here first!"

- Jesus comes into the room and sits down at His place.
- The disciples get quiet and sit still immediately.
- Jesus welcomes the disciples and they start to eat.
- Jesus gets up and starts to wash the disciples' feet.
- Jesus tells the disciples that they should serve or help others.

You may want to use a wet washcloth instead of a basin of water for this dramatization. Give each family member the chance to play the part of Jesus. When you have finished acting out the Bible Drama ask these questions:
- How were the disciples acting when Jesus first came in? Do we ever act this way?
- How does Jesus want the disciples to act? How does He want them to treat one another?

One-Sided Volleyball

For the first activity you will need a balloon and a long piece of string. Tie the string across two chairs. The chairs should be placed approximately eight feet apart. This string will serve as your net for this game. Instruct all the family members to kneel on one side of the net. They are to pass the balloon among themselves by hitting it volleyball-style. As soon as each person hits the balloon to another player on the starting side of the net he crawls or rolls under the net. He then waits on the other side for the rest of the family members to join him. If the balloon touches the floor at any time you must start over. The last player left on the first side must hit the balloon over the net before he can join the others. Then the game begins again. Your task is to change sides as many times as possible without letting the balloon touch the floor. If you want to make this game especially challenging, use two balloons instead of one.

Stop the game before your family starts to lose interest. Explain that in order to complete our task or win at this game we had to think of others. We had to carefully hit the balloon so that each person could return it and move to the other side. We had to look out for other people, not just ourselves.

God wants this to be true of our lives every day. He wants us to care about how others feel and not just think about ourselves.

Healing Words or Hurting Words?

Grade schoolers may often forget the feelings of others when words are exchanged. Ask your family to participate in this activity. It addresses the damage of put-downs. Prior to this activity cut out a large, person-shaped figure. If you have access to the large rolls of butcher paper, this size of paper works best. Otherwise, cut out several large figures from construction paper. Give these instructions: I want each of you to think of words that are "put-downs." Think of words that are mean or ugly. (Words such as "You're ugly" or "You're stupid") Pretend that this paper person is a real person. We're going to say these put-downs to the paper person.

We will pass the paper person around the circle. When you are holding the paper, say your put-down and then tear off a piece of the paper person's body. Pass the paper person around the circle until everyone has torn the paper twice. (Save the paper pieces. You will need them again.)

Stop and ask your family these questions: How did you feel when you said your put-downs and then tore the paper person? How would you feel if someone said these words to you? How do you think others feel if we say these words?

Finally, ask your family if they have ever heard these words: "Sticks and stones can break my bones, but words can never hurt me." Ask children if they agree with this statement. Explain that words can't hurt us on the outside. Words can't hurt our bodies like sticks and stones, but words can hurt us on the inside. Some words hurt our feelings and make us feel sad. There are times when people say things to us that hurt our feelings. We feel like we have been "torn" on the inside, just like the paper person. We need to remember that our words can hurt others too. The things we say can hurt people's feelings. If we put someone down with our words, we make them feel "torn" or sad inside.

Let's demonstrate what we need to say instead of put-downs. Pass the torn pieces of paper around the circle, but this time say words that are kind. As each person holds the pieces of paper, they use a piece of tape to reconstruct the paper person. Family members might say words such as, "Thank you" or "You look nice today."

After you have taped the paper person back together, ask your family these questions: How did you feel when you said kind words? Which words were easier to say, the kind words or the mean words? Explain that sometimes the kind words are harder to say. But the kind words make us feel good and make others feel good. If we are going to treat others the way we want to be treated, then we need to use words that are kind.

(Adapted from *Do It! Active Learning in Youth Ministry,* Thomas Schultz Publications, 1990)

Giving and Getting

Invite your family to join you in two activities that will help you practice thinking of others first. This activity will give us practice in treating others the way we want to be treated. Write these ten items on a piece of paper so that everyone can see them.

I would like:

1. a hug
2. something to drink
3. someone to say, "I love you"
4. someone to write me a note giving me a compliment
5. someone to notice that I've done a good job
6. someone to tickle me or wrestle with me
7. a kiss on the cheek
8. someone to ask about my day
9. a back rub
10. someone to tell me one reason that I am special

Give each family member a piece of paper and something to write with. Give these instructions: Look at this list. Pick the two items that you would like for someone to do for you. Which of these would you like most? Write these two sentences on your paper. Be sure to keep your answers a secret. When you are finished fold your paper twice and place it in the paper sack.

Now, explain that the Bible tells us how we are to treat other people. God says, *Do unto others as you would have them do unto you.* In other words, we are to treat others the way we would like to be treated. Let's practice doing what God says.

Pass the paper sack to each person and ask them to take out one piece of paper. They are to look at the paper to see if it is their own. If the paper belongs to them, they are to put it back in the sack and choose another. If they choose someone else's paper, they keep it. After all the papers have been removed from the sack, each person should have a paper written by another family member. Now as one family member reads the sentences on the paper out loud, the family tries to guess the author of the paper. When the owner is identified read the next paper.

For the next ten minutes I want you to take the piece of paper that you've drawn from the sack and do the things that are written on it. Complete the requests of the family member whose paper you selected. For instance, if someone would like a back rub then give that person a back rub. If another person wanted a drink from the kitchen you will get them a drink. The important thing to remember is that you are treating this person the way you want to be treated. You will want someone to do the things that you have written too.

Give the family plenty of time to complete the lists. When you are all seated together ask these questions: How did it feel when someone did what was on your list? How did it feel when they gave to you? When we treat others like we want to be treated, an exciting thing begins to happen. We start *wanting* to give to others and this makes God very happy. When we give to others we get the privilege of making others happy too.

Closing the Lesson

God wants to remind us to touch others the way we want to be touched. Let's name touches that we don't like. Some responses might be: "I don't like to be hit." "I don't like to be pushed." or "I don't like to be pinched." God wants us to remember that other people don't like these touches either. Now, ask everyone to name a touch that they do like. Some responses might be: "I like handshakes." "I like kisses on the forehead." or "I like to be tickled." Let's practice giving one kind of touch that we like. Let's give a special hug, called a "Jellyroll." Ask everyone to join hands while standing in a straight line. Instruct one of the end people to stand still; he is Person #1. Now ask the person on the opposite end to begin walking around Person #1. The entire group follows. Continue walking in a circle until you have fairly tight concentric circles. Instruct everyone to give one giant squeeze. You've just given a Jellyroll hug!

Making It Real for Middle Schoolers

Materials Needed: String, balloons, newspaper, Koosh ball, several pieces of paper, pens and pencils for everyone, large basin or pan of water and towels

Letting Your Child Know You Begin this lesson by telling your family about some of your dreams and aspirations. You might want to complete this sentence: "When I was young, I wanted to be the greatest. . . ." Think about the dreams you had as a child or pre-teen and share them with your family. Be careful not to exclude the dreams that were "unrealistic." Did you dream about being a professional baseball player? You may have known that the chances of that happening were quite slim, but wasn't it fun to dream about those grand slams and no-hitters? Did you dream about becoming a rock star while you sang into the mirror? You may have known this was pretty far-fetched, but wasn't it fun to sing into that "hairbrush microphone"? Your teens need to hear that it's OK to dream, so let them hear yours.

You may also want to share the more practical dreams. What did you want to be when you grew up? What did you want to accomplish? What or who was your inspiration? What were your plans for career, family, or education? What ambitions filled your daydreams? Describe these to your family.

Getting to Know Your Child Ask your family to finish this sentence: "If I could be or do anything, I would be the greatest. . . ." Give your teens the opportunity to share their dreams. Provide a safe and accepting atmosphere as your family shares. Your kids need to know that they won't be made fun of for sharing their dreams. Make certain you communicate that no dream is too silly or too far-fetched. Talk about each person's dream. Help each person imagine for a moment what it would actually be like to reach that dream. If you did become a professional basketball player, what team would you want to play for? What position would you play? Would you want a certain number for your jersey?

Close the discussion by explaining that our dreams give us goals to strive toward. Even the dreams that seem far-reaching give us an idea about what we enjoy about life. We may or may not ever become a famous musician, but through our dreams we learn what we like about life. We find enjoyment in our dreams.

This lesson lets us peek into a private scene in the life of the disciples. They too wanted to be the greatest. But their desires went past dreams and hopes. The disciples each wanted to be the most famous, most talked about men of their day. There was just one problem. The ministry of a disciple wasn't about fame or fortune, it was about serving people. The disciples let their selfish desires push out the real reason why Jesus had called them. The disciples weren't acting quite like the future leaders of the church. This Bible Drama begins more like the chaos in a second-grade classroom.

Becoming Caringly Involved Read the Bible Drama to your family or invite one of the teens to read for you. As you finish reading, invite your family to participate in this discussion:

- How do you think the disciples felt when Jesus first walked into the room? How do you think they felt as He washed their feet? How would you have felt?
- You may have heard the phrase, "Look out for number one!" Would Jesus say these words? Would this be advice that He would give? Why or why not?
- Is it easy or difficult for you to serve others? Please explain why.

One-Sided Volleyball

See Grade School section.

Sticks and Stones

Middle schoolers can be quite brutal in their verbal attacks toward one another. Ask your family to participate in this activity that is designed to address put-downs. Form a circle with your chairs. Ask one person to sit in the middle of the circle. This person places a Koosh ball or similarly weighted object on top of his head. Instruct the other members of the family to imagine that this person has a certain identity or characteristic. You will need to pick an identity or characteristic that is not true about the person in the middle. You may also need to be sensitive to other members of the family as well. Some categories may include: girls, boys, elderly, very thin people, people who are overweight, someone of a different race, individuals with a handicap, people who are interested in sports, the arts, or science, etc.

The group's task will be to think of put-downs that are often said to these individuals. The group then throws crumpled up newspaper at the person in the middle, trying to knock the Koosh ball off the person's head. At the same time the group is throwing newspaper, they are also "throwing" insults to the person in the middle. While remaining seated, the person in the middle may try to dodge the newspaper, but may not respond to the insults. The game is stopped when the Koosh ball falls off.

Give each family member an opportunity to sit in the middle. When you have finished ask these questions: How did you feel when you were throwing the insults? How did it feel to be in the middle, hearing the insults?

Ask your teens if they are familiar with the saying, "Sticks and stones will break my bones, but words will never hurt me." Do you agree with this statement? Why or why not? How does the game we just played relate to this saying? Explain that the saying is partially true; words cannot hurt us physically. But we all have experienced times when the words that someone said hurt our feelings. Words can hurt us inside. God wants us to remember that words can hurt. *Our* words can hurt. God wants us to say the words to other people that we would like to hear ourselves.
(Adapted from *Do It—Active Learning Youth Ministry*, Thomas Schultz, 1990)

Giving and Getting
See Grade School section.

His Challenge, Our Example
This activity can be a powerful reminder of servanthood. Invite your family to be seated in the living room together. You will

need a pan of warm water, a clean bath sponge, and several towels.

Start this activity with a quiet, sincere tone. You might want to play soft, relaxing music as a background for this activity. Explain that you would like your family to join you in demonstrating Christ's challenge to us. Foot-washing had three purposes in the days of Christ:

- First was the cleansing needed for the priests in the temple. These times were lessons in physical cleanliness and symbolized steps of obedience for the priests.
- Foot-washing was also done as a demonstration of courtesy, usually the responsibility of the host. He or his servants would provide water for guests to wash their feet. This gesture was not mandatory, but only done by the polite host for weary travelers.
- Last, foot-washing symbolized humility. It was an act of sincere affection and proclamation of gratitude. Jesus demonstrated this love and affection for His disciples. He gives us this challenge: "If I then, the Lord and the Teacher, washed your feet, you also ought to wash one another's feet."

Without any other explanation, the father of the household needs to quietly begin to wash each person's feet. If Dad is not living at home, then Mom needs to begin this process. Kneel before each family member. Remove their shoes and socks for them. Place their feet gently into the warm water and then use the sponge for washing. Dry each person's feet with a towel and then you might want to give a brief word of blessing or gesture of affection. Move to each person and repeat the process. Continue to say very few words. Keep the atmosphere quiet and thought-provoking.

If both parents are in the home then Mom needs to go next. She will want to change the water at this point. Mom washes each person's feet in the same way and then returns to her seat. Remain seated and quiet in order to give your teens the opportunity to participate. Do not ask them directly to participate. You will want their gesture to be sincere and not out of obligation.

When everyone has had an opportunity to participate in the foot-washing, close the time in prayer.

Closing the Lesson

Close the lesson by holding hands and thanking Christ for His challenge and His example. Each parent will want to verbalize his or her own commitment to make the attitude of foot-washing a lasting one. Invite your teens to pray if they wish. End this prayer with a hug and an "I love you" for each family member.

High School Happenings

Materials Needed: One deck of playing cards, several spoons, string, balloons, several pieces of paper, pen or pencil for each person, large basin or pan of water, towels

Letting Your Child Know You Begin this lesson by telling your family about some of your dreams and aspirations. You might want to complete this sentence: "When I was young, I wanted to be the greatest. . . ." Think about the dreams you had as a child or pre-teen and share them with your family. Be careful not to exclude the dreams that were "unrealistic." Did you dream about being a professional baseball player? You may have known that the chances of that happening were quite slim, but wasn't it fun to dream about those grand slams and no-hitters? Did you dream about becoming a rock star while you sang into the mirror? You may have known this was pretty far-fetched, but wasn't it fun to sing into that "hairbrush microphone"? Your teens need to hear that it's OK to dream, so let them hear yours.

You may also want to share the more practical dreams. What did you want to be when you grew up? What did you want to be sure to accomplish? What or who was your inspiration? What were your plans for career, family, or education? What ambitions filled your daydreams? Describe these to your family.

Getting to Know Your Child Ask your family to finish this sentence: "If I could be or do anything, I would be the greatest. . . ." Give your teens the opportunity to share their dreams. Provide a safe and accepting atmosphere as your family shares. Your kids need to know that they won't be made fun of. Make certain you communicate that no dream is too silly or too far-fetched. Talk about each person's dream. Help each person imagine for a moment what it would actually be like to reach that dream. If you did become a professional basketball player, what team would you want to play for? What position would you play? Would you want a certain number for your jersey?

Close the discussion by explaining that our dreams give us goals to strive for. Even the dreams that seem far-reaching give us an idea about what we enjoy about life. We may or may not ever become a famous musician, but through our dreams we learn what we like about life. We find enjoyment in our dreams.

This lesson lets us peek into a private scene in the life of the disciples. They too wanted to be the greatest. But their desires went past dreams and hopes. The disciples each wanted to be the most famous, most talked about men of their day. There was just one problem. The ministry of a disciple wasn't about fame or fortune, it was about serving people. The disciples let their selfish desires push out the real reason why Jesus had called them. The disciples aren't acting quite like the future leaders of the church. This Bible Drama begins more like the chaos in a second-grade classroom.

Becoming Caringly Involved Read the Bible Drama to your family or invite one of the teens to read for you. As you finish reading, invite your family to participate in this discussion:

- How do you think the disciples felt when Jesus first walked into the room? How do you think they felt as He washed their feet? How would you have felt?
- You may have heard the phrase, "Look out for number one!" Would Jesus say these words? Would this be advice that He would give? Why or why not?
- Is it easy or difficult for you to serve others? Please explain why.

Spoons

Begin the activity portion of this lesson by playing the card game called "Spoons." Use a regular deck of playing cards. Distribute four cards to each player. Keep the remainder of the cards facedown in front of you. Place several spoons in the center of the table. You should have one spoon less than the number of players.

Give these instructions: There are two objectives for this game. You want to be the first person to have four cards of the same number or four face cards. The second objective is to make sure that you always get a spoon. You'll notice that there is one less spoon than there are people. After each turn one player will be without a spoon.

I will begin the game by drawing one card at a time from this deck. I will decide whether to keep the card or pass it to the player beside me. I keep the card if it is one of the numbers or face cards I hope to match. If I decide to keep this card, I must discard one of my other cards. I can only keep four cards in my hand. I pass any card that does not match. The player beside me does the same. He/she picks up the cards that I pass, looks at them, and must decide whether to keep or pass. This same process continues around the table. As you get the hang of this game, increase the speed at which you pass cards. This will increase the challenge of the game. The last player to get the cards passed to him discards any unwanted cards into a pile beside him. You may only keep four cards in your hand at any one time.

When someone does acquire four cards of the same number or four face cards, that person reaches for a spoon. When the rest of the players see someone going for the spoons, they stop passing cards and immediately go for the spoons too. As soon as one player reaches for the spoon it is OK for all players to reach for the spoon. The other players do not have to have four matching cards.

The one person who is left without a spoon gets a letter counted against him. He gets an "S." The second time this player is left without a spoon, he gets a "P." Play continues until one person has all five letters, S-P-O-O-N. The player with the fewest letters against him wins.

As you finish playing, make these comments. This game illustrates our natural tendency to be selfish. We have a natural inclination to look out for ourselves, to look out for number one! This game demonstrates selfishness because a selfish person only thinks about himself/herself. A selfish person rarely thinks about how others feel or how their actions might impact other people. Let's play a game that demonstrates a different perspective.

One-Sided Volleyball

See Grade School section.

Mother, May I?
(revised)

Give your family this challenge. Invite them to personalize the two ideas of selfishness and unselfishness. This activity shows who can best distinguish between a selfish and unselfish attitude. Tell your family that you're going to play a game that is similar to "Mother, May I?" Ask your family to stand in a line at one end of the room. You are the judge for the first round of the game.

Explain that the object of the game is to reach the judge. But I am the only one who can give you permission to move. I will give you permission to move based on how convincing you are at showing a selfish attitude. You might complete sentences such as: "I am so selfish that . . ." "I look out for 'number one' because . . ." "You gotta take care of yourself because . . ." and "I only think about other people when. . . ."

The first person to reach the judge becomes the judge for the next round. Remember that you want to sound so selfish that I can't help but notice you. The more selfish you pretend to be, the more likely you are to move. I will acknowledge you by calling your name and then telling you what kind of steps to take. I might say things like, "Take two giant steps" or "Take two leap frogs."

Remember that before you move, you must ask permission by saying, "Mother, may I?" I will respond by saying, "Yes, you may." If you move without asking permission, you must go back to the starting line.

Play two rounds of this game. Then ask your family to demonstrate what unselfishness might sound like. For the purpose of this game you and your family will exaggerate the unselfish attitude. Some of your statements might sound like: "I think of others so often that . . ." "I am so unselfish that . . ." and "I'm the gift that keeps on giving because. . . ."

After you've played the game two more times, invite your family to participate in this discussion: How did you feel giving selfish statements? How did you feel giving unselfish statements? Which kind of statements came more easily? Explain that many times it is much easier to respond in selfish ways. The unselfish attitudes and behaviors take much more determination. To be truly unselfish, we need God's help. He's the only one who's unselfish by nature.

Giving and Getting

Invite your family to join you in an activity that will help you practice thinking of others first. This activity will give us practice in treating others the way we want to be treated. Write these ten items on a piece of paper so that everyone can see them.

I would like:

1. a hug
2. a snack from the kitchen
3. someone to say, "I appreciate you"
4. someone to write me a note, giving me a compliment
5. someone to notice that I've done a good job
6. someone to encourage me about my schoolwork
7. someone to help me with a specific chore
8. someone to ask about my day and then listen without interrupting
9. a back rub
10. someone to tell me one reason that I am unique

See Grade School section for continued explanation of this activity.

His Challenge, Our Example

See Middle School section.

Closing the Lesson

Close the lesson by holding hands and thanking Christ for His challenge and His example. Each parent will want to verbalize his or her own commitment to make the attitude of foot-washing a lasting one. Invite your teens to pray if they wish. End this prayer with a hug and an "I love you" for each family member.

Lesson **12**

Temporal priorities can be replaced by eternal

Key Scripture Passage *A certain man had two sons; and the younger of them said to the father, "Father, give me the share of the estate that falls to me." And he divided his wealth between them. And not many days later, the younger son gathered everything together and went on a journey into a distant country, and there he squandered his estate with loose living. . . .*

But when he came to his senses, he said, "How many of my father's hired men have more than enough bread, but I am dying here with hunger! I will get up and go to my father, and will say to him, 'Father, I have sinned against heaven, and in your sight; I am no longer worthy to be called your son; make me as one of your hired men.' " And he got up and came to his father. But while he was still a long way off, his father saw him, and felt compassion for him, and ran and embraced him, and kissed him. . . . But the father said to the slaves, "Quickly bring out the best robe and put it on him, and put a ring on his hand and sandals on his feet; and bring the fattened calf, kill it, and let us eat and be merry...."

Now his older son was in the field, and when he came and approached the house, he heard music and dancing. And he summoned one of the servants and began inquiring what these things might be. And he said to him, "Your brother has come, and your father has killed the fattened calf, because he has received him back safe and sound." But he [the brother] became angry, and was not willing to go in.
—Luke 15:11-13, 17-20, 22-23, 25-28

Bible Drama

When he left, he hoped that he would never again have to see the hill that hid the valley where his father's house lay. Many times he had stood at the foot of the hill and dreamed of the day that he would never again have to walk it.

But that was before. That was before he greedily demanded his inheritance, before he spit on the door of his father's house, and before he walked over the hill vowing to never return.

And now he was standing on top of the little rise again. As he stood and looked over the beautiful valley, he practiced the words he would say to his father. "I'm not worthy to be your son. Just let me be a slave." With his eyes on the door of his father's home and his heart seeming to rise all the way to his throat, the ragged young man walked through the fields of wheat. He walked past the barns filled with cattle and past the servants who stared in unbelief. They most surely thought him to be dead.

Suddenly, he saw him! He looked so much older than when he left. His hair had grayed. His face was sullen and drawn with the look of heartfelt pain. Frozen in their places, the two stared in unbelief. Overwhelmed by both love and sorrow, they wanted only to heal the other's pain.

It was the father who took the first slow step. "Son? Is that you? Is it really you?" And then he began to run. Down the path and through the gate the father ran. He was running toward this unkempt young man who stood overcome with the grief of his sin.

"No, Father! I'm not worthy to be your son. Let me be. . . ." But his voice was lost in the folds of his father's robe. Both stood weeping.

The rest of the day was a blur. There were new clothes, special jewelry, and new sandals brought for his bare feet. A feast was declared in honor of the son's return. Over the hill you could hear the rejoicing for the lost son.

The sound reached the band of workers traveling in from the farthest field. His older brother was in charge of all the hired help now, and cared for little else but the success of the farm. When his rebellious brother left, it meant that it would all be his someday. Now the sound of rejoicing was coming over the hill. The older brother called out to one of the hired hands, "What is all the rejoicing about? Why the big party at the house?"

"It's your brother, sir! He has returned. He's alive and well and home for good. It's now time to rejoice!"

"My brother? That no good, lazy thief has returned? No doubt, he's here to take my inheritance too. No doubt at all!" The older brother refused to go another step. He would not join in any celebration for the return of his brother.

The servant returned to the house. "Sir, it's your other son. He refused to come in from the field. He said something about how you have never given him a party. Then he mumbled something about how he has always been the one who's obeyed. Maybe you should talk to him yourself."

Out the gate and into the field, the old man walked. He realized that all his wealth and riches had almost cost him the loss of one son. He was not about to allow possessions to become more important than people again.

"He's come to steal what is mine, Father!" the brother yelled. "All my life I have faithfully served you and now that son of yours has returned to steal from...." Then he stopped. That was all he could say, because he saw the tears. He saw the tears that came to his father's eyes and he knew his words were the cause.

"Father, don't you understand? Can't you see that...." The shame of hurting his father made him stop again in mid-sentence. What had been a day of great rejoicing had been turned into a day of great sadness.

"My son, my son! Don't you realize that possessions will never take the place of people? Your brother was thought to be dead and he is alive! You and your brother are more important than anything I own. And so it should be with you. Put away your anger, son. Your brother's life is more important than any inheritance."

The older brother understood. Together they returned to the father's house. There on the steps was the younger brother. He stood waiting to greet the two. Embracing both of his sons, the old man cried out loud, "My sons have both returned home. This is a great day indeed! Let the rejoicing begin!"

Goal for Lesson 12: Families will learn that people are more important than things.

Intimacy Principle: We can assist and encourage others to experience intimacy.

Disclosure Goal: Parents will share statements of approval and empathy.

Projects with Preschoolers

Materials Needed: Ring from a gumball machine, magazines, family photos, string, paper clips or magnetic tape, one magnet, a large stick or pole that is approximately two feet long, large sheet of butcher paper, drawing paper, markers or crayons, tape, two of your children's favorite toys

Letting Your Child Know You Begin this lesson by sharing statements of approval with your children. Look at each child and complete these sentences: "I'm glad you're my son/daughter because. . . ." and "I'm so proud of you for. . . ." Be sure to complete these sentences with very specific responses. The more specific you are in your statements of approval, the more impact they will make on your children. Some responses might sound like, "I'm so glad you're my daughter because I like being able to hear you laugh. I like having someone who will share my popcorn with me." or "I'm so proud of you for the way you are learning to take turns with Bradley." End this time by giving each child a toy ring. Rings from a gumball machine would be appropriate. Explain that in today's Bible Drama we are going to hear about a father and his two sons. The father in this story gives his son a special ring because he is so glad to see him. I am giving you this ring. It can remind you that I am glad you're my child.

Getting to Know Your Child Ask your child to think of a time when he/she broke a favorite toy or lost something that was very important. Ask your child to describe the toy that was broken or lost. Why was that toy special? Why did you like that toy best? What happened to the toy? How did you feel when you lost it or broke it? At this point, parents will want to share statements of empathy with your child. Communicate that you hear their feelings, their feelings are important, and you care about them. Your statement of empathy might sound like, "I know you were sad when you lost Raggedy Ann. She was a special doll. I remember feeling sad because you had trouble going to sleep that night."

Let each child share her story and then give appropriate statements of empathy. As you end the discussion, explain that in today's lesson we are going to learn about a father and his two sons. These two sons probably had lots of toys when they were growing up. This family had a lot of money and a big house, but they found out that people are more important than things.

Becoming Caringly Involved Read the Bible Drama to your family, then ask them to join you in acting out the story. Tell your family to listen to your words and follow the actions as you retell the story. You will want to include these points of action:

- The young son comes home after a long trip. He looks toward home. (*put hand over eyes as if you're shading your eyes from the sun*)
- He was happy and sad at the same time. He was happy (*make a big smile*) because he was glad to be home. He was sad (*make a big frown*) because he knew that he had hurt his father's feelings when he went away.
- The father sees his son a long way off. (*put hand over your eyes as if you're shading your eyes from the sun*) The father was very surprised! (*eyes are wide with mouth dropped open*)
- The father runs to the son and hugs him. (*run in place and hug a partner*)
- The young son says that he is sorry for going away. He asks his father if he can be one of the family's servants. (*kneel down and pretend to plead with the father*)
- The father hugs him again and says they're going to have a party in the son's honor. (*hug a partner and then make silly dance moves to indicate a party*)
- The young son gets a special robe and a ring. (*pretend to put on a robe and admire it; pretend to put on a ring and admire it*)
- The older brother asks one of the servants what the party is all about. (*cup your hand around your ear as if you're listening closely*)

- The servant says that the party is for the younger brother. The family thought the younger brother was dead *(put hands to throat as if choking)* but now he has returned. *(make silly dance moves)*
- The older brother refuses to come to the party. *(put hands on your hips and look away indignantly)*
- The father goes out to talk to the older brother. *(put your arm around a partner's shoulders as if you're having a quiet chat)*
- The father explains that his two sons are much more important than any of his possessions. *(give thumbs up to your partner; show thumbs down as you point to possessions in the room)*

After your family has acted out this story invite them to participate in this discussion:
- Why was the older brother mad? Why did he not want to come to the party?
- What did the father say was most important?

Fishers of Men

For the first activity you will need several old magazines, family photos, paper clips or magnetic tape, one magnet, string, and a stick approximately two feet long. Invite your children to go through magazines and tear out pictures of people and toys that they like. When they have torn approximately ten pictures of toys and five pictures of people, ask your children to separate the pictures into two piles. Put the pictures of people in one pile and the pictures of toys in another. Add several pictures of family members to the pile of people.

Next, poke paper clips through the pictures of people only. You may want to put a piece of magnetic tape on the back of the family photos. Once all the pictures of people have magnetic tape or paper clips, put these pictures along with the pictures of toys, into a large empty trash can. The trash can should have a clean trash bag in it.

Make a fishing pole by tying a magnet onto a piece of string and then tying the other end of the string to a stick. Let each child take turns "fishing." As they catch their "fish," ask children to notice what kind of pictures they are catching. "Are you catching people or toys?" When all the pictures of people have been caught, make these closing comments. Which kind of pictures were you able to catch? Which kind of pictures are still left in the trash can? We could only pick up the people pictures. This game helps us remember that people are more important than toys. Jesus wants us to learn the same lesson as the two brothers in the Bible Drama. The brothers learned that people are more important than things Jesus wants us to remember that people are more important than toys. (You may want to save some of the pictures for the next activity.)

First, Second, and Third

Ask your family to help you with the next activity. Explain that you are going to show what things are important in your home. Pin a large piece of butcher paper to one wall in your home. Draw the outline of a large house on the butcher paper. The roof of the house should almost touch the top of the butcher paper. The house should extend down the length of the paper. Divide the house into these sections: roof, first story, and second story.

Ask each family member to draw a picture of their two favorite toys. Draw these pictures onto sheets of construction paper. One adult will need to draw a picture of the Bible on one sheet of paper, and write the word "God" in large print on a second sheet of paper. You will also use the pictures of family members and magazine pictures from the previous activity. When all pictures have been drawn and assembled, make these comments:

We are going to put these pictures in order. The pictures that we put in the roof of our house should be the most important. The pictures we put on the second story should be next in importance. The pictures that are in the bottom story are the least important. Look at the pictures we have here. We have pictures of God, the Bible, of people, and of toys. Which of these is most important? Guide children to the thought that God and His Bible are most important. Ask a child to tape the picture of the Bible to the "roof" section of the butcher paper. Ask another child to tape the paper that says "God" to the top section of the house as well. Look at the pictures we have left. Which of these is most important? We have pictures of people and pictures of toys. Are people or toys most important? Explain that having toys is fun and God wants us to have fun things to play with. He just wants us to remember that people are more important than toys. Ask each child to tape one picture of a family member or one magazine picture on to the second story.

For the final step of this activity, ask each child to look at the pictures that are left. Which toy is most important to you? Which toy is your very favorite? Tape that toy on to the bottom section of the house. Which toy is your next favorite? Tape that toy on to the very bottom of the house.

Make these closing comments: God wants us to make choices with these things in mind. He wants us to remember that God and the Bible are the most important in our home. Family, friends, and other people are second in importance. Our toys and the things we have are third. God wants us to keep these things in order. He's first, people are second, and toys are third.

People First

We make good choices when we remember that people are more important than things. Invite everyone to sit with you on the floor. I am going to read some short stories. If you think this person is putting people first, then give everyone around you a "high five." If you think that the person in the story is making toys most important, then sit on your hands. Model each of these movements for your children. Read the first situation:

- Suzy decided to put her money in the offering plate instead of buying the new clothes for her Barbie doll. Her money is going to help the children who don't have much food. Is she putting people first or toys?
- Jake has been fighting with his friend over who gets to play Nintendo. Jake's mom says that Jake and his friend can't play anymore today, because they're fighting over toys. Is Jake putting people first or toys?
- Travis goes outside to ride his bike. He notices that his neighbor, Mrs. Jones, needs help taking out the trash. Travis gets off his bike and helps Mrs. Jones. Is Travis putting people first or things?

- Carey pushes and shoves other kids out of the way. She wants to get to the jump rope first. Is Carey making people or things most important?
- Tiffany is playing house with her friend. Her friend accidentally breaks Tiffany's tea set and says she's very sorry. Tiffany says, "It's OK. I know that you didn't mean to. We can still have fun." Is Tiffany putting people first or toys?

End this activity by making these comments: God wants us to remember that people are more important than things. We make the best choices when we put people first.

Closing the Lesson

Close the lesson by inviting each person to bring their two favorite toys into the living room. Parents should have two of their "toys" as well. Mom might bring the cover to her sewing machine and a favorite dress. Dad might bring his car keys and one of his golf clubs. Ask everyone to stand in a circle and place their toys on the floor in front of them. Sing the following verses to the tune of "Mary Had a Little Lamb." This song will serve as part of a dedication. You will dedicate your toys to God as you declare that people are most important. Sing the first verse of the song as you're holding one of the toys.

God, I thank You for my toys, for my toys, for my toys.
God, I thank You for my toys.
You gave them all to me.

Sing the next verse with your toy behind your back. As you finish singing, place the toy on the floor behind you.

I'll be kind to girls and boys, girls and boys, girls and boys.
I'll be kind to girls and boys.
They're most important, you see.

Pick up the second toy and hold it as you sing the first verse again. Then sing the last verse of this song with the second toy behind your back. As you finish singing, place the second toy on the floor behind you too.

I will share with all my friends, all my friends, all my
  friends.
I will share with all my friends.
They're most important, you see.

When you finish singing, join hands and pray together. Thank
God for the toys that He has given. Ask Him to help you remember that the toys are fun, but people are more important than toys.

Great Fun for Grade Schoolers

Materials Needed: One bar of soap for each person, table knives,
small toys, large bucket or container of water, red, white, and black
construction paper, two paper sacks, one pair of white socks for
each person, one bed sheet, small slips of paper and pencil

Letting Your Child Know You Begin this lesson by sharing statements
of approval with your children. Look at each child and complete
these sentences: "I'm glad you're my son/daughter because . . ."
and "I'm so proud of you for. . . ." Be sure to complete these sentences with very specific information. The more specific you are in
your statements of approval, the more impact they will make on
your children. Some responses might sound like, "I'm so glad
you're my daughter because I like being able to hear you laugh. I
like having someone to pray with me at night." or "I'm so proud of
you for the way you are learning to play with fairness."

Getting to Know Your Child Ask your child to think of a time when
he/she broke a favorite toy or lost something that was very important. Ask your child to describe the toy that was broken or lost.
Why was that toy special? Why did you like that toy best? What
happened to the toy? How did you feel when you lost it or broke
it? At this point, parents will want to share statements of empathy
with your child. Communicate that you hear their feelings, their
feelings are important, and you care about them. Your statement
of empathy might sound like, "I know you were sad when your favorite model airplane was broken. You worked so hard on that
plane. I remember feeling sad because you were so disappointed."

Temporal priorities can be replaced by eternal 315

Let each child share her story and then give appropriate statements of empathy. As you end the discussion, explain that in today's lesson we are going to learn about a father and his two sons. These two sons probably had many toys when they were growing up. This family had a great deal of money and a big house, but they found out that people are more important than things.

Becoming Caringly Involved Read the Bible Drama, then act out the story. Tell your family to listen to your words and follow the actions as you retell the story. You will want to include these points of action:

- The young son comes home after a long trip. He looks toward home. *(put hand over eyes as if you're shading your eyes from the sun)*
- He was happy and sad at the same time. He was happy *(make a big smile)* because he was glad to be home. He was sad *(make a big frown)* because he knew that he had hurt his father's feelings when he went away.
- The father sees his son a long way off. *(put hand over your eyes as if you're shading your eyes from the sun)* The father was very surprised! *(eyes are wide with mouth dropped open)*
- The father runs to the son and hugs him. *(run in place and hug a partner)*
- The young son says that he is sorry for going away. He asks his father if he can be one of the family's servants. *(kneel down and pretend to plead with the father)*
- The father hugs him again and says they're going to have a party in the son's honor. *(hug a partner and then make silly dance moves to indicate a party)*
- The young son gets a special robe and a ring. *(pretend to put on a robe and admire it; pretend to put on a ring and admire it)*
- The older brother asks one of the servants what the party is all about. *(cup your hand around your ear as if you're listening closely)*
- The servant says that the party is for the younger brother. The family thought the younger brother was dead *(put hands to throat as if choking)* but now he has returned. *(make silly dance moves)*

- The older brother refuses to come to the party. *(put hands on your hips and look away indignantly)*
- The father goes out to talk to the older brother. *(put your arm around a partner's shoulders as if you're having a quiet chat)*
- The father explains that his two sons are much more important than any of his possessions. *(give thumbs up to your partner; show thumbs down as you point to possessions in the room)*

After your family has acted out this story invite them to participate in this discussion:
- Why was the older brother mad? Why did he not want to come to the party?
- What did the father say was most important?

Top Priority

For the first activity of the lesson give each person a new bar of soap. Select a brand of soap that can be carved or cut easily and that floats. Ivory soap works well for this activity. Give each person a marker or crayon and ask them to draw the shape of a large gingerbread man on the bar of soap. Show your children an example. Draw the gingerbread shape as large as possible onto the face of the soap. Cover the table with several layers of newspaper or a plastic tablecloth.

Give each person a table knife. Tell your family to use the table knife to carve the gingerbread shape out of the soap. Chip and cut the soap with the knife until only the gingerbread shape is left. One adult should remain at the table at all times. Children will need supervision for this activity.

When everyone has completed their gingerbread carvings, place them into a large bucket or container for water. Ask children to find several of their small toys and drop them into the bucket as well. Make sure the toys that the children have selected do not float. As you pour water into the bucket, ask children to predict which objects will come to the top of the water. Which objects will float?

When your children have clearly seen that the soap is at the top of the water, make these final comments. This activity reminds us of the Bible Drama. You see the people-shapes came to the top of the water. They floated to the top and the toys stayed on the bottom of the bucket. God wants us to remember that people are more important than things. People should be at the top of our list and toys near the bottom.

Priority Baseball

Invite your family to play a game of Priority Baseball. Cut strips of red, white, and black construction paper. You will need two sets of fifteen strips of red and white paper, and six strips of black paper. Put all three colors into a paper bag. You will have two bags that contain thirty-six strips of paper (fifteen red, fifteen white, and six black). Make two baseball diamonds on the floor with masking tape and divide your family into two teams.

Give these instructions: We are going to play a baseball game. This game has nine innings and each team bats three times per inning. Each player takes his turn at bat by selecting one colored strip from the paper bag. You must choose a strip of paper without looking in the paper bag. The colors represent different plays:

white:	home run	You decide to put God first.
red:	double	You decide that people are more important than things.
black:	out	You decide that toys or things are more important than people

Play the game for nine innings, which means you will draw twenty-seven strips of paper out of the sack. You might want to play for a specified period of time instead. The team with the most runs at the end of the nine innings or specified time wins the game.

As you finish playing the game, ask these questions: Which color scored the home run? Which decision did this color represent? Which color was for the double? Which decision did this represent? God wants us to remember that people are more important than things. He wants us to put Him first. When we remember these things we can make good decisions. Let's practice identifying good decisions.

Red, White, and Black

Invite your family to join you in the next activity. Each person will need to be wearing white socks in order to participate. Ask each person to pull their socks down, so that the toes of the socks are "floppy." Give these instructions: I am going to read five situations. Please listen carefully to each of these situations. You must decide if this is an example of someone putting God first, making people more important than things, or making things more important than people.

You will indicate your decision in the following ways. If you think that the person is putting God first, then you will raise your **white** socks and wave your feet in the air.

If you think that the person is making people more important than things, then you will pucker your (**red**) lips and kiss the hand of the person next to you.

If you think that the person in the situation is making things more important than people, then you will cover your eyes with both hands till you see only **black.**

Read the situations:

- John is anxious to play with his new football. John's grandmother comes over for dinner. He hasn't seen her in a long time. He decides to sit and talk with her before he goes out to play.
- Elizabeth decides to obey the Bible. She gives the first part of her baby-sitting money to God. She places her money in the offering plate on Sunday morning.
- Haley decides to go over to Jennifer's house just because Jennifer got a new trampoline. Haley doesn't even talk with her friend very much. In fact, Haley is quite rude to Jennifer.
- Travis pushes and shoves his way to the front of the line. He doesn't pay any attention to the rest of his classmates. All Travis cares about is getting to the soccer ball first.
- Chris just got a new remote control car. Chris is outside playing with the car, when he notices the new kid who lives next door. Chris is really protective of his new car, but decides to invite the neighbor over to play with him. This neighbor looks like he could use a friend.

Close this activity by reviewing the two situations where people were more important than things. How did each person show that he considered people more important? Consider the two situations where things were more important than people. How could each person have behaved differently?

Closing the Lesson

Prior to this closing you will need to have each person write the names of at least three family members and close friends on small sheets of paper (i.e., grandparents, aunts, uncles, stepparents, neighbors, siblings, school friends, teachers, church leaders). Close the lesson by asking family members to bring two of their favorite toys to the living room. Parents will want to bring two of their favorite possessions as well. Lay all the possessions in a pile in the middle of the floor. Ask family members to stand in a circle around the toys.

Explain that we are going to close this lesson by dedicating our toys and our decisions to God. We are going to thank Him for giving us people to love and these possessions. God wants us to have fun things to play with and He wants us to enjoy them. But God wants us to remember that people are more important than these possessions.

Unfold a bed sheet and ask every family member to hold one side of the sheet. Hold the sheet over the toys and invite each person to say this sentence prayer. "Thank You, God, for giving me my _____. I know You like for me to have fun." When each person has said their prayer, lay the sheet over the toys.

Distribute the papers that contain the names of family and friends. Ask each person to place their papers on top of the sheet and say this sentence prayer: "God, help me to remember that people are more important than things."

Making It Real for Middle Schoolers

Materials Needed: Xerox copies of the Bible Drama, masking tape, paper and pens for everyone, video or Polaroid camera, scavenger hunt list, transportation for the scavenger hunt, two water guns, balloons, markers, Energizer batteries

Letting Your Child Know You Begin this lesson by sharing statements of approval with your children. Look at each child and complete these sentences: "I'm glad you're my son/daughter because. . . ." and "I'm so proud of you for. . . ." Be sure to complete these sentences with very specific information. The more specific you are in your statements of approval, the more impact they will make on your child. Your statements might sound like: "I'm glad you're my son because I like skiing with you and getting to have fun with you." or "I'm so proud of you for standing up for what you believe in. It sounds like you handled the discussion in class with a great deal of courage."

Getting to Know Your Child Ask your teen to think of a time when he/she broke a favorite possession or lost something that was very important. Ask your teen to describe the item that was broken or lost. Why was that item special? Why did you like that possession best? What happened to the item? How did you feel when you lost it or broke it? At this point, parents will want to share statements of empathy with your child. Communicate that you hear their feelings, their feelings are important, and you care about them. Your statement of empathy might sound like, "I know you were disappointed when your T-shirt from the concert was stolen. You looked forward to that concert for such a long time. I felt sad because you were upset."

Explain that this lesson contains a story about a family who had a great deal of money. The father provided his two sons with many possessions and even saved money that was to be their inheritance. This story puts these possessions in perspective. The Bible Drama suggests we prioritize people rather than things.

Becoming Caringly Involved Read the Bible Drama once to your family. Then divide into pairs and give these instructions. Pretend that you and your partner have been hired to provide the sound track for this story. This Bible Drama will be aired on national radio in two weeks. You must provide the sound effects and/or music to go along with the narrator's retelling of the story.

If possible, provide each pair of family members with a copy of the Bible Drama. They will use this to plan out their sound track. Here are a few suggestions to get your groups started:

- Gather several coins and make the sound of jingling coins as the narrator explains how the young son demanded his inheritance.
- Hum the theme song of *Chariots of Fire* as the father and son are running toward each other.
- Make sounds like a crowd cheering when the young son finally reaches his father.
- Play a contemporary "party" song as the family celebrates the son's return.
- Sing the words to Aretha Franklin's "R-E-S-P-E-C-T" as the older brother complains about his younger brother's return.

Allow fifteen minutes for your family to plan out their sound effects. As you work, instruct each group to decide where the pauses should occur. Designate the places that you want the narrator to pause so that you can give the appropriate sound effect. Write these pauses on the written copy of the Bible Drama.

When everyone is ready, perform these sound effects for one another. Decide on a narrator and let him begin reading the story. As he reads, the narrator pauses so that sound effects can be introduced. Enjoy making each other laugh. You might even want to record this activity and keep it as a record of this family memory.

As you finish performing, invite your family to participate in this discussion:

- How do you think you would have reacted if you had been the father or the older brother?
- Did the father's response surprise you? Tell why or why not. If you knew the story already, tell why this father's response might be considered unusual.
- What order of priorities does the Bible Drama suggest?

Line Up

For the first activity make a long line of masking tape on the floor. At one end of the line make a sign that says, "Not Important." On the other end of the line, make a sign that says, "Very Important." Write the six sentences below on a large sheet of blank paper so that everyone can see them. Make sure each person has her own sheet of paper and pen. Give these instructions: Draw a line like the one that is on the floor. On one end of your line write the words, "Not Important." On the other end of your line write the words, "Very Important." Now look at these six sentences. Read the six sentences and then put them in order according to how important they are to you. If sentence #1 is most important to you then write a #1 closest to the words, "Very Important." If sentence #2 is the least important to you, then write a #2 close to the words, "Not Important." By the time you finish, you should have the numbers 1–6 written on the line that you've drawn on the paper.

After everyone has completed this step, give these instructions. Find the sentence that was most important to you. Where is that number on your line? Get up and stand at the same spot on the line that is taped on the floor. Stand at the point that represents the sentence that was most important to you. As family members find their positions, ask them to tell which sentence was most important to them. Which numbered sentence is written closest to the words, "Very Important"?

Continue asking family members to find the sentence that was next in importance. Then ask them to move to that point on the taped line. Allow each person to share their responses. Give each person the freedom to choose and express reasons for their choices. Make this a lighthearted activity and discussion. Here are the sentences:

- I want to be incredibly, insanely, undoubtedly rich.
- I want to have a family that loves me.
- I want to have good friends that I can trust.
- I would like to have an unlimited supply of music CDs and video games.
- I want to get along with all my teachers.
- I would like to have a lifetime membership in the "Make-up of the Month Club."

Close the activity by asking each person to look at the six sentences again. Ask each person to name the sentence that is most important to them and the sentence that is least important. Explain that we are going to participate in an activity that shows us how God would order these sentences.

People 'N Things Scavenger Hunt

For this activity you will need a Polaroid camera or video camera. If you do not own one of these items yourself, you may be able to borrow one from another family. Additionally, this activity will be most successful if you build in a little competition. Ask another family to join you in this scavenger hunt. Families compete against one another for the most points accumulated on the scavenger hunt. The losing team must make dinner for the winning family.

Explain to your family that the scavenger hunt will take place over the next two hours. Each team will be given this list of possible pictures and the points associated. You and your team must decide which pictures you will try to get within the two-hour time frame. The team that accumulates the most points and arrives back at the house on time, wins the scavenger hunt. Happy Hunting!

People 'N Things List

Find pictures of:	*Point Value*
an open cash register	10
a fortune cookie	10
the television and electronics section of a local department store	30
a mannequin wearing a red shirt	50
a basketball, football, and Ping-Pong ball (all together)	50
any truck that has a bumper sticker	50
one of your team members holding a box of Depends undergarments	75
one of your team members and a restaurant chef	100
one of your team members and a police officer	100
one of your team members behind the counter in a hotel lobby	100
your entire team demonstrating a church service while inside or outside a church	100
two of your group members in wedding attire	100

At the end of the two-hour time limit, total up the points for both teams. The team that has the most points and obtained them within the two-hour time limit, wins the scavenger hunt. You'll want to share your pictures or videotape with the other family. Spend time retelling your adventures. Invite your family (and perhaps the other family) to join you in this discussion: Which pictures were the most difficult to obtain? Which pictures had the greatest point value? Were the pictures of people or things worth the most points?

Give these closing comments: The easiest way to win this scavenger hunt was to obtain pictures of people. The people were more important than the things. God has these same priorities. He considers people more important than things too. God wants us to remember this order of priorities when we make decisions. Let's practice making good choices.

People 'N Things Decision-making

Ask your family to join you at the dinner table. Give everyone a balloon and ask them to blow it up and tie it. Hand each person a marker and ask them to write the word "people" at the top of their balloon and the word "things" at the bottom of the balloon. Then ask everyone to draw a circle around the word "things" and draw a slash through the circle. Each person should have the symbol that stands for "not" or "no" around the word "things."

Second, place at least two water guns filled with water on the table. Give these instructions: I am going to read a particular situation for each person. You must tell us what you would do in this situation. When you have given your response, the rest of the family will decide if your answer reflects an attitude of putting people first or things first. If family members think that you are putting people first they will shower you with "blessings." The family will take turns shooting this water gun. God showers us with blessings when we think of people first. But if family members think that you are putting things first, they will shower you with their balloons. Family members will show you the truth that "people are more important than things," by throwing or volleying their balloons at you. Here are the situations:

- Your sister's graduation is Saturday. You had planned to rebuild your bike that day. What do you do?
- You have saved $200. You have to decide how you will

spend this money. You can either buy new speakers for your stereo or use the money to go on the missions trip with the youth group. Which will you choose?

- Your best friend invites you to come to her dad's wedding. She's worried that things could get really uncomfortable and she might need your support. Your sister offers to take you to your favorite clothing store. They're having a one-day sale. Both events are on the same day. What would you do?
- Your mom asks you to help her carry in groceries from the car. You have just reached a new level on your video game. It has taken you months to reach this level. What do you do?
- You've had a great time with your family at Disneyland and Epcot Center. Your family's vacation is about to end and your parents say that there's not going to be enough cash to buy souvenirs. How do you respond to this news?
- Your girlfriend/boyfriend accidentally spills red punch all over your new jacket. How do you respond?

As family members finish giving their responses, close this activity with this discussion. How easy or difficult is it for you to put people first? Can you think of times when you have had to decide between people or things? What did you decide? How do you feel about that choice now? Explain that God wants to challenge us to keep our priorities in order. God wants to be first, people come second, and possessions third.

Closing the Lesson

Close the lesson by giving everyone a piece of paper and an Energizer battery. Ask everyone to lay these two items in front of them. Explain that God wants us to make people more important than things, because people are eternal. They keep going and going. The commercials for the Energizer battery show us the pink rabbit that keeps going and going. In the same way, our bodies die but we keep going. People are eternal. Let's make this battery represent people.

Now on the paper, draw your two most important possessions.

Draw a picture of the things that you value the most. Once everyone has drawn their pictures and shared them with one another, make these comments: God wants us to make people more important than things because things are not eternal. Crumple up your paper, then ask each family member to do the same. God wants us to enjoy life and having these possessions is certainly enjoyable. But He does want us to remember that these possessions don't last. They eventually become one giant garbage dump. Place all the crumpled-up paper in the middle of the table.

God wants us to prioritize the things that last—people. Close the lesson by inviting each person to say a sentence prayer, thanking God for giving us our possessions. Then ask everyone to place their batteries next to the pieces of paper and say a second sentence prayer. Ask God to help you remember that people are more important than things.

High School Happenings

Materials Needed: Energizer batteries, paper and pens for each person, video or Polaroid camera, scavenger hunt list, transportation for scavenger hunt, two water guns, balloons, markers

Letting Your Child Know You Begin this lesson by sharing statements of approval with your children. Look at each child and complete these sentences: "I'm glad you're my son/daughter because . . ." and "I'm so proud of you for. . . ." Be sure to complete these sentences with very specific responses. The more specific you are in your statements of approval, the more impact they will make on your teenager. Your responses might sound like: "I'm glad you're my daughter because I enjoy getting to go to your volleyball games to watch you play." Or, "I'm so proud of your willingness to try new things. I admire you for taking the karate class."

Getting to Know Your Child Ask your teen to think of a time when he/she broke a favorite possession or lost something that was very important. Ask your teen to describe the item that was broken or lost. Why was that item special? Why did you like that possession best? What happened to the item? How did you feel when you lost it or broke it? At this point, parents will want to share statements of empathy with your child. Communicate that you hear their feelings, their feelings are important, and you care about them. Your statement of empathy might sound like, "I know you were disappointed when your T-shirt from the concert was stolen. You looked forward to that concert for such a long time. I felt sad because you were upset."

Explain that this lesson contains a story about a family who had a great deal of money. The father provided his two sons with many possessions and even saved money that was to be their inheritance. This story puts these possessions in perspective. The Bible Drama suggests we prioritize people rather than things.

Becoming Caringly Involved Read the Bible Drama once to your family. Then divide into pairs and give these instructions. Pretend that you and your partner have been hired to provide the sound track for this story. This Bible Drama will be aired on national radio in two weeks. You must provide the sound effects and/or music to go along with the narrator's retelling of the story.

If possible, provide each pair of family members with a copy of the Bible Drama. They will use this to plan out their sound track. Here are a few suggestions to get your groups started:

- Gather several coins and make the sound of jingling coins as the narrator explains how the young son demanded his inheritance.
- Hum the theme song of *Chariots of Fire* as the father and son are running toward each other.
- Make sounds like a crowd cheering when the young son finally reaches his father.
- Play a contemporary "party" song as the family celebrates the son's return.
- Sing the words to Aretha Franklin's "R-E-S-P-E-C-T" as the older brother complains about his younger brother's return.

Allow fifteen minutes for your family to plan out their sound effects. As you work, instruct each group to decide where the pauses should occur. Designate the places that you want the narrator to pause so that you can give the appropriate sound effect. Write these pauses on the written copy of the Bible Drama.

When everyone is ready, perform these sound effects for one another. Decide on a narrator and let him begin reading the story. As he reads, the narrator pauses so that sound effects can be introduced. Enjoy making each other laugh. You might even want to record this activity and keep it as a record of this family memory.

As you finish performing, invite your family to participate in this discussion:

- How do you think you would have reacted if you had been the father or the older brother?
- Did the father's response surprise you? Tell why or why not. If you knew the story already, tell why this father's response might be considered unusual.
- What order of priorities does the Bible Drama suggest?

Keeps on Going

For the first activity ask each family member to draw several pictures on separate sheets of paper. Give these instructions: Draw a picture of your favorite possession/toy when you were five years old. Draw pictures of your favorite possessions when you were eight years old, ten years old, twelve years old, and your most prized possession now. When you have finished you should have five pictures on five different sheets of paper.

Ask these questions of each family member. As they give their answers ask them to crumple up their papers and throw them in the middle of the table or floor. What happened to the toy you liked when you were five? What happened to the toy that you liked when you were eight, ten, and twelve? What do you think will happen to the most prized possession you have now? Explain that eventually all these *things* end up broken, thrown away, given away, or trashed. These possessions don't last.

Give each person three Energizer batteries. Ask everyone to hold their batteries and consider these thoughts. What do the commercials about this battery tell us? The commercials show a pink bunny that is powered by the Energizer batteries. What's the slogan attached to these commercials? The commercials tell us that the Energizer batteries keep going and going. The advertisers want us to think this battery will never die. God has told us about three things that really do keep going and going. He tells us that there are only three things that will last forever. Three things are eternal: God, His Word, and people.

Ask each family member to place their three batteries on the dinner table. Next, ask everyone to pick up their crumpled pieces of paper and put them in a pile in the center of the table. Ask teens to explain the contrast between the possessions and what the batteries represent. Leave these items on the table. You will return to these items at the end of the lesson.

People 'N Things Scavenger Hunt
See Middle School section.

People 'N Things Decision-making
See Middle School section for explanation of this activity. The situations for this activity are as follows:

- Your girlfriend/boyfriend calls and would like to spend time with you. The two of you haven't seen each other for a week. You planned to spend the day washing your car. What do you do?
- You are supposed to celebrate your mom's birthday on Friday. Your entire family will be at this event. One of your friends asks you to take his shift at work on Friday. You could really use the extra money. What will you do?
- You have saved $50. You can either buy that new shirt you've been wanting or use the money for the Student Council trip. The Student Council is sponsoring an event to take underprivileged kids to the zoo. What will you do?
- Your grandfather gave you part of his stamp collection just before he passed away. He wanted you to have the collection because you will carry on the family name. One of your friends suggests that you sell the collection for the money. What will you decide?
- Your best friend wants you to come to opening night of the senior musical. You have been waiting all week to get your new car alarm installed. What will you do?
- Your little brother accidentally spills red punch all over

your favorite CD. How will you respond?

As family members finish giving their responses, close this activity with this discussion. How easy or difficult is it for you to put people first? Can you think of times when you have had to decide between people or things? What did you decide? How do you feel about that choice now? Explain that God wants to challenge us to keep our priorities in order. God wants to be first; people come second and possessions third.

Closing the Lesson

Close the lesson by asking every family member to bring two of their most valuable possessions to the dinner table. Some individuals may need to bring something that represents their possession. For instance, Dad may want to bring his car keys. One of your teens may want to bring the speaker wires instead of the entire speaker. Place all these items in the middle of the table. You should have the crumpled pieces of paper from the first activity as well.

Explain that God wants us to enjoy our lives. He has given us many gifts and allowed us to have the money to buy nice things. There is nothing wrong with having these things. God just wants us to keep them in perspective. Ask each person to say a sentence prayer, thanking God for giving you these gifts. Thank Him for His provision.

Next, lay a sheet over the items that are on the table. Ask each person to pick up the three Energizer batteries again. Remind your family that these batteries represent things that keep going. These batteries represent things that are eternal. We are going to let each battery represent one specific person.

Adults will want to model the next step of the closing. Hold up one of the batteries, name a specific name, a specific thing, and then place the battery on top of the sheet. Your statement might sound like: God help me to remember that Paula is more important than my car. Paula is more important than things. Invite each family member to complete this same step with each of their three batteries.

Close the lesson by asking God to help each family member keep these priorities in mind. Ask Him to help you make choices that reflect people as more important than things.

Appendix **A**

Intimacy Principles

Key elements in the Intimate Life message include our need for intimacy with both God and meaningful others, our fundamental need to experience biblical truth, and God's provision for both our "fallen-ness" and our aloneness.

Intimacy Principles

1. Man is viewed from a Judeo-Christian worldview as being created in God's image and having existence in three dimensions—spirit, soul, and body. These dimensions give rise to various human functions, namely: the body functions through the five senses and we are "world conscious"; the soul functions through our thoughts, feelings, and choices and we are "self-conscious"; the spirit functions through conscience, intuition, and worship and we are God-conscious.

2. Man is by nature "fallen," separated from God, and is motivated out of a need for intimacy with God and intimacy through meaningful relationships ordained by God, i.e., marriage, the family, and the church (the body of Christ).

3. Fulfillment and abundance in life are considered from a biblical perspective as coming by grace through faith in personal intimacy with Jesus Christ and in intimate relationships with meaningful others as ordained by Him.

4. Man's need to relate to Jesus Christ and meaningful others is viewed as a personal challenge to express humility, exercise faith, and experience intimacy. In contrast, man's fallen condition prompts a selfish, self-reliant, and self-condemning

response to this neediness.

5. Individual problems in living and relational conflict are considered from an object-relations/developmental framework, in the context of unmet intimacy needs which result in unhealthy thinking, unhealed emotions, and unproductive behaviors. God's concern for both our "fallen-ness" (Gen. 3) as well our neediness/aloneness (Gen. 2) is considered foundational.

6. This pattern of unmet needs, unhealthy thinking, unhealed emotions, and unproductive behaviors outlines the major hindrances to intimacy and thus the focus of the Spirit's sanctifying work. God is viewed as the ultimate provision for all human neediness and the Bible as giving complete and adequate instruction for mature living and fulfilling relationships.

7. A systems perspective seeks to address the personal, relational, and intergenerational origins of the intimacy hindrances noted above. Thus, in marriage and family relationships, a premise of Genesis 2:24 would be to "leave father and mother, cleave to one another, and the two shall become one flesh." In other words, since "leaving" precedes "cleaving," one would expect intergenerational issues to hinder the relational issues involved in marital "cleaving" and these issues to directly impact parenting and family relationships.

8. Intimacy is enhanced through receiving of God's manifold grace. His grace is experienced as intimacy needs are met across the spectrum of four major ingredients or intimacy processes, namely: affectionate caring, vulnerable communication, joint accomplishment, and mutual giving. For intimacy to be maintained, these intimacy processes become linked to one another in a repeated spiral over the family life cycle.

9. The family life cycle is considered as bringing predictable challenges to relational intimacy, and thus the need to repeat the "spiral" of intimacy ingredients, beginning with affectionate caring. Thus, the marital stage of mutual giving is challenged by the addition of children to return to affectionate caring, followed by vulnerable communication, joint accomplishment, and again, mutual giving.

10. Intimacy is built upon man's need to experience biblical truth. The experience of biblical truth leads to emotionally

focused freedom, cognitive renewal, and behavioral discipline. The "empathic comforting of identified hurts and needs" is a pivotal element in the affectionate-caring ingredient of intimacy. Because a fundamental breakdown or hindrance to intimacy results from a lack of empathic comfort, this connection serves as the beginning point of experienced intimacy.

11. A "staged" approach to address individual, marriage, and family issues seeks to address in Stage 1: Initial Assessment (or self-inventory) of the individuals, the marriage and family relationships and intergenerational dynamics; in Stage 2: Increased Stability of the individual and relationships as a basis for improved functioning and additional maturity; in Stage 3: the Leave-Cleave issues of intergenerational significance which contribute to personal problems in living and relational discord; in Stage 4: the Becoming One Disciplines with both God and others which help ensure relational intimacy, personal maturity, and life fulfillment.

12. A working definition and goal of intimacy in relationships draws upon the biblical model of God "knowing" us, allowing us to "know" Him, and His caring involvement in our lives. Thus, mature personality development and fulfilling relationships are based upon this mutual knowing and caring involvement.

13. Significant ministry occurs as we serve a God-intended role within the body of Christ to assist and encourage others along a journey toward experiencing "life and life abundant" (John 10:10). Key elements in this ministry include imparting our very life to others (1 Thes. 2:8-9) along with encouraging them to encounter the working of God's Spirit at the point of His Word. Specifically, this ministry role is fivefold as a believer lives and shares biblical truth within the framework of eliminating hindrances and enhancing intimacy. He/she is to assist the individual, couple, or family in their need for intimacy with God and with others by:

Eliminating Hindrances
a. Identifying and Interrupting Unproductive Behaviors
b. Resolving Unhealed Emotions

c. Identifying and Countering Unhealthy Thinking
d. Identifying Unmet Intimacy Needs
e. Exposing and Resisting Selfishness, Self-Reliance, and Self-Condemnation

Enhancing Intimacy
a. Modeling and Reinforcing Productive Behaviors
b. Experiencing Positive Emotions
c. Internalizing Healthy Thinking
d. Modeling and Encouraging the Meeting of Intimacy Needs
e. Encouraging Expressions of Humility, Exhortation to Express Faith, and Rejoicing in Experienced Intimacy

Appendix **B**

Intimacy Disclosures

-Letting Your Child Know You-

Stages

1. Infancy
   0–18 Months
   Trust versus Mistrust

2. Early Childhood
   18–36 Months
   Autonomy versus
   Shame/Doubt

3. Middle Childhood
   3–5 Years
   Initiative versus Guilt

Disclosure at Each Stage

● Acceptance
● Care
● Joy
  *continue these disclosures, then
  share your—*

● Approval
● Empathy
● Faith
● Protection
  *continue these disclosures, then
  share your—*

● Affirmation
● Confession
● Remembrances
  *continue these disclosures, then
  share your—*

4. Late Childhood
   6–12 Years
   Industry versus
   Inferiority

   - Dreams
   - Decision-Making
   - Struggles
   - Hopes
   - Individuality
   - Remembrances of Same-Sex Friends
   - Experiences of Delayed Gratification
     continue these disclosures, then share your—

5. Adolescence
   13–18 Years
   Identity versus Role
   Confusion

   - Negative Feelings
   - Temptations
   - Dating Experiences
   - Inadequacies
     continue these disclosures, then share your—

6. Young Adult
   19–30 Years
   Intimacy versus Isolation

   - Enjoyment of Common Interests
   - Remembrances (Painful)
   - Need for Mutual Giving
   - Confession

Appendix C

Fifty Selected Character Qualities

1. **Alertness** — Learning to pay attention to all the lessons God is teaching through authorities, friends, and experiences.

2. **Attentiveness** — Learning who to be attentive to, what to listen for, and who not to listen to.

3. **Availability** — Learning to reject distractions that hinder me from fulfilling my responsibilities.

4. **Boldness** — Demonstrating the confidence that following the principles of Scripture will bring ultimate victory regardless of present opposition.

5. **Cautiousness** — Gaining adequate counsel before making decisions. Recognizing temptations and fleeing them.

6. **Compassion** — Reliving the hurts of others and doing all that is possible to relieve them.

7. **Contentment** — Learning to enjoy present possessions rather than desiring new or additional ones.

8. **Creativity** — Finding ways to overcome seemingly impossible obstacles; discovering practical applications for spiritual principles.

9. **Decisiveness** — Learning to finalize difficult decisions on the basis of God's ways, Word, and will.

10. **Deference** — Limiting my freedom in order not to offend the personal tastes of those God has called me to serve.

11. **Dependability** — Learning to be true to your word even when it is difficult to carry out what you promised to do.

12. **Determination** — Learning to give whatever energy is necessary to complete a project.

13. **Diligence** — Seeing every task as an assignment from the Lord and applying energy and concentration to accomplish it.

14. **Discernment** — Knowing what to look for in evaluating people, problems, and things.

15. **Discretion** — Knowing what is appropriate and what is inappropriate. Seeing the consequences of words and actions down the road.

16. **Endurance** — Maintaining commitment to a goal during times of pressure. Recognizing and laying aside hindrances.

17. **Enthusiasm** — Learning what actions and attitudes please God and becoming excited about them.

18. **Fairness** — Looking at a situation through the eyes of each one involved in it.

19. **Faith** — Developing an unshakable confidence in God and His Word. Identifying God's will and acting on it.

20. **Flexibility** — Learning how to cheerfully change plans when unexpected conditions require it.

21. **Forgiveness** — Learning to demonstrate Christ's love toward others, remembering how much God has forgiven us.

22. **Generosity** — Recognizing that all possessions belong to God. Learning how to be a wise steward of time, money, and possessions.

23. **Gentleness** — Learning to respond to needs with kindness and love. Knowing what is appropriate for the emotional needs of others.

24. **Gratefulness** — Learning to recognize the benefits which God and others have provided; looking for appropriate ways to express genuine appreciation.

25. **Hospitality** — Learning how to provide an atmosphere which contributes to the physical and spiritual growth of those around us.

26. **Humility** — Recognizing my total inability to accomplish anything for God apart from His grace.

27. **Initiative** — Taking steps to seek after God with our whole heart. Assuming responsibility for the physical, emotional, and spiritual encouragement of those around us.

28. **Joyfulness** — Learning to be happy regardless of outside circumstances.

29. **Love** — Learning how to give to the basic needs of others without motive of personal reward; an unconditional commitment to an imperfect person.

30. **Loyalty** — Adopting as your own the wishes and goals of those you are serving.

31. **Meekness** — Learning how to yield rights and possessions to God. Learning to earn the right to be heard rather than demanding a hearing.

32. **Neatness** — Learning to organize and care for personal possessions.

33. **Obedience** — Yielding the right to have the final decision.

34. **Patience** — Learning to accept difficult situations as from God without giving Him a deadline to remove the problem.

35. **Persuasiveness** — Effectively presenting our case while demonstrating commitment to our convictions by the example of our lives.

36. **Punctuality** — Showing esteem for other people and their time by not keeping them waiting.

37. **Resourcefulness** — Seeing value in that which others overlook. Learning to make wise use of things which others would discard.

38. **Responsibility** — Learning to establish personal restrictions and guidelines that are necessary to fulfill what you know you should do.

39. **Reverence** — Learning to respect the authority and position of God and others.

40. **Security** — Learning to exhibit a freedom from fear.

41. **Self-control** — Learning to quickly identify and obey the initial promptings of the Holy Spirit. Bringing my thoughts, words, and actions under the control of the Holy Spirit.

42. **Sensitivity** — Being alert to the promptings of the Holy Spirit. Avoiding danger by sensing wrong motives in others. Knowing how to give the right words at the right time.

43. **Sincerity** — Having motives that are transparent. Having a genuine concern to benefit the lives of others.

44. **Thoroughness** — Learning what details are important for the success of a project.

45. **Thriftiness** — Knowing how to accomplish the most with what's available.

46. **Tolerance** — Learning how to respond to the immaturity of others without accepting their standard of immaturity.

47. **Truthfulness** — Learning to share that which is right without misrepresenting the facts. Facing the consequences of a mistake.

48. **Understanding** — Viewing life from another's perspective; looking past life's obvious disappointments to find the comfort of God.

49. **Virtue** — Learning to build personal moral standards which will cause others to desire a more godly life.

50. **Wisdom** — Learning to see life from God's perspective. Learning how to apply principles of life in daily situations.

Appendix D

Top Ten Intimacy Needs

Acceptance – deliberate and ready reception with a favorable positive response.

Affection – to communicate care and closeness through physical touch and verbalized love.

Appreciation – to communicate with words and feelings a personal gratefulness for another.

Approval – expressed commendation; to think and speak well of.

Attention – to take thought of another and convey appropriate interest and support; to enter into another's world.

Comfort (empathy) – to come alongside with word, feeling, and touch; to give consolation with tenderness.

Encouragement – to urge forward and positively persuade toward a goal.

Respect – to value and regard highly; to convey great worth.

Security – confidence of harmony in relationships; free from fear and harm.

Support – come alongside and gently help carry a load.

About the Authors

Dr. David and Teresa Ferguson serve as Directors of Intimate Life Ministries and Professional Associates with the Center for Marriage and Family Intimacy. David's doctoral work at Oxford Graduate School focused on the development of Intimacy Therapy, a biblically centered counseling approach.

David and Teresa appear regularly on the Intimate Life radio program and have coauthored several books including *The Pursuit of Intimacy, Intimate Moments*, and *Intimate Encounters*. Married for thirty-two years, they are the parents of three children—Terri, Robin, and Eric.

Dr. Paul Warren is the Medical Director of the Child and Adolescent Division of the Minirth-Meier New Life Clinic in Richardson, Texas, as well as a Professional Associate of the Center for Marriage and Family Intimacy. He is the co-author of several books including *Kids Who Carry Our Pain, Things That Go Bump in the Night,* and *The Father Book.* **Vicky Warren,** a graduate of UCLA, has held staff positions with Campus Crusade for Christ, Minirth-Meier Clinics, and *Today's Better Life* magazine before joining the Center for Marriage and Family Intimacy.

Paul and Vicky have been married for fifteen years and have a son, Matthew.

Terri Ferguson is a certified teacher and has taught children of all ages in both church and academic settings. While pursuing an M.A. in counseling, Terri develops curriculum for the Center for Marriage and Family Intimacy and serves as a seminar speaker.